Hands-On Web Scraping with Python

Perform advanced scraping operations using various Python
libraries and tools such as Selenium, Regex, and others

Anish Chapagain

BIRMINGHAM - MUMBAI

Hands-On Web Scraping with Python

Commissioning Editor: Sunith Shetty
Acquisition Editor: Aniruddha Patil
Content Development Editor: Roshan Kumar
Senior Editor: Ayaan Hoda
Technical Editor: Sushmeeta Jena
Copy Editor: Safis Editing
Project Coordinator: Namrata Swetta
Proofreader: Safis Editing
Indexer: Tejal Daruwale Soni
Production Designer: Alishon Mendonsa

First published: June 2019

Production reference: 2120619

Published by Packt Publishing Ltd.
Livery Place
35 Livery Street
Birmingham
B3 2PB, UK.

ISBN 978-1-78953-339-2

www.packtpub.com

To my daughter, Aasira, and my family and friends. Special thanks to Ashish Chapagain, Peter, and Prof. W.J. Teahan. This book is dedicated to you all.

`Packt.com`

Subscribe to our online digital library for full access to over 7,000 books and videos, as well as industry leading tools to help you plan your personal development and advance your career. For more information, please visit our website.

Why subscribe?

- Spend less time learning and more time coding with practical eBooks and Videos from over 4,000 industry professionals

- Improve your learning with Skill Plans built especially for you

- Get a free eBook or video every month

- Fully searchable for easy access to vital information

- Copy and paste, print, and bookmark content

Did you know that Packt offers eBook versions of every book published, with PDF and ePub files available? You can upgrade to the eBook version at `www.packt.com` and as a print book customer, you are entitled to a discount on the eBook copy. Get in touch with us at `customercare@packtpub.com` for more details.

At `www.packt.com`, you can also read a collection of free technical articles, sign up for a range of free newsletters, and receive exclusive discounts and offers on Packt books and eBooks.

Contributors

About the author

Anish Chapagain is a software engineer with a passion for data science, its processes, and Python programming, which began around 2007. He has been working with web scraping and analysis-related tasks for more than 5 years, and is currently pursuing freelance projects in the web scraping domain. Anish previously worked as a trainer, web/software developer, and as a banker, where he was exposed to data and gained further insights into topics including data analysis, visualization, data mining, information processing, and knowledge discovery. He has an MSc in computer systems from Bangor University (University of Wales), United Kingdom, and an Executive MBA from Himalayan Whitehouse International College, Kathmandu, Nepal.

About the reviewers

Radhika Datar has more than 5 years' experience in software development and content writing. She is well versed in frameworks such as Python, PHP, and Java, and regularly provides training on them. She has been working with Educba and Eduonix as a training consultant since June 2016, while also working as a freelance academic writer in data science and data analytics. She obtained her master's degree from the Symbiosis Institute of Computer Studies and Research and her bachelor's degree from K. J. Somaiya College of Science and Commerce.

Rohit Negi completed his bachelor of technology in computer science from Uttarakhand Technical University, Dehradun. His bachelor's curriculum included a specialization in computer science and applied engineering. Currently, he is working as a senior test consultant at Orbit Technologies and provides test automation solutions to LAM Research (USA clients). He has extensive quality assurance proficiency working with the following tools: Microsoft Azure VSTS, Selenium, Cucumber/BDD, MS SQL/MySQL, Java, and web scraping using Selenium. Additionally, he has a good working knowledge of how to automate workflows using Selenium, Protractor for AngularJS-based applications, Python for exploratory data analysis, and machine learning.

Packt is searching for authors like you

If you're interested in becoming an author for Packt, please visit `authors.packtpub.com` and apply today. We have worked with thousands of developers and tech professionals, just like you, to help them share their insight with the global tech community. You can make a general application, apply for a specific hot topic that we are recruiting an author for, or submit your own idea.

Table of Contents

Preface

Web scraping is an essential technique used in many organizations to scrape valuable data from web pages. Web scraping, or web harvesting, is done with a view to extracting and collecting data from websites. Web scraping comes in handy with model development, which requires data to be collected on the fly. It is also applicable for the data that is true and relevant to the topic, in which the accuracy is desired over the short-term, as opposed to implementing datasets. Data collected is stored in files including JSON, CSV, and XML, is also written a the database for later use, and is also made available online as datasets. This book will open the gates for you in terms of delving deep into web scraping techniques and methodologies using Python libraries and other popular tools, such as Selenium. By the end of this book, you will have learned how to efficiently scrape different websites.

Who this book is for

This book is intended for Python programmers, data analysts, web scraping newbies, and anyone who wants to learn how to perform web scraping from scratch. If you want to begin your journey in applying web scraping techniques to a range of web pages, then this book is what you need!

What this book covers

Chapter 1, *Web Scraping Fundamentals*, explores some core technologies and tools that are relevant to WWW and that are required for web scraping.

Chapter 2, *Python and the Web – Using URLlib and Requests*, demonstrates some of the core features available through the Python libraries such as `requests` and `urllib`, in addition to exploring page contents in various formats and structures.

Chapter 3, *Using LXML, XPath, and CSS Selectors*, describes various examples using LXML, implementing a variety of techniques and library features to deal with elements and ElementTree.

Chapter 4, Scraping Using pyquery – a Python Library, goes into more detail regarding web scraping techniques and a number of new Python libraries that deploy these techniques.

Chapter 5, *Web Scraping Using Scrapy and Beautiful Soup*, examines various aspects of traversing web documents using Beautiful Soup, while also exploring a framework that was built for crawling activities using spiders, in other words, Scrapy.

Chapter 6, *Working with Secure Web*, covers a number of basic security-related measures and techniques that are often encountered and that pose a challenge to web scraping.

Chapter 7, *Data Extraction Using Web-Based APIs*, covers the Python programming language and how to interact with the web APIs with regard to data extraction.

Chapter 8, *Using Selenium to Scrape the Web*, covers Selenium and how to use it to scrape data from the web.

Chapter 9, *Using Regex to Extract Data*, goes into more detail regarding web scraping techniques using regular expressions.

Chapter 10, *Next Steps*, introduces and examines basic concepts regarding data management using files, and analysis and visualization using pandas and matplotlib, while also providing an introduction to machine learning and data mining and exploring a number of related resources that can be helpful in terms of further learning and career development.

To get the most out of this book

Readers should have some working knowledge of the Python programming language.

Download the example code files

You can download the example code files for this book from your account at www.packt.com. If you purchased this book elsewhere, you can visit www.packt.com/support and register to have the files emailed directly to you.

You can download the code files by following these steps:

1. Log in or register at www.packt.com.
2. Select the **SUPPORT** tab.
3. Click on **Code Downloads & Errata**.
4. Enter the name of the book in the **Search** box and follow the onscreen instructions.

Once the file is downloaded, please make sure that you unzip or extract the folder using the latest version of:

- WinRAR/7-Zip for Windows
- Zipeg/iZip/UnRarX for Mac
- 7-Zip/PeaZip for Linux

The code bundle for the book is also hosted on GitHub at `https://github.com/PacktPublishing/Hands-On-Web-Scraping-with-Python`. In case there's an update to the code, it will be updated on the existing GitHub repository.

We also have other code bundles from our rich catalog of books and videos available at `https://github.com/PacktPublishing/`. Check them out!

Download the color images

We also provide a PDF file that has color images of the screenshots/diagrams used in this book. You can download it here: `https://www.packtpub.com/sites/default/files/downloads/9781789533392_ColorImages.pdf`.

Conventions used

There are a number of text conventions used throughout this book.

`CodeInText`: Indicates code words in text, database table names, folder names, filenames, file extensions, pathnames, dummy URLs, user input, and Twitter handles. Here is an example: "The <p> and <h1> HTML elements contain general text information (element content) with them."

A block of code is set as follows:

```
import requests
link="http://localhost:8080/~cache"

queries= {'id':'123456','display':'yes'}

addedheaders={'user-agent':''}
```

When we wish to draw your attention to a particular part of a code block, the relevant lines or items are set in bold:

```
import requests
link="http://localhost:8080/~cache"

queries= {'id':'123456','display':'yes'}

addedheaders={'user-agent':''}
```

Any command-line input or output is written as follows:

```
C:\> pip --version

pip 18.1 from c:\python37\lib\site-packages\pip (python 3.7)
```

Bold: Indicates a new term, an important word, or words that you see on screen. For example, words in menus or dialog boxes appear in the text like this. Here is an example: "If accessing **Developer tools** through the Chrome menu, click **More tools** | **Developer tools**"

Warnings or important notes appear like this.

Tips and tricks appear like this.

Get in touch

Feedback from our readers is always welcome.

General feedback: If you have questions about any aspect of this book, mention the book title in the subject of your message and email us at customercare@packtpub.com.

Errata: Although we have taken every care to ensure the accuracy of our content, mistakes do happen. If you have found a mistake in this book, we would be grateful if you would report this to us. Please visit www.packt.com/submit-errata, selecting your book, clicking on the Errata Submission Form link, and entering the details.

Piracy: If you come across any illegal copies of our works in any form on the internet, we would be grateful if you would provide us with the location address or website name. Please contact us at copyright@packt.com with a link to the material.

If you are interested in becoming an author: If there is a topic that you have expertise in, and you are interested in either writing or contributing to a book, please visit authors.packtpub.com.

Reviews

Please leave a review. Once you have read and used this book, why not leave a review on the site that you purchased it from? Potential readers can then see and use your unbiased opinion to make purchase decisions, we at Packt can understand what you think about our products, and our authors can see your feedback on their book. Thank you!

For more information about Packt, please visit packt.com.

Section 1: Introduction to Web Scraping

In this section, you will be given an overview of web scraping (scraping requirements, the importance of data), web contents (patterns and layouts), Python programming and libraries (the basics and advanced), and data managing techniques (file handling and databases).

This section consists of the following chapter:

- Chapter 1, *Web Scraping Fundamentals*

Web Scraping Fundamentals

In this chapter, we will learn about and explore certain fundamental concepts related to web scraping and web-based technologies, assuming that you have no prior experience of web scraping.

So, to start with, let's begin by asking a number of questions:

- Why is there a growing need or demand for data?
- How are we going to manage and fulfill the requirement for data with resources from the **World Wide Web (WWW)**?

Web scraping addresses both these questions, as it provides various tools and technologies that can be deployed to extract data or assist with information retrieval. Whether its web-based structured or unstructured data, we can use the web scraping process to extract data and use it for research, analysis, personal collections, information extraction, knowledge discovery, and many more purposes.

We will learn general techniques that are deployed to find data from the web and explore those techniques in depth using the Python programming language in the chapters ahead.

In this chapter, we will cover the following topics:

- Introduction to web scraping
- Understanding web development and technologies
- Data finding techniques

Introduction to web scraping

Scraping is the process of extracting, copying, screening, or collecting data. Scraping or extracting data from the web (commonly known as websites or web pages, or internet-related resources) is normally termed *web scraping*.

Web scraping is a process of data extraction from the web that is suitable for certain requirements. Data collection and analysis, and its involvement in information and decision making, plus research-related activities, make the scraping process sensitive for all types of industry.

The popularity of the internet and its resources is causing information domains to evolve every day, which is also causing a growing demand for raw data. Data is the basic requirement in the fields of science, technology, and management. Collected or organized data is processed with varying degrees of logic to obtain information and gain further insights.

Web scraping provides the tools and techniques used to collect data from websites as appropriate for either personal or business-related needs, but with a number of legal considerations.

There are a number of legal factors to consider before performing scraping tasks. Most websites contain pages such as *Privacy Policy*, *About Us*, and *Terms and Conditions*, where legal terms, prohibited content policies, and general information are available. It's a developer's ethical duty to follow those policies before planning any crawling and scraping activities from websites.

 Scraping and crawling are both used quite interchangeably throughout the chapters in this book. Crawling, also known as spidering, is a process used to browse through the links on websites and is often used by search engines for indexing purposes, whereas scraping is mostly related to content extraction from websites.

Understanding web development and technologies

A web page is not only a document container. Today's rapid developments in computing and web technologies have transformed the web into a dynamic and real-time source of information.

At our end, we (the users) use web browsers (such as Google Chrome, Firefox Mozilla, Internet Explorer, and Safari) to access information from the web. Web browsers provide various document-based functionalities to users and contain application-level features that are often useful to web developers.

Web pages that users view or explore through their browsers are not only single documents. Various technologies exist that can be used to develop websites or web pages. A web page is a document that contains blocks of HTML tags. Most of the time, it is built with various sub-blocks linked as dependent or independent components from various interlinked technologies, including JavaScript and CSS.

An understanding of the general concepts of web pages and the techniques of web development, along with the technologies found inside web pages, will provide more flexibility and control in the scraping process. A lot of the time, a developer can also employ reverse engineering techniques.

Reverse engineering is an activity that involves breaking down and examining the concepts that were required to build certain products. For more information on reverse engineering, please refer to the GlobalSpec article, *How Does Reverse Engineering Work?*, available at `https://insights.globalspec.com/article/7367/how-does-reverse-engineering-work`.

Here, we will introduce and explore a few of the techniques that can help and guide us in the process of data extraction.

HTTP

Hyper Text Transfer Protocol (HTTP) is an application protocol that transfers resources such as HTML documents between a client and a web server. HTTP is a stateless protocol that follows the client-server model. Clients (web browsers) and web servers communicate or exchange information using HTTP **Requests** and HTTP **Responses**:

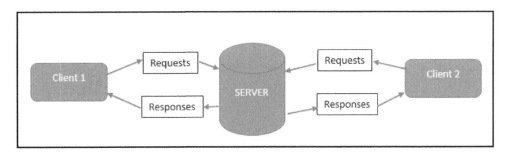

HTTP (client-server communication)

With HTTP requests or HTTP methods, a client or browser submits requests to the server. There are various methods (also known as HTTP request methods) for submitting requests, such as GET, POST, and PUT:

- GET: This is a common method for requesting information. It is considered a safe method, as the resource state is not altered. Also, it is used to provide query strings such as http://www.test-domain.com/, requesting information from servers based on the id and display parameters sent with the request.
- POST: This is used to make a secure request to a server. The requested resource state *can* be altered. Data posted or sent to the requested URL is not visible in the URL, but rather transferred with the request body. It's used to submit information to the server in secure way, such as for login and user registration.

Using the browser developer tools shown in the following screenshot, the **Request Method** can be revealed, along with other HTTP-related information:

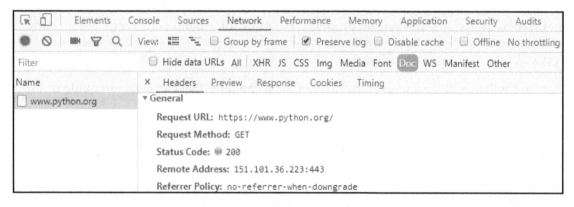

General HTTP headers (accessed using the browser developer tools)

We will explore more about HTTP methods in Chapter 2,
Python and the Web – Using urllib and Requests, in the *Implementing HTTP methods* section.

HTTP headers pass additional information to a client or server while performing a request or response. Headers are generally name-value pairs of information transferred between a client and a server during their communication, and are generally grouped into request and response headers:

- **Request Headers**: These are headers that is used for making requests. Information such as language and encoding requests – *, that is referrers, cookies, browser-related information, and so on, is provided to the server while making the request. The following screenshot displays the **Request Headers** obtained from browser developer tools while making a request to `https://www.python.org`:

```
▼ Request Headers
  :authority: www.python.org
  :method: GET
  :path: /
  :scheme: https
  accept: text/html,application/xhtml+xml,application/xml;q=0.9,image/webp,image/apng,*/*;q=0.8,application/signed-exchange;v=b3
  accept-encoding: gzip, deflate, br
  accept-language: en-US,en;q=0.9
  cache-control: max-age=0
  cookie: __utma=32101439.1496736712.1557543879.1557543879.1557543879.1; __utmc=32101439; __utmz=32101439.1557543879.1.1.utmcsr=(direct)|utmccn=(direct)|utmcmd=(none); __utmt=1;
  upgrade-insecure-requests: 1
  user-agent: Mozilla/5.0 (Windows NT 10.0; Win64; x64) AppleWebKit/537.36 (KHTML, like Gecko) Chrome/74.0.3729.131 Safari/537.36
```

Request headers (accessed using the browser developer tools)

- **Response Headers**: These headers contain information about the server's response. Information regarding the response (including size, type, and date) and the **server status** is generally found in **Response Headers**. The following screenshot displays the **Response Headers** obtained from the browser developer tools after making a request to `https://www.python.org`:

```
▼ Response Headers
  accept-ranges: bytes
  age: 0
  content-length: 48995
  content-type: text/html; charset=utf-8
  date: Sat, 11 May 2019 03:09:34 GMT
  server: nginx
  status: 200
  strict-transport-security: max-age=63072000; includeSubDomains
  vary: Cookie
  via: 1.1 vegur
```

Response headers (accessed using the browser developer tools)

The information seen in the previous screenshots was captured during the request made to https://www.python.org.

HTTP Requests can also be provided with the required **HTTP Headers** while making requests to the server. Information related to the request URL, request method, status code, request headers, query string parameters, cookies, POST parameters, and server details can generally be explored using **HTTP Headers** information.

With **HTTP responses**, the server processes the requests, and sometimes the specified HTTP headers, that are sent to it. When requests are received and processed, it returns its response to the browser.

A response contains status codes, the meaning of which can be revealed using developer tools, as seen in the previous screenshots. The following list contains a few status codes along with some brief information:

- 200 (OK, request succeeded)
- 404 (Not found; requested resource cannot be found)
- 500 (Internal server error)
- 204 (No content to be sent)
- 401 (Unauthorized request was made to the server)

 For more information on HTTP, HTTP responses, and status codes, please consult the official documentation at https://www.w3.org/Protocols/ and https://developer.mozilla.org/en-US/docs/Web/HTTP/Status.

HTTP cookies are data sent by server to the browser. Cookies are data that's generated and stored by websites on your system or computer. Data in cookies helps to identify HTTP requests from the user to the website. Cookies contain information regarding session management, user preferences, and user behavior.

The server identifies and communicates with the browser based on the information stored in the cookie. Data stored in cookies helps a website to access and transfer certain saved values such as session ID, expiration date and time, and so on, providing quick interaction between the web request and the response:

Cookies set by a website (accessed using the browser developer tools)

For more information on cookies, please visit AboutCookies at `http://www.allaboutcookies.org/`, and allaboutcookies at `http://www.allaboutcookies.org/`.

With **HTTP proxies**, a proxy server acts as an intermediate server between a client and the main web server. The web browser sends requests to the server that are actually passed through the proxy, and the proxy returns the response from the server to the client.

Proxies are often used for monitoring/filtering, performance improvement, translation, and security for internet-related resources. Proxies can also be bought as a service, which may also be used to deal with cross-domain resources. There are also various forms of proxy implementation, such as web proxies (which can be used to bypass IP blocking), CGI proxies, and DNS proxies.

Cookie-based parameters that are passed in using GET requests, HTML form-related POST requests, and modifying or adapting headers will be crucial in managing code (that is, scripts) and accessing content during the web scraping process.

Details on HTTP, headers, cookies, and so on will be explored more in the upcoming *Data finding techniques for the web* section. Please visit MDN web docs-HTTP (`https://developer.mozilla.org/en-US/docs/Web/HTTP`) for more detailed information on HTTP.

HTML

Websites are made up of pages or documents containing text, images, style sheets, and scripts, among other things. They are often built with markup languages such as **Hypertext Markup Language (HTML)** and **Extensible Hypertext Markup Language (XHTML)**.

HTML is often termed as the standard markup language used for building a web page. Since the early 1990s, HTML has been used independently, as well as in conjunction with server-based scripting languages such as PHP, ASP, and JSP.

XHTML is an advanced and extended version of HTML, which is the primary markup language for web documents. XHTML is also stricter than HTML, and from the coding perspective, is an XML application.

HTML defines and contains the contents of a web page. Data that can be extracted, and any information-revealing data sources can be found inside HTML pages within a predefined instruction set or markup elements called **tags**. HTML tags are normally a named placeholder carrying certain predefined attributes.

HTML elements and attributes

HTML elements (also referred to as document nodes) are the building block of web documents. HTML elements are built with a start tag, `<..>`, and an end tag, `</..>`, with certain contents inside them. An HTML element can also contain attributes, usually defined as `attribute-name = attribute-value`, that provide additional information to the element:

```
<p>normal paragraph tags</p>
<h1>heading tags there are also h2, h3, h4, h5, h6</h1>
<a href="https://www.google.com">Click here for Google.com</a>
<img src="myphoto1.jpg" width="300" height="300" alt="Picture" />
<br />
```

The preceding code can be broken down as follows:

- The `<p>` and `<h1>` HTML elements contain general text information (element content) with them.
- `<a>` is defined with an `href` attribute that contains the actual link, which will be processed when the text `Click here for Google.com` is clicked. The link refers to `https://www.google.com/`.

- The `<img>` image tag also contains a few attributes, such as `src` and `alt`, along with their respective values. `src` holds the resource, that is, the image address or image URL as an value, whereas `alt` holds value for alternative text for `<img>`.
- `<br />` represents a line break in HTML, and has no attribute or text content. It is used to insert a new line in the layout of the document.

HTML elements can also be nested in a tree-like structure with a parent-child hierarchy:

```
<div>
    <p id="mainContent" class="content">
        <i> Paragraph contents </i>
        <img src="mylogo.png" id="pageLogo" class="logo"/>
        ....
    </p>
    <p class="content" id="subContent">
        <i style="color:red"> Sub paragraph content </i>
        <h1 itemprop="subheading">Sub heading Content! </h1>
        ....
    </p>
</div>
```

As seen in the preceding code, two `<p>` child elements are found inside an HTML `<div>` block. Both child elements carry certain attributes and various child elements as their contents. Normally, HTML documents are built with this aforementioned structure.

Global attributes

HTML elements can contain some additional information, such as key/value pairs. These are also known as HTML element attributes. Attributes holds values and provide identification, or contain additional information that can be helpful in many aspects during scraping activities such as identifying exact web elements and extracting values or text from them, traversing through elements and more.

There are certain attributes that are common to HTML elements or can be applied to all HTML elements as follows. These attributes are identified as global attributes (https://developer.mozilla.org/en-US/docs/Web/HTML/Global_attributes):

- `id`
- `class`
- `style`
- `lang`

HTML elements attributes such as id and class are mostly used to identify or format individual elements, or groups of elements. These attributes can also be managed by CSS and other scripting languages.

id attribute values should be unique to the element they're applied to. class attribute values are mostly used with CSS, providing equal state formatting options, and can be used with multiple elements.

Attributes such as id and class are identified by placing # and . respectively in front of the attribute name when used with CSS, traversing, and parsing techniques.

 HTML element attributes can also be overwritten or implemented dynamically using scripting languages.

As displayed in following examples, itemprop attributes are used to add properties to an element, whereas data-* is used to store data that is native to the element itself:

```
<div itemscope itemtype ="http://schema.org/Place">
    <h1 itemprop="univeristy">University of Helsinki</h1>
     <span>Subject:
         <span itemprop="subject1">Artificial Intelligence</span>
    </span>
     <span itemprop="subject2">Data Science</span>
</div>

<img class="dept" src="logo.png" data-course-id="324" data-
title="Predictive Aanalysis"  data-x="12345" data-y="54321" data-z="56743"
onclick="schedule.load()">
</img>
```

HTML tags and attributes are a major source of data when it comes to extraction.

 Please visit https://www.w3.org/html/ and https://www.w3schools.com/html/ for more information on HTML.

In the chapters ahead, we will explore these attributes using different tools. We will also perform various logical operations and use them to extract content.

XML

Extensible Markup Language (**XML**) is a markup language used for distributing data over the internet, with a set of rules for encoding documents that are readable and easily exchangeable between machines and documents.

XML can use textual data across various formats and systems. XML is designed to carry portable data or data stored in tags that is not predefined with HTML tags. In XML documents, tags are created by the document developer or an automated program to describe the content they are carrying.

The following code displays some example XML content. The <employees> parent node has three <employee> child nodes, which in turn contain the other child nodes <firstName>, <lastName>, and <gender>:

```
<employees>
    <employee>
        <firstName>Rahul</firstName>
        <lastName>Reddy</lastName>
        <gender>Male</gender>
    </employee>
    <employee>
        <firstName>Aasira</firstName>
        <lastName>Chapagain</lastName>
        <gender>Female</gender>
    </employee>
    <employee>
        <firstName>Peter</firstName>
        <lastName>Lara</lastName>
        <gender>Male</gender>
    </employee>
</employees>
```

XML is an open standard, using the Unicode character set. XML is used for sharing data across various platforms and has been adopted by various web applications. Many websites use XML data, implementing its contents with the use of scripting languages and presenting it in HTML or other document formats for the end user to view.

Extraction tasks from XML documents can also be performed to obtain the contents in the desired format, or by filtering the requirement with respect to a specific need for data. Plus, behind-the-scenes data may also be obtained from certain websites only.

Please visit `https://www.w3.org/XML/` and `https://www.w3schools.com/ xml/` for more information on XML.

JavaScript

JavaScript is a programming language that's used to program HTML and web applications that run in the browser. JavaScript is mostly preferred for adding dynamic features and providing user-based interaction inside web pages. JavaScript, HTML, and CSS are among the most commonly used web technologies, and now they are also used with headless browsers. The client-side availability of the JavaScript engine has also strengthened its position in application testing and debugging.

JavaScript code can be added to HTML using `<script>` or embedded as a file. `<script>` contains programming logic with JavaScript variables, operators, functions, arrays, loops, conditions, and events, targeting the HTML **Document Object Model (DOM)**:

```
<!DOCTYPE html>
<html>
<head>
    <script>
        function placeTitle() {
            document.getElementById("innerDiv").innerHTML = "Welcome to
WebScraping";
        }
    </script>
</head>
<body>
    <div>Press the button: <p id="innerDiv"></p></div>
    <br />
    <button id="btnTitle" name="btnTitle" type="submit"
onclick="placeTitle()">
        Load Page Title!
    </button>
</body>
</html>
```

The HTML DOM is a standard for how to get, change, add, or delete HTML elements. JavaScript HTML DOM, W3Schools can be referred to the URL `https://www.w3schools.com/js/js_htmldom.asp`.

Dynamic manipulation of HTML contents, elements, attribute values, CSS, and HTML events with accessible internal functions and programming features makes JavaScript very popular in web development. There are many web-based technologies related to JavaScript, including JSON, jQuery, AngularJS, and AJAX, among many more.

jQuery is a JavaScript library that addresses incompatibilities across browsers, providing API features to handle the HTML DOM, events, and animations.

jQuery has been acclaimed globally for providing interactivity to the web and the way JavaScript was used to code. jQuery is lightweight in comparison to JavaScript framework, it is also easy to implement, with a short and readable coding approach.

For more information on jQuery, please visit `https://www.w3schools.com/jquery/` and `http://jquery.com/`.

Asynchronous JavaScript and XML (AJAX) is a web development technique that uses a group of web technologies on the client side to create asynchronous web applications. JavaScript **XMLHttpRequest (XHR)** objects are used to execute AJAX on web pages and load page content without refreshing or reloading the page. Please visit AJAX W3Schools (`https://www.w3schools.com/js/js_ajax_intro.asp`) for more information on AJAX.

From a scraping point of view, a basic overview of JavaScript functionality will be valuable to understanding how a page is built or manipulated, as well as identifying the dynamic components used.

Please visit `https://developer.mozilla.org/en-US/docs/Web/JavaScript` and `https://www.javascript.com/` for more information on JavaScript.

JSON

JavaScript Object Notation (JSON) is a format used for storing and transporting data from a server to a web page. It is language independent and is popular in web-based data-interchange actions due to its size and readability.

JSON data is normally a name/value pair that is evaluated as a JavaScript object and follows JavaScript operations. JSON and XML are often compared, as they both carry and exchange data between various web resources. JSON is also ranked higher than XML for its structure, which is simple, readable, self-descriptive, understandable, and easy to process. For web applications using JavaScript, AJAX, or RESTful services, JSON is preferred over XML due to its fast and easy operation.

JSON and JavaScript objects are interchangeable. JSON is not a markup language and it doesn't contain any tags or attributes. Instead, it is a text-only format that can be sent to/accessed through a server, as well as being managed by any programming language. JSON objects can also be expressed as arrays, dictionary, and lists as seen in the following code:

```
{"mymembers":[
    { "firstName":"Aasira",  "lastName":"Chapagain","cityName":"Kathmandu"},
    { "firstName":"Rakshya", "lastName":"Dhungel","cityName":"New Delhi"},
    { "firstName":"Shiba",   "lastName":"Paudel","cityName":"Biratnagar"},
    { "firstName":"Rahul",   "lastName":"Reddy","cityName":"New Delhi"},
    { "firstName":"Peter",   "lastName":"Lara","cityName":"Trinidad"}
]}
```

JSON Lines: This is a JSON-like format where each line of a record is a valid JSON value. It is also known as newline-delimited JSON, that is, individual JSON records separated by newline (\n) characters. JSON Lines formatting can be very useful when dealing with a large volume of data.

Data sources in the JSON or JSON Lines formats are preferred to XML because of the easy data pattern and code readability, which can also be managed with minimum programming effort:

```
{"firstName":"Aasira",  "lastName":"Chapagain","cityName":"Kathmandu"}
{"firstName":"Rakshya", "lastName":"Dhungel","cityName":"New Delhi"}
{"firstName":"Shiba",   "lastName":"Paudel","cityName":"Biratnagar"}
{"firstName":"Rahul",   "lastName":"Reddy","cityName":"New Delhi"}
{"firstName":"Peter",   "lastName":"Lara","cityName":"Trinidad"}
```

From the perspective of data extraction, because of the lightweight and simple structure of the JSON format, web pages use JSON content with their scripting technologies to add dynamic features.

Please visit `http://www.json.org/`, `http://jsonlines.org/`, and `https://www.w3schools.com/js/js_json_intro.asp` for more information regarding JSON and JSON Lines.

CSS

The web-based technologies we have introduced so far deal with content, content binding, content development, and processing. **Cascading Style Sheets (CSS)** describes the display properties of HTML elements and the appearance of web pages. CSS is used for styling and providing the desired appearance and presentation of HTML elements.

Developers/designers can control the layout and presentation of a web document using CSS. CSS can be applied to a distinct element in a page, or it can be embedded through a separate document. Styling details can be described using the <style> tag.

The <style> tag can contain details targeting repeated and various elements in a block. As seen in the following code, multiple <a> elements exist and also possess the class and id global attributes:

```html
<html>
<head>
     <style>
       a{color:blue; }
       h1{color:black; text-decoration:underline; }
       #idOne{color:red; }
       .classOne{color:orange; }
     </style>
</head>
<body>
     <h1> Welcome to Web Scraping </h1>
     Links:
     <a href="https://www.google.com"> Google </a>
     <a class='classOne' href="https://www.yahoo.com"> Yahoo </a>
     <a id='idOne' href="https://www.wikipedia.org"> Wikipedia </a>
</body>
</html>
```

Attributes that are provided with CSS properties or have been styled inside <style> tags in the preceding code block will result in the output seen here:

HTML output (with the elements styled using CSS)

CSS properties can also appear in in-line structure with each particular element. In-line CSS properties override external CSS styles. The CSS `color` property has been applied in-line to elements. This will override the `color` value defined inside `<style>`:

```
<h1 style ='color:orange;'> Welcome to Web Scraping </h1>
Links:
<a href="https://www.google.com" style ='color:red;'> Google </a>
<a class='classOne' href="https://www.yahoo.com"> Yahoo </a>
<a id='idOne' href="https://www.wikipedia.org" style ='color:blue;'>
Wikipedia </a>
```

CSS can also be embedded in HTML using an external stylesheet file:

```
<link href="http://..../filename.css" rel="stylesheet" type="text/css">
```

Although CSS is used for the appearance of HTML elements, CSS selectors (patterns used to select elements) often play a major role in the scraping process. We will be exploring CSS selectors in detail in the chapters ahead.

 Please visit `https://www.w3.org/Style/CSS/` and `https://www.w3schools.com/css/` for more detailed information on CSS.

AngularJS

We have introduced few selected web-related technologies so far in this chapter. Let's get an overview of web frameworks by introducing AngularJS. Web frameworks deal with numerous web-related tools and are used to develop web-related resources while adopting the latest methodologies.

AngularJS (also styled as *Angular.js* or *Angular*) is mostly used to build client-side web applications. This is a framework based on JavaScript. AngularJS is added to HTML using the `<script>` tag, which extends HTML attributes as directives and binds data as expressions. AngularJS expressions are used to bind data to HTML elements retrieved from static or dynamic JSON resources. AngularJS directives are prefixed with `ng-`.

AngularJS is used with HTML for dynamic content development. It provides performance improvement, a testing environment, manipulation of elements, and data-binding features, and helps to build web applications in the **model-view-controller** (**MVC**) framework by offering a more dynamic and flexible environment across documents, data, platforms, and other tools.

We can link external JavaScript files to our HTML document as follows:

```
<!doctype html>
<html ng-app>
    <head>
        <script
src="https://ajax.googleapis.com/ajax/libs/angularjs/1.7.5/angular.min.js">
        </script>
    </head>
    <body>
        <div>
            <label> Place: </label>
            <input type="text" ng-model="place" placeholder="Visited
place!">
            <label> Cost :</label>
            <input type="text" ng-model="price" placeholder="Ticket
Price!">
            <br>
            <b>Wow! {{place}} for only {{price}}</b>
        </div>
    </body>
</html>
```

Also, we can include the script and element blocks together on a page, as seen here:

```
<script>
    var app = angular.module('myContact', []);
    app.controller('myDiv', function($scope) {
        $scope.firstName = "Aasira";
        $scope.lastName = "Chapagain";
        $scope.college= "London Business School";
        $scope.subject= "Masters in Analytics and Management";
    });
</script>
<div ng-app="myContact" ng-controller="myDiv">
    First Name: <input type="text" ng-model="firstName"><br>
    Last Name: <input type="text" ng-model="lastName"><br>
    College Name: <input type="text" ng-model="college"><br>
    Subjects: <input type="text" ng-model="subject"><br>
    <br>
    Full Name: {{firstName + " " + lastName}}
    <br>
    Enrolled on {{college + " with " + subject}}
</div>
```

The general overview that we've provided here of AngularJS and its working methodology allows more flexibility in tracing and traversing data.

 Please visit AngularJS (`https://angularjs.org/` and `https://angular.io/`) for more detail information on AngularJS.

The technologies discussed previously are a few core components of the web; they are linked, dependent on each other to produce the websites or web documents that end users interact with. In the chapters ahead, we will identify scripts and further analyze the code contained within.

In the following section, we will explore web content and look for the data that can be found inside web pages, which we will be extracting in the chapters ahead using the Python programming language.

Data finding techniques for the web

There are various technologies that can be used for developing a website. The content presented to end users using web browsers can also exist in various other formats and patterns.

As discussed earlier, dynamic generation or manipulation of the contents of web page are also possible. Page content can also include static content rendered with HTML and associated technologies, or presented and created on the fly. Content can also be retrieved using third-party sources and presented to end users.

HTML page source

Web browsers are used for client-server based GUI interaction exploring web content. The browser address bar is supplied with the web address or URL, and the requested URL is communicated to the server (host) and response is received, that is, loaded by the browser. This obtained response or page source can be further explored, and the desired content can be searched in raw format.

Users are free to choose their web browser. We will be using Google Chrome for most of the book, installed on the Windows **operating system (OS)**.

The HTML source for pages will be frequently opened and investigated for required content and resources during scraping process. Right click the web page. A menu will then appear where you can find the **View page source** option. Alternatively, press *Ctrl + U*.

Case 1

Let's look at an example of web scraping by following these steps:

1. Go to `https://www.google.com` on in your chosen browser
2. Enter `Web Scraping` in the search box
3. Press *Enter* or click the Google search button on the page
4. You should see something similar to the following screenshot:

Search results for web scraping from Google

Google has provided us with the search information we have asked for. This information is displayed in paragraphs and numerous links are also presented. The information displayed is interactive, colorful, and presented in maintained structure with the search contents adopted in the layout.

This is the frontend content we are viewing. This content is provided to us dynamically based on our interaction with Google. Let's now view the raw content that has been provided to us.

5. Right-click the web page. A menu will then appear where you can find the **View page source** option. Alternatively, press *Ctrl + U*. Here, a new tab will be opened with the HTML source of the page. Check for `view-source` at the start of the URL in the browser:

HTML page source: search results for web scraping from Google

We are now accessing the HTML source of the page displayed in the previous screenshot. HTML tags and JavaScript codes can be easily seen, but are not presented in the proper format. These are the core contents that the browser has rendered to us.

Search for some text, displayed on the normal page view, in the page source. Identify how and where the text, links, and images are found in the page source. You will be able to find the text in the page source within HTML tags (but not always, as we shall see!)

Web development can be done using various technologies and tools, as we discussed in the previous sections. Web page content displayed by browsers might not always be available inside HTML tags when its source is explored. Content can also exist inside scripts or even on third-party links. This is what makes web scraping often challenging, and thus demands the latest tools and technologies that exist for web development.

Case 2

Let's explore another case, with the browsing procedure that we applied in the *Case 1* section:

1. Search for `Top Hotels in USA for 2018` on Google and choose any hotel name you like.
2. Search for the hotel name in Google directly (or you can ignore the preceding step). For example, try `The Peninsula Chicago`.
3. Google will load the searched hotel's details' along with a map and booking and reviews sections. The result of this will be similar to the following screenshot:

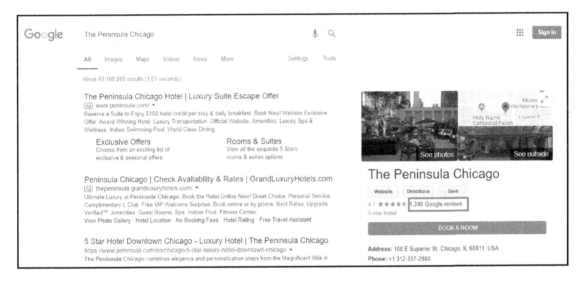

Google search result for The Peninsula Chicago

4. On the left-hand side, you can find the link for **Google reviews**. After clicking the link, a new page will pop up, as seen in the following screenshot:

Google reviews page from the search page

5. Right-click on the pop-up review page and select **View page source**, or press *Ctrl + U* for the page source.

Try to find the reviews and response texts by users from the page source.

Developer tools

Developer tools (or *DevTools*) are found embedded within most browsers on the market today. Developers and end users alike can identify and locate resources and search for web content that is used during client-server communication, or while engaged in an HTTP request and response.

DevTools allow a user to examine, create, edit, and debug HTML, CSS, and JavaScript. They also allow us to handle performance problems. They facilitate the extraction of data that is dynamically or securely presented by the browser.

DevTools will be used for most data extraction cases, and for cases similar to *Case 2* from the *page source* section previously mentioned. For more information on developer tools, please explore these links:

- Chrome DevTools (`https://developers.google.com/web/tools/chrome-devtools/`)
- Firefox DevTools (`https://developer.mozilla.org/son/docs/Tools/`)

In Google Chrome, we can load DevTools by following any of these instructions:

- Simply press *Ctrl + Shift + I*
- Another option is to right-click on the page and press the **Inspect** option
- Alternatively, if accessing **Developer tools** through the Chrome menu, click **More tools | Developer tools**:

Loading the Chrome DevTools for a reviews page

The preceding screenshot displays the **Developer Tools** panels: **Elements**, **Console**, **Network**, **Sources**, and so on. In our case, let's look for some text from the review page. Following these steps will allow us to find it:

1. Open the **Network** panel inside **Developer Tools**.
2. Select the **XHR** filter option. (Multiple resources such as HTML files, images, and JSON data will be found listed under the **Name** panel.)
3. We need to traverse through the resources under the **Name** pane looking for the chosen text fragment we seek. (The **Response** tab displays the content of chosen resources.)
4. A resource beginning with `reviewDialog?` is found, containing the searched-for text.

The steps outlined here for searching review text form one of the most commonly used techniques for locating exact content. These steps are followed normally when the content is obtained dynamically and is not found inside the page source.

There are various panels in **Developer tools** that are related to specific functions provided to web resources or for analysis, including **Sources**, **Memory**, **Performance**, and **Networks**. We will be exploring a few panels found in Chrome DevTools, as follows:

The specific names of panels found in browser-based DevTools might not be the same across all browsers.

- **Elements**: Displays the HTML content of the page viewed. This is used for viewing and editing the DOM and CSS, and also for finding CSS selectors and XPath.

HTML elements displayed or located from the **Elements** panel may not be available in the page source.

- **Console**: Used to run and interact with JavaScript code, and view log messages:

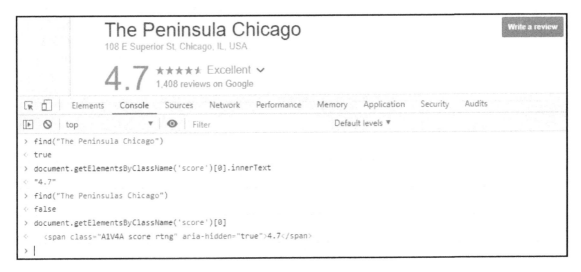

The Console panel inside Chrome DevTools

- **Sources**: Used to navigate pages, view available scripts and documents sources. Script-based tools are available for tasks such as script execution (that is, resuming, pausing), stepping over function calls, activating and deactivating breakpoints, and also handling the exceptions such as pausing exceptions, if encountered:

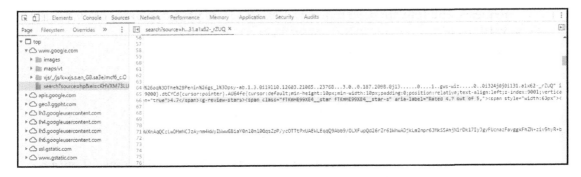

The Sources panel from Chrome DevTools

- **Network**: Provides us with HTTP request and response-related resources, and shows the network resources used while loading a page. Resources found inside **Network** feature options such as recording data to network logs, capturing screenshots, filtering web resources (JavaScript, images, documents, and CSS), searching web resources, and grouping web resources, and can be used for debugging tasks too:

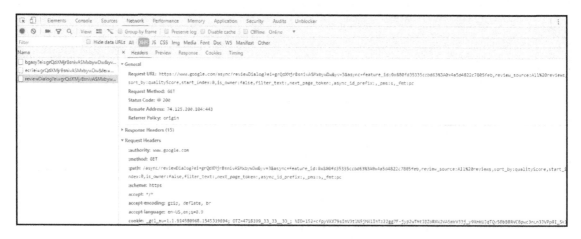

The Chrome DevTools Network panel

Requests can also be filtered by type:

- **All**: Lists all requests related to the network, including document requests, image requests, and font and CSS requests. Resources are placed in order of loading.
- **XHR**: Lists `XmlHttpRequest` objects load AJAX content on the fly
- **JS**: Lists requested scripts files
- **CSS**: Lists requested style files
- **Img**: Lists requested image files
- **Doc**: Lists requested HTML or web documents
- **Other**: Any unlisted type of request related resources

For filter options listed previously, there are tabs (**Headers, Preview, Response, Timing, Cookies**) for selected resources in the **Name** panel:

- **Headers**: Loads HTTP header data for a particular request. Information revealed includes request URLs, request methods, status codes, request headers, query string parameters, and `POST` parameters.
- **Preview**: Loads a formatted preview of the response.

- **Response**: Loads the response to a particular request.
- **Timing**: To view time breakdown information.
- **Cookies**: Loads cookie information for the resources selected in the **Name** panel.

From the scraping point of view, the DevTools **Network** panel is useful for finding and analyzing web resources. This information can be useful for retrieving data and choosing methods to process these resources.

> For more information on the **Network** panel, please visit `https://developers.google.com/web/tools/chrome-devtools/network-performance/reference/` and `https://developer.mozilla.org/en-US/docs/Tools/Network_Monitor/`.

There are various elements provided on the Network panel which are explained below:

- **Performance**: The **Screenshots** page and **Memory** timeline can be recorded. The visual information obtained is used to optimize website speed, improving load times and analyzing runtime performance. In earlier Chrome versions, information provided by the **Performance** panel used to exist inside a panel named **Timeline**:

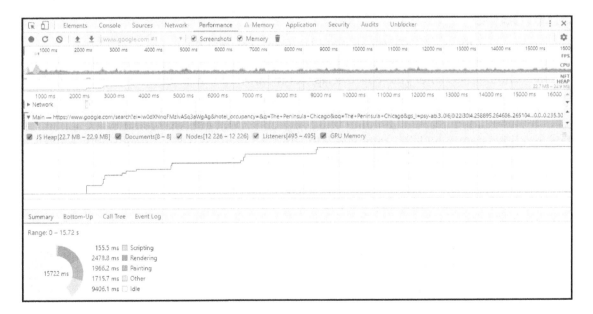

The Performance panel in Chrome DevTools

- **Memory**: This panel was also known as panel profiles in earlier Chrome versions. Information obtained from this panel is used to fix memory problems and track down memory leaks. The **Performance** and **Memory** panels are also used by developers to analyze overall website performance.
- **Application**: The end user can inspect and manage storage for all loaded resources, including cookies, sessions, application cache, images, and databases.

After exploring the HTML page source and **DevTools**, we now have a general idea of where data can be explored or searched for. Overall, scraping involves extracting data from web pages, and we need to identify or locate the resource carrying the data we want to extract. Before proceeding with data exploration and content identification, it will be beneficial to plan and identify page's URLs or links that contain data.

Users can pick any URL for scraping purposes. Page links or URLs that point to a single page might also contain pagination links or links that redirect the user to other resources. Content distributed across multiple pages needs to be crawled individually by identifying the page URL. There exist sitemaps and `robots.txt` files, made available by websites, that contain links and directives for crawling-related activities.

Sitemaps

A `sitemap.xml` file is an XML file that holds the information related to page URLs. Maintaining a sitemap is an easy way to inform search engines about the URLs the website contains. Search-engine-based scripts crawl the links in sitemaps and use the links found for indexing and various purposes such as **search engine optimization (SEO)**.

URLs found inside a sitemap generally exist with additional information such as created date, modified date, new URL, removed URL, and many more. These are normally found wrapped in XML tags. In this case, we have `<sitemap>` with `<loc>`, as shown in the following screenshot:

Sitemap content from https://www.samsclub.com/

Sitemaps are accessed by adding `sitemap.xml` to the URL, for example, `https://www.samsclub.com/sitemap.xml`.

There's no obligation for `sitemap.xml` to exist for all websites. Sitemaps might carry individual URLs for pages, products, categories, and inner sitemap files that can be processed easily for scraping purposes, instead of exploring web pages for links and collecting all of them from each website, one by one.

The robots.txt file

`robots.txt`, also known as the robots exclusion protocol, is a web-based standard used by websites to exchange information with automated scripts. In general, `robots.txt` carries instructions regarding URLs, pages, and directories on their site to web robots (also known as **web wanderers**, **crawlers**, or **spiders**) using directives such as **Allow**, **Disallow**, **Sitemap**, and **Crawl-delay** to direct their behavior:

The robots.txt file from https://www.samsclub.com/

For any provided website addresses or URLs, the `robots.txt` file can be accessed by adding `robots.txt` to the URL,
for example, `https://www.samsclub.com/robots.txt` or
`https://www.test-domainname.com/robots.txt`.

As seen in the preceding screenshot (*The robots.txt file from https://www.samsclub.com/*), there are **Allow**, **Disallow**, and **Sitemap** directives listed inside `https://www.samsclub.com/robots.txt`:

- **Allow** permits web robots to access the link it carries
- **Disallow** conveys restriction of access to a given resource
- **User-agent: *** shows that the listed directives are to be followed by all agents

For access violation caused by web crawlers and spammers, the following steps can be taken by website admins:

- Enhance security mechanisms to restrict any unauthorized access to the website
- Impose a block on the traced IP address
- Take necessary legal action

Web crawlers should obey the directives mentioned in the file, but for normal data extraction purposes, there's no restriction imposed until and unless the crawling scripts hamper website traffic, or if they access personal data from the web. Again, it's not obligatory that a `robots.txt` file should be available on each website.

 For more information on directives and `robots.txt`, please visit `http://www.robotstxt.org/`.

Summary

In this chapter, we have explored some core technologies and tools that are relevant to the World Wide Web and that are required for web scraping.

Identifying and exploring content via an introduction to web development tools, and seeking page URLs for target data, were the main focus of this chapter.

In the next chapter, we will be using the Python programming language to interact with the web, and exploring major web-related Python libraries, which we'll use to examine web contents.

Further reading

- AngularJS: `https://www.angularjs.org`, `https://www.angular.io`
- AJAX: `http://api.jquery.com/jquery.ajax/`, `https://www.w3schools.com/js/js_ajax_intro.asp`
- Browser developer tools: `https://developers.google.com/web/tools/chrome-devtools/`, `https://developer.mozilla.org/son/docs/Tools`
- CSS: `https://www.w3schools.com/css/`, `https://www.w3.org/Style/CSS/`

- Cookies: `https://www.aboutcookies.org/, www.allaboutcookies.org`
- HTTP: `https://www.w3.org/Protocols/, https://developer.mozilla.org/en-US/docs/Web/HTTP`
- HTTP methods: `https://restfulapi.net/http-methods/`
- Quick reference to HTTP headers: `http://jkorpela.fi/http.html`
- Web technology for developers: `https://developer.mozilla.org/en-US/docs/Web`
- Markup systems and the future of scholarly text processing: `http://xml.coverpages.org/coombs.html`
- JSON Lines: `http://jsonlines.org/`
- jQuery: `https://jquery.com/, https://www.w3schools.com/jquery/`
- JavaScript: `https://developer.mozilla.org/en-US/docs/Web/JavaScript, https://www.javascript.com/`
- Robots Exclusion Protocol: `http://www.robotstxt.org/`
- Reverse engineering: `https://insights.globalspec.com/article/7367/how-does-reverse-engineering-work`
- Sitemaps: `https://www.sitemaps.org/`
- XML: `https://www.w3schools.com/xml/, https://www.w3.org/XML/`

Section 2: Beginning Web Scraping 2

In this section, you will learn how to plan, analyze, and process the required data from a target website via the use of web scraping and Python programming. Information regarding effective tools and various data collecting techniques will be explored.

This section consists of the following chapters:

- Chapter 2, *Python and the Web – Using urllib and Requests*
- Chapter 3, *Using LXML, XPath, and CSS Selectors*
- Chapter 4, *Scraping Using pyquery – a Python Library*
- Chapter 5, *Web Scraping Using Scrapy and Beautiful Soup*

Python and the Web – Using urllib and Requests

2

From the previous chapter, we now have an idea about what web scraping is, what the core development technologies that exist are, and where or how we can plan to find the information we are looking for.

Web scraping requires tools and techniques to be implemented and deployed using scripts or programs. The Python programming language consists of a huge set of libraries that are fit for interacting with the web and for scraping purposes. In this chapter, we will communicate with web resources using Python; we'll also explore and search for the contents to be extracted from the web.

This chapter will also provide a detailed overview of using Python libraries such as `requests` and `urllib`.

In particular, we will learn about the following topics:

- Setting Python and its required libraries, `requests` and `urllib`, to load URLs
- A detailed overview of `requests` and `urllib`
- Implementing HTTP methods (GET/POST)

We assume that you have some prior basic experience of using the Python programming language. If not, then please refer to Python tutorials from W3schools (`https://www.w3schools.com/python/default.asp`), Python course (`https://python-course.eu/`), or search Google for *learn Python programming*.

Technical requirements

We will be using Python 3.7.0, which has been installed on the Windows operating system. There are plenty of choices for code editors; choose one that is convenient to use and deal with the libraries that are used in this chapter's code examples. We will be using PyCharm (Community Edition `https://www.jetbrains.com/pycharm/download/download-thanks.html?platform=windowscode=PCC`) from JetBrains and Python IDLE (`https://www.python.org/downloads/`) side by side.

To follow along with this chapter, you will need to install the following applications:

- Python 3.7.* or the latest version that's appropriate for your OS: `https://www.python.org/downloads/`
- The `pip` Python package management: `https://packaging.python.org/tutorials/installing-packages/`
- Either Google Chrome or Mozilla Firefox
- JetBrains PyCharm or Visual Studio Code

The Python libraries that are required for this chapter are as follows:

- `requests`
- `urllib`

The code files for this chapter are available online on GitHub: `https://github.com/PacktPublishing/Hands-On-Web-Scraping-with-Python/tree/master/Chapter02`.

Accessing the web with Python

Python is a programming language that's used to code various types of applications, from simple scripts to AI algorithms and web frameworks. We will be writing scripts in Python to access the URLs that we are interested in from a data extraction or scraping perspective.

A number of Python libraries exist for HTTP communication and web-related purposes (including `http`, `cookielib`, `urllib`, `requests`, `html`, `socket`, `json`, `xmlrpc`, `httplib2`, and `urllib3`). We will explore and use a few of them that have been praised by the programmers' community for HTTP access or client-server communication. The `urllib` and `requests` Python modules are the ones we are interested in using. These libraries possess various functions that can be used to communicate with the web using Python and deal with HTTP requests and responses.

In order to start a few coding tasks and explore the Python-based modules straightaway, let's verify that we have installed all the Python resources we want before moving on.

Setting things up

It is assumed that Python has been preinstalled. If not, please visit `https://www.python.org/downloads/` and `https://www.python.org/download/other/` for the latest Python version for your operating system. Regarding the general setup and installation procedure, please visit `https://realpython.com/installing-python/` to find out how to install Python on your chosen platform. We will be using the Windows operating system here.

To verify that we have all the required tools available, let's check that Python and `pip` are installed and are up to date.

 `pip` package management system is used to install and manage software packages written in Python. More on installing Python packages and `pip` can be found at `https://packaging.python.org/tutorials/installing-packages/`.

We will be using Python 3.7 on the Windows operating system. Press Windows + *R* to open the **Run** box and type `cmd` to get the command-line interface:

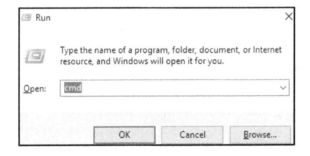

Opening the command-line interface on the Windows operating system

Now, move to your root directory and type the following command:

```
C:\> python –version
Python 3.7.0
```

The preceding command will provide us with the Python version that we currently have on our system. Let's get some information on the `pip` version that we are using. The following command will display the current `pip` version, as well as its location:

```
C:\> pip --version

pip 18.1 from c:\python37\lib\site-packages\pip (python 3.7)
```

We are happy to proceed after seeing the preceding responses. If you encounter an error stating **Application not found** or `not recognized as an internal or external command`, then we need to reinstall Python or check for the proper drive that was used during installation.

It's always advisable to check for the system and library version and keep them updated unless a specific version is required.

To update `pip` to its latest release, use the following command:

```
C:\> python -m pip install --upgrade pip
```

You can verify the libraries we wish to use, that is, `requests` and `urllib`, either from the command line or by importing the Python IDE and getting details on the package using the `help()` method:

```
C:\> pip install requests

Requirement already satisfied: requests in c:\python37\lib\site-packages
(2.19.1)
```

As shown in the preceding code, we are trying to install `requests`, but the command returns `Requirement already satisfied`. The `pip` command checks for an existing installation on the system before installing a fresh library.

In the following code block, we will be using the Python IDE to import `urllib`. We'll view its details using Python's built-in `help()` method.

The >>> symbol in code represents use of the Python IDE; it accepts the code or instructions and displays the output on the next line:

```
>>> import urllib
>>> help(urllib) #display documentation available for urllib
```

The following is the output:

```
Help on package urllib:
NAME
 urllib
PACKAGE CONTENTS
 error
 parse
 request
 response
 robotparser
FILE
 c:\python37\lib\urllib\__init__.py
```

Similar to the previous code, lets import requests using the Python IDE:

```
>>> import requests
>>> requests.__version__ #display requests version

'2.21.0'

>>> help(requests)    #display documentation available for requests

Help on package requests:
NAME
 requests
DESCRIPTION
 Requests HTTP Library
 ~~~~~~~~~~~~~~~~~~
 Requests is an HTTP library, written in Python, for human beings.
```

If we import urllib or requests and these libraries don't exist, the result will throw an error:

```
ModuleNotFoundError: No module named 'requests'
```

For missing modules or in the previous case, install the module first; use pip as follows to install or upgrade. You can install it from your command line, as follows:

```
C:\> pip install requests
```

You can also upgrade the module version using the --upgrade argument:

```
C:\> pip install requests --upgrade
```

Loading URLs

Now that we've confirmed the required libraries and system requirements, we will proceed with loading the URLs. While looking for contents from a URL, it is also necessary to confirm and verify the exact URL that has been chosen for the required content. Contents can be found on single web pages or scattered across multiple pages, and it might not always be the HTML sources we are looking for.

We will load some URLs and explore the content using a couple of tasks.

Before loading URLs using Python script, it's also advisable to verify the URLs are working properly and contain the detail we are looking for, using web browsers. Developer tools can also be used for similar scenarios, as discussed in Chapter 1, *Web Scraping Fundamentals*, in the *Developer tools* section.

Task 1: To view data related to the listings of the most popular websites from Wikipedia. We will identify data from the **Site**, **Domain**, and **Type** columns in the page source.

We will follow the steps at the following link to achieve our task (a data extraction-related activity will be done in Chapter 3, *Using LXML, XPath and CSS Selectors*): https://en.wikipedia.org/wiki/List_of_most_popular_websites.

Search Wikipedia for the information we are looking for. The preceding link can be easily viewed in a web browser. The content is in tabular format (as shown in the following screenshot), and so the data can be collected by repeatedly using the select, copy, and paste actions, or by collecting all the text inside the table.

However, such actions will not result in the content that we are interested in being in a desirable format, or it will require extra editing and formatting tasks being performed on the text to achieve the desired result. We are also not interested in the page source that's obtained from the browser:

Site ⬦	Domain ⬦	Alexa top 50 global sites (As of May 16, 2018)[3] ⬦	SimilarWeb top 50 sites (As of March 2018)[4] ⬦	Type ⬦	Principal country ⬦
Google	google.com	1 (—)	1 (—)	Internet services and products	U.S.
YouTube	youtube.com	2 (—)	3 (—)	Video sharing	U.S.
Facebook	facebook.com	3 (—)	2 (—)	Social network	U.S.
Baidu	baidu.com	4 (—)	4 (▲11)	Search engine	China
Wikipedia	wikipedia.org	5 (—)	5 (—)	Encyclopedia	U.S.
Reddit	reddit.com	6 (▲13)	37 (▼6)	Social news and entertainment	U.S.
Yahoo!	yahoo.com	7 (▼1)	7 (▼3)	Portal and media	U.S.
Tencent QQ	qq.com	8 (▲1)	11 (▲27)	Portal	China
Taobao	taobao.com	9 (▲3)	35 (▲16)	Online shopping	China
Google India	google.co.in	10 (▼3)	6 (▲4)	Internet services and products	India
Amazon	amazon.com	11 (▼3)	23 (▼12)	E-commerce and cloud computing	U.S.
Tmall	tmall.com	12 (▲10)	51 (▲31)	Online shopping	China
Twitter	twitter.com	13 (▲1)	10 (▼4)	Social network	U.S.
Sohu	sohu.com	14 (▲3)	84 (▲120)	Portal	China
Instagram	instagram.com	15 (—)	20 (▼2)	Photo sharing and social media	U.S.
VK	vk.com	16 (▼3)	21 (▼9)	Social network	Russia
Windows Live	live.com	17 (▼6)	19 (▼12)	Software plus services	U.S.
Jingdong Mall	jd.com	18 (▲1)	69	E-commerce	China
Sina Corp	sina.com.cn	19 (▼1)	122 (▼12)	Portal and instant messaging	China
Sina Weibo	weibo.com	20 (▲4)	97 (▼1)	Social network	China
Yandex	yandex.ru	21 (▲9)	16 (▼2)	Internet services and products	Russia
Haosou	360.cn	22 (▲4)	124 (▼35)	Internet security and search engine	China
Google Japan	google.co.jp	23 (—)	25 (▲2)	Internet services and products	Japan
Google UK	google.co.uk	24 (▼3)	15 (▼7)	Internet services and products	UK

List of websites

Changes in ranking are since December 28, 2016.

Page from Wikipedia, that is, https://en.wikipedia.org/wiki/List_of_most_popular_websites

After finalizing the link that contains the content we require, let's load the link using Python. We are making a request to the link and willing to see the response returned by both libraries, that is, `urllib` and `requests`:

1. Let's use `urllib`:

```
>>> import urllib.request as req #import module request from urllib
>>> link =
"https://en.wikipedia.org/wiki/List_of_most_popular_websites"
>>> response = req.urlopen(link)  #load the link using method
urlopen()

>>> print(type(response))    #print type of response object
    <class 'http.client.HTTPResponse'>

>>> print(response.read()) #read response content
b'<!DOCTYPE html>\n<html class="client-nojs" lang="en"
dir="ltr">\n<head>\n<meta charset="UTF-8"/>\n<title>List of most
popular websites –
Wikipedia</title>\n<script>.....,"wgCanonicalSpecialPageName":false,
"wgNamespaceNumber":0,"wgPageName":"List_of_most_popular_websites",
"wgTitle":"List of most popular websites",......
```

The `urlopen()` function from `urllib.request` has been passed with the selected URL or request that has been made to the URL and `response` is received, that is, `HTTPResponse.response` that's received for the request made can be read using the `read()` method.

2. Now, let's use `requests`:

```
>>> import requests
>>> link =
"https://en.wikipedia.org/wiki/List_of_most_popular_websites"
>>> response = requests.get(link)

>>> print(type(response))
    <class 'requests.models.Response'>

>>> content = response.content #response content received
>>> print(content[0:150])   #print(content) printing first 150
character from content

b'<!DOCTYPE html>\n<html class="client-nojs" lang="en"
dir="ltr">\n<head>\n<meta charset="UTF-8"/>\n<title>List of most
popular websites - Wikipedia</title>'
```

Here, we are using the `requests` module to load the page source, just like we did using `urllib.requests` with the `get()` method, which accepts a URL as a parameter. The `response` type for both examples has also been checked.

The output that's displayed in the preceding code blocks has been shortened. You can find the code files for this at `https://github.com/PacktPublishing/Hands-On-Web-Scraping-with-Python`.

In the preceding examples, the page content—or the `response` object—contains the details we were looking for, that is, the **Site**, **Domain**, and **Type** columns.

We can choose any one library to deal with the HTTP request and response. Detailed information on these two Python libraries with examples is provided in the next section, *URL handling and operations with urllib and requests*.

Let's have a look at the following screenshot:

Wikipedia.com page content, viewed using Python libraries

Further activities like processing and parsing can be applied to content like this in order to extract the required data. More details about further processing tools/techniques and parsing can be found in Chapter 3, *Using LXML, XPath, and CSS Selectors*, Chapter 4, *Scraping Using pyquery – a Python Library*, and Chapter 5, *Web Scraping Using Scrapy and Beautiful Soup*.

Task 2: Load and save the page content from https://www.samsclub.com/robots.txt and https://www.samsclub.com/sitemap.xml using urllib and requests.

Generally, websites provide files in their root path (for more information on these files, please refer to Chapter 1, *Web Scraping Fundamentals*, the *Data finding techniques for the web* section):

- robots.txt: This contains information for the crawler, web agents, and so on

- sitemap.xml: This contains links to recently modified files, published files, and so on

From *Task 1*, we were able to load the URL and retrieve its content. Saving the content to local files using libraries methods and using file handling concepts will be implemented in this task. Saving content to local files and working on content with tasks like parsing and traversing can be really quick and even reduce network resources:

1. Load and save the content from `https://www.samsclub.com/robots.txt` using `urllib`:

   ```
   >>> import urllib.request

   >>>
   urllib.request.urlretrieve('https://www.samsclub.com/robots.txt')
   ('C:\\Users\\*****\AppData\\Local\\Temp\\tmpjs_cktnc',
   <http.client.HTTPMessage object at 0x04029110>)

   >>> urllib.request.urlretrieve(link,"testrobots.txt")
   #urlretrieve(url, filename=None)
   ('testrobots.txt', <http.client.HTTPMessage object at 0x04322DF0>)
   ```

   The `urlretrieve()` function, that is, `urlretrieve(url, filename=None, reporthook=None, data=None)`, from `urllib.request` returns a tuple with the filename and HTTP headers. You can find this file in the `C:\\Users..Temp` directory if no path is given; otherwise, the file will be generated in the current working directory with the name provided to the `urlretrieve()` method as the second argument. This was `testrobots.txt` in the preceding code:

   ```
   >>> import urllib.request
   >>> import os
   >>> content =
   urllib.request.urlopen('https://www.samsclub.com/robots.txt').read(
   ) #reads robots.txt content from provided URL

   >>> file =
   open(os.getcwd()+os.sep+"contents"+os.sep+"robots.txt","wb")
   #Creating a file robots.txt inside directory 'contents' that exist
   under current working directory (os.getcwd())

   >>> file.write(content) #writing content to file robots.txt opened
   in line above. If the file doesn't exist inside directory
   'contents', Python will throw exception "File not Found"

   >>> file.close() #closes the file handle
   ```

   In the preceding code, we are reading the URL and writing the content found using a file handling concept.

2. Load and save the content from `https://www.samsclub.com/sitemap.xml` using `requests`:

```
>>> link="https://www.samsclub.com/sitemap.xml"
>>> import requests
>>> content = requests.get(link).content
>>> content

b'<?xml version="1.0" encoding="UTF-8"?>\n<sitemapindex
xmlns="http://www.sitemaps.org/schemas/sitemap/0.9">\n<sitemap><loc
>https://www.samsclub.com/sitemap_categories.xml</loc></sitemap>\n<
sitemap><loc>https://www.samsclub.com/sitemap_products_1.xml</loc><
/sitemap>\n<sitemap><loc>https://www.samsclub.com/sitemap_products_
2.xml</loc></sitemap>\n<sitemap><loc>https://www.samsclub.com/sitem
ap_locators.xml</loc></sitemap>\n</sitemapindex>'

>>> file =
open(os.getcwd()+os.sep+"contents"+os.sep+"sitemap.xml","wb")
#Creating a file robots.txt inside directory 'contents' that exist
under current working directory (os.getcwd())

>>> file.write(content) #writing content to file robots.txt opened
in line above. If the file doesn't exist inside directory
'contents', Python will throw exception "File not Found"

>>> file.close() #closes the file handle
```

In both cases, we were able to find the content from the respective URL and save it to individual files and locations. The contents from the preceding code was found as bytes literals, for example, `b'<!DOCTYPE` ... or `b'<?xml`. Page content can also be retrieved in a text format, such as `requests.get(link).text`.

We can use the `decode()` method to convert bytes into a string and the `encode()` method to convert a string into bytes, as shown in the following code:

```
>>> link="https://www.samsclub.com/sitemap.xml"
>>> import requests
>>> content = requests.get(link).text   #using 'text'
>>> content

'<?xml version="1.0" encoding="UTF-8"?>\n<sitemapindex
xmlns="http://www.sitemaps.org/schemas/sitemap/0.9">\n<sitemap><loc>https:/
/www.samsclub.com/sitemap_categories.xml</loc></sitemap>\n<sitemap><loc>htt
ps://www.samsclub.com/sitemap_products_1.xml</loc></sitemap>\n<sitemap><loc
>https://www.samsclub.com/sitemap_products_2.xml</loc></sitemap>\n<sitemap>
<loc>https://www.samsclub.com/sitemap_locators.xml</loc></sitemap>\n</sitem
apindex>'
```

```
>>> content = requests.get(link).content
>>> content.decode() # decoding 'content' , decode('utf-8')

'<?xml version="1.0" encoding="UTF-8"?>\n<sitemapindex
xmlns="http://www.sitemaps.org/schemas/sitemap/0.9">\n<sitemap><loc>https:/
/www.samsclub.com/sitemap_categories.xml</loc></sitemap>\n<sitemap><loc>htt
ps://www.samsclub.com/sitemap_products_1.xml</loc></sitemap>\n<sitemap><loc
>https://www.samsclub.com/sitemap_products_2.xml</loc></sitemap>\n<sitemap>
<loc>https://www.samsclub.com/sitemap_locators.xml</loc></sitemap>\n</sitem
apindex>'
```

Identifying a proper character set or `charset` is important when dealing with various domains and type of documents. To identify a proper `charset` encoding type, we can seek help from the page source for the `<meta>` tag by using `content-type` or `charset`.

The `<meta>` tag with the `charset` attribute, that is, `<meta charset="utf-8"/>`, is identified from the page source, as shown in the following screenshot (or `<meta http-equiv="content-type" content="text/html; charset=utf-8">`:

Identifying charset from the document response or page source

Also, the content for `<meta http-equiv="content-type" content="text/html; charset=utf-8">` can be obtained from the response header, as highlighted in the following screenshot:

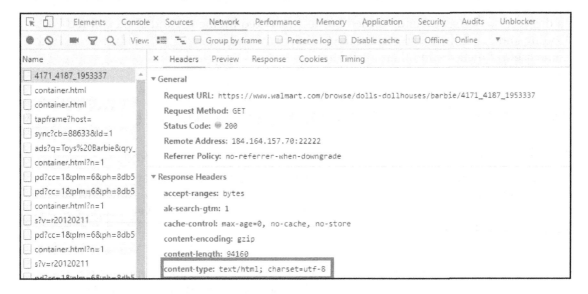

Identifying charset through the browser DevTools, Network panel, Headers tab, and response headers

Using Python code, we can find `charset` in the HTTP header:

```
>>> import urllib.request
>>> someRequest = urllib.request.urlopen(URL) #load/Open the URL
>>> urllib.request.getheaders() #Lists all HTTP headers.

>>> urllib.request.getheader("Content-Type") #return value of header
'Content-Type'

'text/html; charset=ISO-8859-1' or 'utf-8'
```

`charset` that was identified will be used to encode and decode with `requests.get(link).content.decode('utf-8')`.

Python 3.0 uses the concepts of *text* and (binary) *data* instead of Unicode strings and 8-bit strings. All text is Unicode; however, *encoded* Unicode is represented as binary data. The type that's used to hold text is `str` (https://docs.python.org/3/library/stdtypes.html#str), and the type that's used to hold data is bytes (https://docs.python.org/3/library/stdtypes.html#bytes). For more information on Python 3.0, please visit https://docs.python.org/3/whatsnew/3.0.html.

In this section, we set up and verified our technical requirements, and also explored URL loading and content viewing. In the next section, we will explore Python libraries to find some useful functions and their attributes.

URL handling and operations with urllib and requests

For our primary motive of extracting data from a web page, it's necessary to work with URLs. In the examples we've seen so far, we have noticed some pretty simple URLs being used with Python to communicate with their source or contents. The web scraping process often requires the use of different URLs from various domains that do not exist in the same format or pattern.

Developers might also face many cases where there will be a requirement for URL manipulation (altering, cleaning) to access the resource quickly and conveniently. URL handling and operations are used to set up, alter query parameters, or clean up unnecessary parameters. It also passes the required request headers with the appropriate values and identification of the proper HTTP method for making requests. There will be many cases where you will find URL-related operations that are identified using browser **DevTools** or the **Network** panel.

The `urllib` and `requests` Python libraries, which we will be using throughout this book, deal with URL and network-based client-server communication. These libraries provide various easy to use functions and attributes, and we will be exploring a few important ones.

urllib

The `urllib` library is a standard Python package that collects several modules to work with HTTP-related communication models. Modules inside `urllib` are specially designed and contain functions and classes that deal with various types of client-server communication.

 Similarly named packages also exist, like `urllib2`, an extensible library, and `urllib3`, a powerful HTTP client that addresses missing features from Python standard libraries.

Two of the most important `urllib` modules that deal with URL requests and responses are as follows. We will be using these modules in this and upcoming chapters:

- `urllib.request`: Used for opening and reading URLs and requesting or accessing network resources (cookies, authentication, and so on)
- `urllib.response`: This module is used to provide a response to the requests that are generated

There are a number of functions and public attributes that exist to handle request information and process response data that's relevant to HTTP requests, such as `urlopen()`, `urlretrieve()`, `getcode()`, `getheaders()`, `getheader()`, `geturl()`, `read()`, `readline()`, and many more.

We can use Python's built-in `dir()` function to display a module's content, such as its classes, functions, and attributes, as shown in the following code:

```
>>> import urllib.request
>>> dir(urllib.request) #list features available from urllib.request

['AbstractBasicAuthHandler', 'AbstractDigestAuthHandler',
'AbstractHTTPHandler', 'BaseHandler', 'CacheFTPHandler',
'ContentTooShortError', 'DataHandler', 'FTPHandler', 'FancyURLopener',
'FileHandler', 'HTTPBasicAuthHandler', 'HTTPCookieProcessor',....'Request',
'URLError', 'URLopener',......'pathname2url', 'posixpath', 'proxy_bypass',
'proxy_bypass_environment', 'proxy_bypass_registry', 'quote', 're',
'request_host', 'socket', 'splitattr', 'splithost', 'splitpasswd',
'splitport', 'splitquery', 'splittag', 'splittype', 'splituser',
'splitvalue', 'ssl', 'string', 'sys', 'tempfile', 'thishost', 'time',
'to_bytes', 'unquote', 'unquote_to_bytes', 'unwrap', 'url2pathname',
'urlcleanup', 'urljoin', 'urlopen', 'urlparse', 'urlretrieve', 'urlsplit',
'urlunparse', 'warnings']
```

The `urlopen()` function accepts a URL or an `urllib.request.Request` object, such as `requestObj`, and returns a response through the `urllib.response read()` function, as shown in the following code:

```
>>> import urllib.request
>>> link='https://www.google.com'

>>> linkRequest = urllib.request.urlopen(link) #open link
>>> print(type(linkRequest)) #object type
    <class 'http.client.HTTPResponse'>

>>> linkResponse = urllib.request.urlopen(link).read() #open link and read
content
>>> print(type(linkResponse))
```

```
    <class 'bytes'>

>>> requestObj =
urllib.request.Request('https:/www.samsclub.com/robots.txt')
>>> print(type(requestObj)) #object type
    <class 'urllib.request.Request'>

>>> requestObjResponse = urllib.request.urlopen(requestObj).read()
>>> print(type(requestObjResponse))  #object type
    <class 'bytes'>
```

The object types that are returned are different in the case of linkRequest and
requestObj from the urlopen() function and class request, respectively.
The linkResponse and requestObjResponse objects were also created, which holds the
urllib.response information of the read() function.

> Generally, urlopen() is used to read a response from the URL, while
> urllib.request.Request is used to send extra arguments like
> data or headers, and even to specify the HTTP method and retrieve a
> response. It can be used as follows:
>
> ```
> urllib.request.Request(url, data=None, headers={},
> origin_req_host=None, unverifiable=False, method=None)
> ```

urllib.response and its functions, such as read() and readline(), are used with
the urllib.request objects.

If the request that was made was successful and received a response from the proper URL,
we can check the HTTP status code, the HTTP method that was used, as well as the
returned URL to view a description:

- getcode() returns a HTTP status code. The same result can also be achieved
  using the code and status public attributes, as shown in the following code:

  ```
  >>> linkRequest.getcode()  #can also be used as: linkRequest.code
  or linkRequest.status

     200
  ```

- geturl() returns current the URL. It is sometimes handy to verify whether any
  redirection occurred. The url attribute can be used for a similar purpose:

  ```
  >>> linkRequest.geturl()   # can also be used as: linkRequest.url

  'https://www.google.com'
  ```

- `_method` returns a HTTP method; `GET` is the default response:

```
>>> linkRequest._method
'GET'
```

- `getheaders()` returns a list with tuples that contains HTTP headers. As we can see from the following code, we can determine values regarding cookie, content type, date, and so on from the output:

```
>>> linkRequest.getheaders()

[('Date','Sun, 30 Dec 2018 07:00:25 GMT'),('Expires',
'-1'),('Cache-Control','private, max-age=0'),('Content-
Type','text/html; charset=ISO-8859-1'),('P3P', 'CP="This is not a
P3P policy! See g.co/p3phelp for more info."'),('Server',
'gws'),('X-XSS-Protection', '1; mode=block'),('X-Frame-
Options','SAMEORIGIN'),('Set-Cookie', '1P_JAR=.....; expires=Tue,
29-Jan-2019 07:00:25 GMT; path=/; domain=.google.com'),('Set-Cookie
'NID=152=DANr9NtDzU_glKFRgVsOm2eJQpyLijpRav7OAAd97QXGX6WwYMC59dDPe.
; expires=Mon, 01-Jul-2019 07:00:25 GMT; path=/;
domain=.google.com; HttpOnly'),('Alt-Svc', 'quic=":443";
ma=2592000; v="44,43,39,35"'),('Accept-Ranges', 'none'),('Vary',
'Accept-Encoding'),('Connection', 'close')]
```

- Individual request-based headers can also be retrieved when `getheader()` is passed with desired header element, as shown in the following code. Here, we can see we can obtain the value for the **Content-Type** header. The same result can also be achieved using the `info()` function:

```
>>> linkRequest.getheader("Content-Type")

'text/html; charset=ISO-8859-1'
```

```
>>> linkRequest.info()["content-type"]
'text/html; charset=ISO-8859-1'
```

We have used code blocks and found the output that's relevant to our request and response. Web browsers also allow us to trace request/response-related information using browser DevTools (browser-based developer tools).

The following screenshot displays the **Network** panel and the **Doc** tab, which includes the **Headers** option. This contains various sections, such as **General**, **Response Headers**, and **Request Headers**. Basic request and response-related information can be found inside the **Headers** option:

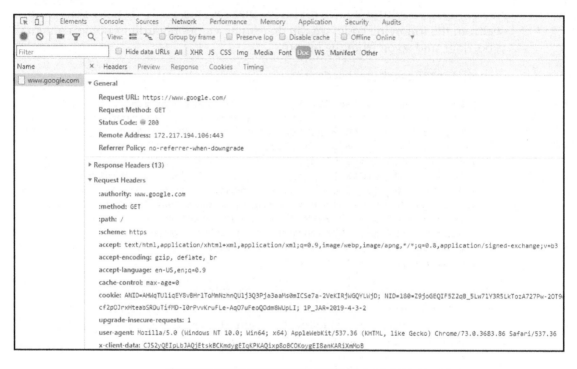

Network panel and Document tab with General and Request header information

Note `urllib.error` deals with the exceptions raised by `urllib.request`. Exceptions like `URLError` and `HTTPError` can be raised for a request.The following code demonstrates the use of `urllib.error`:

 Exception handling deals with error handling and management in programming. Code that uses exception handling is also considered an effective technique and is often prescribed to adapt.

```
>>> import urllib.request as request
>>> import urllib.error as error

>>> try:  #attempting an error case
        request.urlopen("https://www.python.ogr") #wrong URL is passed to
urlopen()
```

```
    except error.URLError as e:
        print("Error Occurred: ",e.reason)
Error Occurred: [Errno 11001] getaddrinfo failed #output
```

urllib.parse is used to encode/decode request(data) or links, add/update headers, and analyze, parse, and manipulate URLs. Parsed URL strings or objects are processed with urllib.request.

Furthermore, urlencode(), urlparse(), urljoin(), urlsplit(), quote_plus() are a few important functions that are available in urllib.parse, as shown in the following code:

```
>>> import urllib.parse as urlparse
>>> print(dir(urlparse)) #listing features from urlparse
```

We get the following output:

```
['DefragResult', 'DefragResultBytes', 'MAX_CACHE_SIZE', 'ParseResult',
'ParseResultBytes', 'Quoter', 'ResultBase', 'SplitResult',
'SplitResultBytes', .........'clear_cache', 'collections', 'namedtuple',
'non_hierarchical', 'parse_qs', 'parse_qsl', 'quote', 'quote_from_bytes',
'quote_plus', 're', 'scheme_chars', 'splitattr', 'splithost', 'splitnport',
'splitpasswd', 'splitport', 'splitquery', 'splittag', 'splittype',
'splituser', 'splitvalue', 'sys', 'to_bytes', 'unquote', 'unquote_plus',
'unquote_to_bytes', 'unwrap', 'urldefrag', 'urlencode', 'urljoin',
'urlparse', 'urlsplit', 'urlunparse', 'urlunsplit', 'uses_fragment',
'uses_netloc', 'uses_params', 'uses_query', 'uses_relative']
```

The urlsplit() function from urllib.parse splits the URL that's passed into the namedtuple object. Each name in tuple identifies parts of the URL. These parts can be separated and retrieved in other variables and used as needed. The following code implements urlsplit() for amazonUrl:

```
>>> amazonUrl
='https://www.amazon.com/s/ref=nb_sb_noss?url=search-alias%3Dstripbooks-int
l-ship&field-keywords=Packt+Books'

>>> print(urlparse.urlsplit(amazonUrl)) #split amazonURL
SplitResult(scheme='https', netloc='www.amazon.com',
path='/s/ref=nb_sb_noss', query='url=search-alias%3Dstripbooks-intl-
ship&field-keywords=Packt+Books', fragment='')

>>> print(urlparse.urlsplit(amazonUrl).query) #query-string from amazonURL
'url=search-alias%3Dstripbooks-intl-ship&field-keywords=Packt+Books'

>>> print(urlparse.urlsplit(amazonUrl).scheme) #return URL scheme
'https'
```

Using the `urlparse()` function from `urllib.parse` results in the `ParseResult` object. It differs in terms of the parameters (`params` and `path`) that are retrieved in he URL compared to `urlsplit()`. The following code prints the object from `urlparse()`:

```
>>> print(urlparse.urlparse(amazonUrl)) #parsing components of amazonUrl

    ParseResult(scheme='https', netloc='www.amazon.com',
path='/s/ref=nb_sb_noss', params='', query='url=search-alias%3Dstripbooks-
intl-ship&field-keywords=Packt+Books', fragment='')
```

Let's confirm the differences between `urlparse()` and `urlsplit()`. The `localUrl` that's created is parsed with both `urlsplit()` and `urlparse()`. `params` is only available with `urlparse()`:

```
import urllib.parse as urlparse
>>> localUrl=
'http://localhost/programming/books;2018?browse=yes&sort=ASC#footer'

>>> print(urlparse.urlsplit(localUrl))
SplitResult(scheme='http', netloc='localhost',
path='/programming/books;2018', query='browse=yes&sort=ASC',
fragment='footer')

>>> parseLink = urlparse.urlparse(localUrl)
ParseResult(scheme='http', netloc='localhost', path='/programming/books',
params='2018', query='browse=yes&sort=ASC', fragment='footer')

>>> print(parseLink.path) #path without domain information
    '/programming/books'

>>> print(parseLink.params) #parameters
    '2018'

>>> print(parseLink.fragment) #fragment information from URL
    'footer'
```

Basically, `urllib.request.Request` accepts data and headers-related information, and `headers` can be assigned to an object using `add_header()`; for example, `object.add_header('host','hostname')` or `object.add_header('referer','refererUrl')`.

In order to request `data`, `Query Information`, or `URL arguments` need to be used as key-value pair of information that are appended to the desired URL. Such a URL is usually processed with the HTTP GET method. Query information that's passed to the request object should be encoded using `urlencode()`.

urlencode() ensures that arguments comply with the W3C standard and are accepted by the server. parse_qs() parses percent-encoded query strings to the Python dictionary. The following code demonstrates an example of using urlencode():

```
>>> import urllib.parse as urlparse
>>> data = {'param1': 'value1', 'param2': 'value2'}

>>> urlparse.urlencode(data)
 'param1=value1&param2=value2'

>>> urlparse.parse_qs(urlparse.urlencode(data))
 {'param1': ['value1'], 'param2': ['value2']}

>>> urlparse.urlencode(data).encode('utf-8')
    b'param1=value1&param2=value2'
```

You may also need to encode the special characters in a URL before processing the request to the server:

Note that urllib.parse contains the quote(), quote_plus(), and unquote() functions, which permit error-free server requests:

- quote() is generally applied to the URL path (listed with urlsplit() or urlparse()) or queried with reserved and special characters (defined by RFC 3986) before it's passed to urlencode() to ensure that the server's acceptable. Default encoding is done with UTF-8.
- quote_plus() also encodes special characters, spaces, and the URL separator, /.
- unquote() and unquote_plus() are used to revert the encoding that's applied by using quote() and quote_plus().

These functions are demonstrated in the following code:

```
>>> import urllib.parse as urlparse
>>> url="http://localhost:8080/~cache/data
file?id=1345322&display=yes&expiry=false"

>>> urlparse.quote(url)
'http%3A//localhost%3A8080/~cache/data%20file%3Fid%3D1345322%26display%3Dye
s%26expiry%3Dfalse'

>>> urlparse.unquote(url)
    'http://localhost:8080/~cache/data
file?id=1345322&display=yes&expiry=false'
```

```
>>> urlparse.quote_plus(url)
'http%3A%2F%2Flocalhost%3A8080%2F~cache%2Fdata+file%3Fid%3D1345322%26displa
y%3Dyes%26expiry%3Dfalse'

>>> urlparse.unquote_plus(url)
    'http://localhost:8080/~cache/data
file?id=1345322&display=yes&expiry=false'
```

The `urljoin()` function from `urllib.parse` helps obtain the URL from the provided arguments, as demonstrated in the following code:

```
>>> import urllib.parse as urlparse

>>> urlparse.urljoin('http://localhost:8080/~cache/','data file') #creating
URL
    'http://localhost:8080/~cache/data file'

>>> urlparse.urljoin('http://localhost:8080/~cache/data
file/','id=1345322&display=yes')
    'http://localhost:8080/~cache/data file/id=1345322&display=yes'
```

`urllib.robotparser`, as its name suggests, helps parse `robots.txt` and identifies agent-based rules. Please refer to Chapter 1, *Web Scraping Fundamentals*, the *Data finding techniques for the web* section, for more detailed information on `robots.txt`.

As we can see in the following code, `par`, which is an object of `RobotFileParser`, can be used to set a URL via the `set_url()` function. It can also read contents with the `read()` function. Functions such as `can_fetch()` can return a Boolean answer for the evaluated condition:

```
>>> import urllib.robotparser as robot
>>> par = robot.RobotFileParser()
>>> par.set_url('https://www.samsclub.com/robots.txt') #setting robots URL
>>> par.read()   #reading URL content

>>> print(par)
User-agent: *
Allow: /sams/account/signin/createSession.jsp
Disallow: /cgi-bin/
Disallow: /sams/checkout/
Disallow: /sams/account/
Disallow: /sams/cart/
Disallow: /sams/eValues/clubInsiderOffers.jsp
Disallow: /friend
Allow: /sams/account/referal/

>>> par.can_fetch('*','https://www.samsclub.com/category') #verify if URL
```

```
is 'Allow' to Crawlers
True

>>> par.can_fetch('*','https://www.samsclub.com/friend')
False
```

As we can see, `https://www.samsclub.com/friend` returns `False` when passed with the `can_fetch()` function, thus satisfying the `Disallow: /friend` directives found in `robots.txt`. Similarly, `https://www.samsclub.com/category` returns `True` as there are no listed directives that restrict the category URL.

However, there are some limitations to using `urllib.request`. Connection-based delays can occur while using functions like `urlopen()` and `urlretrieve()`. These functions return raw data and need to be converted into the required type for the parser before they can be used in the scraping process.

 Deploying threads, or threading, is considered an effective technique when dealing with HTTP requests and responses.

requests

`requests` HTTP Python library released in 2011 and is one of the most renowned HTTP libraries for developers in recent times.

Requests is an elegant and simple HTTP library for Python, built for human beings.
(source: `https://2.python-requests.org/en/master/`).

More information on `requests` can be found at `http://docs.python-requests.org/en/master/`.

Compared to other HTTP libraries in Python, `requests` is rated highly in terms of its functioning capability with HTTP. A few of its capabilities are as follows:

- Short, simple, and readable functions and attributes
- Access to various HTTP methods (GET, POST, and PUT, to name a few)

- Gets rid of manual actions, like encoding form values
- Processes query strings
- Custom headers
- Session and cookie processing
- Deals with JSON requests and content
- Proxy settings
- Deploys encoding and compliance
- API-based link headers
- Raw socket response
- Timeouts and more...

We will be using the `requests` library and accessing some of its properties. The `get()` function from `requests` is used to send a GET HTTP request to the URL provided. The object that's returned is of the `requests.model.Response` type, as shown in the following code:

```
>>> import requests
>>> link="http://www.python-requests.org"
>>> r = requests.get(link)

>>> dir(r)
['__attrs__', '__bool__', '__class__'......'_content', '_content_consumed',
'_next', 'apparent_encoding', 'close', 'connection', 'content', 'cookies',
'elapsed', 'encoding', 'headers', 'history', 'is_permanent_redirect',
'is_redirect', 'iter_content', 'iter_lines', 'json', 'links', 'next', 'ok',
'raise_for_status', 'raw', 'reason', 'request', 'status_code', 'text',
'url']

>>> print(type(r))
<class 'requests.models.Response'>
```

The `requests` library also supports HTTP requests such as PUT, POST, DELETE, HEAD, and OPTIONS using the `put()`, `post()`, `delete()`, `head()`, and `options()` methods, respectively.

The following are some `requests` attributes, along with a short explanation of each:

- `url` outputs the current URL
- The HTTP status code is found using `status_code`
- `history` is used to track redirection:

```
>>> r.url #URL of response object`
 'http://www.python-requests.org/en/master/'

>>> r.status_code #status code
 200

>>> r.history #status code of history event
 [<Response [302]>]
```

We can also obtain some details that are found when we use developer tools, such as **HTTP Header**, **Encoding**, and so on:

- `headers` returns response-related HTTP headers
- `requests.header` returns request-related HTTP headers
- `encoding` displays the `charset` that's obtained from the content:

```
>>> r.headers #response headers with information about server,
date..
{'Transfer-Encoding': 'chunked', 'Content-Type': 'text/html',
'Content-Encoding': 'gzip', 'Last-Modified': '....'Vary': 'Accept-
Encoding', 'Server': 'nginx/1.14.0 (Ubuntu)', 'X-Cname-TryFiles':
'True', 'X-Served': 'Nginx', 'X-Deity': 'web02', 'Date': 'Tue, 01
Jan 2019 12:07:28 GMT'}

>>> r.headers['Content-Type'] #specific header Content-Type
 'text/html'

>>> r.request.headers   #Request headers
{'User-Agent': 'python-requests/2.21.0', 'Accept-Encoding': 'gzip,
deflate', 'Accept': '*/*', 'Connection': 'keep-alive'}

>>> r.encoding   #response encoding
 'ISO-8859-1'
```

Page or response content can be retrieved using the `content` in bytes, whereas `text` returns a `str` string:

```
>>> r.content[0:400]   #400 bytes characters

b'\n<!DOCTYPE html PUBLIC "-//W3C//DTD XHTML 1.0 Transitional//EN"\n
....... <meta http-equiv="Content-Type" content="text/html; charset=utf-8"
/>\n <title>Requests: HTTP for Humans\xe2\x84\xa2 — Requests 2.21.0
documentation'

>>> r.text[0:400]   #sub string that is 400 string character from response

'\n<!DOCTYPE html PUBLIC "-//W3C//DTD XHTML 1.0 Transitional//EN"\n......\n
<meta http-equiv="Content-Type" content="text/html; charset=utf-8" />\n
<title>Requests: HTTP for Humansâ\x84¢ — Requests 2.21.0 documentation'
```

Furthermore, `requests` also returns a `raw` socket response from the server by using the `stream` argument in a `get()` request. We can read a raw response using the `raw.read()` function:

```
>>> r = requests.get(link, stream=True) #raw response

>>> print(type(r.raw))     #type of raw response obtained
    <class 'urllib3.response.HTTPResponse'>

>>> r.raw.read(100)   #read first 100 character from raw response
b"\x1f\x8b\x08\x00\x00\x00\x00\x00\x00\x03\xed}[o\xdcH\x96\xe6{\xfe\x8a\xa8
\xd4\xb4%O\x8bL2/JI\x96\xb2Z\x96e[U\xbe\xa8-
\xb9\xaa\x1b\x85^!\x92\x8c\xcc\xa4\xc5$Y\xbc(\x95\xae)\xa0\x1e\x06\x18\xcc\
xf3\xce\xcb\x00\xbbX`\x16\xd8\xc7\xc5>\xed\xeb\x02\xfb3f_\x16\xf5\x0b\xf6'\
xec9'\x82\x97\xbc\xc9\xb2+#g"
```

 A raw response that's received using the `raw` attribute is raw bytes of characters that haven't been transformed or automatically decoded.

`requests` handles JSON data very effectively with its built-in decoder. As we can see, URLs with JSON content can be parsed with `requests` and used as required:

```
>>> import requests
>>> link = "https://feeds.citibikenyc.com/stations/stations.json"
>>> response = requests.get(link).json()

>>> for i in range(10): #read 10 stationName from JSON response.
        print('Station ',response['stationBeanList'][i]['stationName'])
```

```
Station W 52 St & 11 Ave
Station Franklin St & W Broadway
Station St James Pl & Pearl St
. . . . . . . .
Station Clinton St & Joralemon St
Station Nassau St & Navy St
Station Hudson St & Reade St
```

Note that, requests uses urllib3 for session and for raw socket response. At the time of writing, requests version 2.21.0 was available.

Crawling the script might use any of the mentioned or available HTTP libraries to make web-based communications. Most of the time, functions and attributes from multiple libraries will make this task easy. In the next section, we will be using the requests library to implement the HTTP (GET/POST) methods.

Implementing HTTP methods

Generally, web-based interaction or communication between the web page and the user or reader is achieved as follows:

- The user or reader can access the web page to read or navigate through information that's presented to them
- The user or reader can also submit certain information to the web page using the HTML form, such as by searching, logging in, user registration, password recovery, and so on

In this section, we will be using the requests Python library to implement common HTTP methods (GET and POST) that execute the HTTP-based communication scenario we listed previously.

GET

A command way to request information is to use safe methods since the resource state is not altered. The GET parameters, also known as query strings, are visible in the URL. They are appended to the URL using ? and are available as key=value pairs.

Generally, a processed URLs without any specified HTTP methods are normally GET requests. A request that's made using GET can be cached and bookmarked. There are also length restrictions while making a GET request. Some examples URLs are as follows:

- `http://www.test-domain.com`
- `http://www.test-domain.com/indexes/`
- `http://www.test-domain.com/data file?id=1345322&display=yes`

In the preceding sections, requests were made to normal URLs such as `robots.txt` and `sitemap.xml`, both of which use the HTTP GET method. The `get()` function from `requests` accepts URLs, parameters, and headers:

```
import requests
link="http://localhost:8080/~cache"

queries= {'id':'123456','display':'yes'}

addedheaders={'user-agent':''}

#request made with parameters and headers
r = requests.get(link, params=queries, headers=addedheaders)
print(r.url)
```

This is the output of the preceding code:

`http://localhst:8080/~cache?id=123456+display=yes`

POST

These are known as secure requests that are made to a source. The requested resource state can be altered. Data that's posted or sent to the requested URL is not visible in the URL; instead, it's transferred to the request body. A request that's made using POST isn't cached or bookmarked and has no restrictions in terms of length.

In the following example, a simple HTTP request and response service (source: `http://httpbin.org/`) has been used to make a POST request.

`pageUrl` accepts data to be posted, as defined in `params` to `postUrl`. Custom headers are assigned as `headers`. The `post()` function from the `requests` library accepts URLs, data, and headers, and returns a response in JSON format:

```
import requests
pageUrl="http://httpbin.org/forms/post"
postUrl="http://httpbin.org/post"
```

```
params = {'custname':'Mr.
ABC','custtel':'','custemail':'abc@somedomain.com','size':'small',
'topping':['cheese','mushroom'],'delivery':'13:00','comments':'None'}

headers={
'Accept':'text/html,application/xhtml+xml,application/xml;q=0.9,image/webp,
image/apng,*/*;q=0.8','Content-Type':'application/x-www-form-urlencoded',
'Referer':pageUrl
}

#making POST request to postUrl with params and request headers, response
will be read as JSON
response = requests.post(postUrl,data=params,headers=headers).json()
print(response)
```

The previous code will result in the following output:

```
{
'args': {},
'data': '',
'files': {},
'form': {
'comments': 'None',
'custemail': 'abc@somedomain.com',
'custname': 'Mr. ABC',
'custtel': '',
'delivery': '13:00',
'size': 'small',
'topping': ['cheese', 'mushroom']
},
'headers': {
'Accept':'text/html,application/xhtml+xml,application/xml;q=0.9,image/webp,
image/apng,*/*;q=0.8', 'Accept-Encoding': 'gzip, deflate',
'Connection': 'close',
'Content-Length': '130',
'Content-Type': 'application/x-www-form-urlencoded',
'Host': 'httpbin.org',
'Referer': 'http://httpbin.org/forms/post',
'User-Agent': 'python-requests/2.21.0'
},
'json': None, 'origin': '202.51.76.90',
'url': 'http://httpbin.org/post'
}
```

For the POST request we attempted, we can find detailed information regarding **Request Headers**, **Response Headers**, **HTTP Status**, and POST data (params) using the **DevTools Network** panel, as shown in the following screenshot:

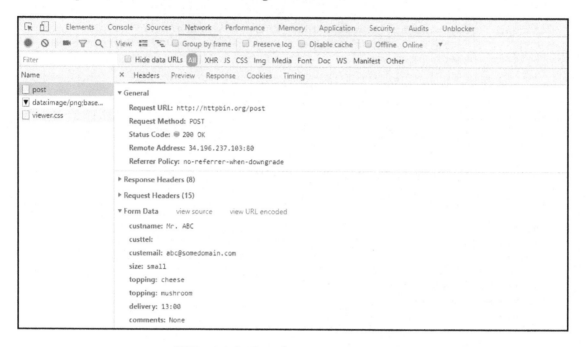

POST data submitted and found as form data in the DevTools Network panel

 It's always beneficial to learn and detect the request and response sequences that are made with URLs through the browser and the available **DevTools**.

Summary

In this chapter, we learned about using Python libraries to make a request to a web resource and collect the response that was returned. This chapter's main objective was to demonstrate core features that are available through the urllib and requests Python libraries, plus exploring page contents that are found in various formats.

In the next chapter, we will learn and use a few techniques to identify and extract data from web contents.

Further reading

- urllib: `https://docs.python.org/3/library/urllib.html`
- Requests: `https://2.python-requests.org/en/master/`
- urllib3 `https://urllib3.readthedocs.io/en/latest/index.html`
- HTTP methods (GET/POST): `https://www.w3schools.com/tags/ref_httpmethods.asp`
- Installing Python packages: `https://packaging.python.org/tutorials/installing-packages/`
- What are DevTools? `https://developer.mozilla.org/en-US/docs/Learn/Common_questions/What_are_browser_developer_tools`
- HTTP request and response service: `http://httpbin.org/`

3
Using LXML, XPath, and CSS Selectors

So far, we have learned about web-development technologies, data-finding techniques, and accessing web content using the Python programming language.

Web-based content exists in parts or elements using some predefined document expressions. Analyzing these parts for patterns is a major task for processing convenient scraping. Elements can be searched and identified with XPath and CSS selectors that are processed with scraping logic for required content. lxml will be used to process elements inside markup documents. We will be using browser-based development tools for content reading and element identification.

In this chapter, we will learn the following:

- Introduction to XPath and CSS selectors
- Using browser developer tools
- Learning and scraping using the Python lxml library

Technical requirements

A web browser (Google Chrome or Mozilla Firefox) is required and we will be using the following Python libraries:

- lxml
- Requests

If the preceding libraries do not exist with the current Python setup, for setting up or installation, refer to the *Setting things up* section in the last chapter.

Code files are available online on GitHub: `https://github.com/PacktPublishing/Hands-On-Web-Scraping-with-Python/tree/master/Chapter03`.

Introduction to XPath and CSS selector

In the *Understanding web development and technologies* section in Chapter 1, *Web Scraping Fundamentals*, we introduced XML as a document that contains data that is exchangeable and distributable across various technologies related to the web and documents. XML carries user-defined tags, also known as nodes, which hold data in a tree-like structure.

A tree-type structure (also known as an element-tree) is a base model for most markup languages and is often referred to as the **Document Object Model** (**DOM**). With the help of the DOM and its defined conventions, we can access, traverse, and manipulate elements.

Elements are structured inside some parent elements, which are inside their own parent and so on; this describes a parent-child relationship that is the most significant feature of markup language. Many applications that support XML or markup language supports the DOM and even contain a parser to use.

For extraction, it is necessary to identify the exact location of information. Information can be found nested inside a tree structure and could possess some additional attributes to represent the content. XPath and CSS selectors are both used to navigate along the DOM and search for desired elements or nodes found in the document.

In the following sections, we will introduce both XPath and CSS selectors, and use them for a web-scraping purpose with a supportive Python library.

XPath

The **XML Path** (**XPath**) language is a part of XML-based technologies (XML, XSLT, and XQuery), which deal with navigating through DOM elements or locating nodes in XML (or HTML) documents using expressions also known as XPath expressions. XPath is normally a path that identifies nodes in documents. XPath is also a **W3C** (short for **World Wide Web Consortium**) recommendation (https://www.w3.org/TR/xpath/all/).

XPath or XPath expressions are also identified as absolute and relative:

- The absolute path is an expression that represents a complete path from the root element to the desired element. It begins with /html and looks like /html/body/div[1]/div/div[1]/div/div[1]/div[2]/div[2]/div/span/ b[1]. Individual elements are identified with their position and represented by an index number.
- The relative path represents an expression chosen from certain selected elements to the desired element. Relative paths are shorter and readable in comparison to absolute paths and look like //*[@id="answer"]/div/span/b[@class="text"]. A relative path is often preferred over an absolute path as element indexes, attributes, logical expressions, and so on can be combined and articulated in a single expression.

With XPath expressions, we can navigate hierarchically through elements and reach the targeted one. XPath is also implemented by various programming languages, such as JavaScript, Java, PHP, Python, and C++. Web applications and browsers also have built-in support to XPath.

Expressions can be built using a number of built-in functions available for various data types. Operations related to general math (+, -, *, /), comparison (<, >, =, !=, >=, <=), and combination operators (and, or, and mod) can also be used to build expression. XPath is also a core block for XML technologies such as XQuery and **eXtensible Stylesheet Language Transformations (XSLT)**.

 XML Query (**XQuery**) is a query language that uses XPath expressions to extract data from XML document.
XSLT is used to render XML in a more readable format.

Let's explore a few XPath expressions from the XML content as seen in the following from the food.xml file:

```xml
<?xml version="1.0" encoding="UTF-8" ?>
<menus>
    <food>
        <name>Butter Milk with Vanilla</name>
        <price>$3.99</price>
        <description>Rich tangy buttermilk with vanilla essence</description>
        <rating>5.0</rating>
        <feedback>6</feedback>
    </food>
    <food...>
    <food...>
    <food>
        <name>Pineapple Cake</name>
        <price>$3.99</price>
        <description>Crushed Pineapple mixed with vanilla, eggs and lemon juice</description>
        <rating>5.0</rating>
        <feedback>9</feedback>
    </food>
    <food>
        <name>Eggs and Bacon</name>
        <price>$5.50</price>
        <description>Served with rice and fresh fruit</description>
        <rating>4.5</rating>
        <feedback>4</feedback>
    </food>
    <food>
        <name>Orange Juice</name>
        <price>$2.99</price>
        <description>Fresh Orange juice served</description>
        <rating>4.9</rating>
        <feedback>10</feedback>
    </food>
</menus>
```

XML content

In the following example, we will be using XPath-Tester from Code Beautify (https://codebeautify.org/Xpath-Tester). Use the XML source URL provided earlier to fetch the XML content and use it with the Code Beautify XPath-Tester.

You can use `https://codebeautify.org/Xpath-Tester`, `https://www.freeformatter.com/xpath-tester.htm`, or any other XPath tester tools that are available free on the web.

Everything is a node in an XML document, for example, `menus`, `food`, and `price`. An XML node can be an element itself (elements are types or entities that have start and end tags).

The preceding XML document can also be read as inherited element blocks. Parent node `menus` contain multiple child nodes `food`, which distinguishes child elements for appropriate values and proper data types. The XPath expression, `//food`, as shown in the following screenshot, displays the result for the selected node `food`. Node selection also retrieves the child nodes within the parents, as seen in the following screenshot:

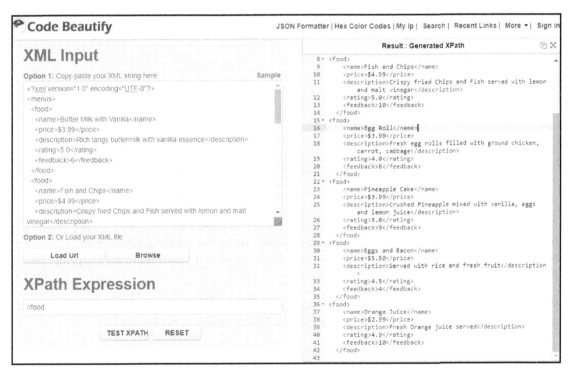

Result for XPath //food (using https://codebeautify.org/Xpath-Tester)

The XPath expression in the following screenshot selects the child node, `price`, found inside all parent nodes `food`. There are six child `food` nodes available, each of them containing `price`, `name`, `description`, `feedback`, and `rating`:

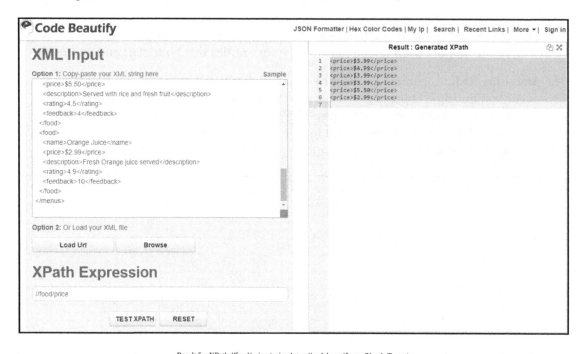

Result for XPath //food/price (using https://codebeautify.org/Xpath-Tester)

As we can see from the two preceding XPaths tested, expressions are created almost like a filesystem (command line or Terminal path), which we use in various OS. XPath expressions contain code patterns, functions, and conditional statements and support the use of predicates.

Predicates are used to identify a specific node or element. Predicate expressions are written using square brackets that are similar to Python lists or array expressions.

A brief explanation of the XPath expression given in the preceding XML is listed in the following table:

XPath expression	Description
`//`	Selects nodes in the document, no matter where they are located
`//*`	Selects all elements in the document
`//food`	Selects the element `food`

`*`	Selects all elements

`//food/name	//food/price`	Selects the `name` and `price` elements found in the `food` node:
		`<name>Butter Milk with Vanilla</name>`
		`<name>Fish and Chips</name>`
		`<price>$5.50</price>`
		`<price>$2.99</price>`

`//food/name`	Selects all the `name` elements inside `food`:
	`<name>Butter Milk with Vanilla</name>`
	`<name>Eggs and Bacon</name>`
	`<name>Orange Juice</name>`

`//food/name/text()`	Selects the `text` only for all `food/name` elements: `Butter Milk with Vanilla Orange Juice`

`//food/name	//rating`	Selects all `name` elements from `food` and `rating` found in document:
		`<name>Butter Milk with Vanilla</name>`
		`<name>Fish and Chips</name><rating>4.5</rating>`
		`<rating>4.9</rating>`

`//food[1]/name`	Selects the `name` element for the first `food` node: `<name>Butter Milk with Vanilla</name>`

`//food[feedback<9]`	Select the `food` node and all of its elements where the predicate condition, `feedback<9`, is true:
	`<food>`
	`<name>Butter Milk with Vanilla</name>`
	`<name>Egg Roll</name>`
	`<name>Eggs and Bacon</name>`
	`</food>`

`//food[feedback<9]/name`	Selects the `food` node and the `name` element that matches the condition:
	`<name>Butter Milk with Vanilla</name>`
	`<name>Egg Roll</name>`
	`<name>Eggs and Bacon</name>`

`//food[last()]/name`	Selects the `name` element from the last `food` node: `<name>Orange Juice</name>`

`//food[last()]/name/text()`	Selects `text` for the `name` element from the last `food` node: `Orange Juice`
`sum(//food/feedback)`	Provides the sum of feedback found in all `food`:nodes: `47.0`

`//food[rating>3 and rating<5]/name`	Selects the `name` of `food` that fulfills the predicate condition:
	`<name>Egg Roll</name>`
	`<name>Eggs and Bacon</name>`
	`<name>Orange Juice</name>`

`//food/name[contains(.,"Juice")]`	Selects the `name` of `food` that contains the `Juice` string: `<name>Orange Juice</name>`

`//food/description[starts-with(.,"Fresh")]/text()`	Selects the node description that starts with `Fresh`:
	`Fresh egg rolls filled with ground chicken, ... cabbage`
	`Fresh Orange juice served`

`//food/description[starts-with(.,"Fresh")]`	Selects `text`
	from `description` node that starts with `Fresh`:
	`<description>Fresh egg rolls filled with..`
	`cabbage</description>`
	` <description>Fresh Orange juice served</description>`

`//food[position()<3]`	Selects the first and second food according to its position:
	`<food>`
	` <name>Butter Milk with Vanilla</name>`
	` <price>$3.99</price>`
	` ...`
	` <rating>5.0</rating>`
	` <feedback>10</feedback>`
	`</food>`

XPath predicates can contain a numeric index that starts from 1 (not 0) and conditional statements, for example, `//food[1]` or `//food[last()]/price`.

Now that we have tested the preceding XML with various XPath expressions, let's consider a simple XML with some attributes. Attributes are extra properties that identify certain parameters for a given node or element. A single element can contain a unique attributes set. Attributes found in XML nodes or HTML elements help to identify the unique element with the value it contains. As we can see in the code in the following XML, attributes are found as a `key=value` pair of information, for example `id="1491946008"`:

```xml
<?xml version="1.0" encoding="UTF-8"?>
<books>
    <book id="1491946008" price='47.49'>
        <author>Luciano Ramalho</author>
        <title>
            Fluent Python: Clear, Concise, and Effective Programming
        </title>
    </book>
    <book id="1491939362" price='29.83'>
        <author>Allen B. Downey</author>
        <title>
  Think Python: How to Think Like a Computer Scientist
        </title>
    </book>
</books>
```

XPath expression accepts `key` attributes by adding the @ character in front of the key name. Listed in the following table are a few examples of XPath using attributes with a brief description.

XPath expression	Description
`//book/@price`	Selects the `price` attribute for a book: price="47.49" price="29.83"

`//book`	Selects the `book` field and its elements:
	`<book id="1491946008" price="47.49">`
	
	`<author>Luciano Ramalho</author>`
	`<title>Fluent Python: Clear, Concise, and Effective Programming`
	` Think Python: How to Think Like a Computer Scientist`
	`</title></book>`

`//book[@price>30]`	Selects all elements in book the price attribute of which is greater than 30:
	`<book id="1491946008" price="47.49">`
	`<author>Luciano Ramalho</author>`
	`<title>Fluent Python: Clear, Concise, and Effective Programming </title> </book>`

//book[@price<30]/title	Selects `title` from books where the `price` attribute is less than 30: `<title>Think Python: How to Think Like a Computer Scientist</title>`

//book/@id	Selects the `id` attribute and its value. The `//@id` expression also results in the same output:
	`id="1491946008"`
	` id="1491939362"`

//book[@id=1491939362]/author	Selects `author` from `book` where `id=1491939362`: `<author>Allen B. Downey</author>`

We have tried to explore and learn a few basic features about XPath and writing expressions to retrieve the desired content. In the *Scraping using lxml - a Python library* section, we will use Python programming libraries to further explore deploying code using XPath to scrape provided documents (XML or HTML) and learn to generate or create XPath expressions using browser tools. For more information on XPaths please refer to the links in the *Further reading* section.

CSS selectors

In `Chapter` 1, *Web Scraping Fundamentals*, under the *Understanding web development and technologies* section, we learned about CSS and its use to style HTML elements plus we learned about using global attributes. CSS is normally used to style HTML and there are various ways to apply CSS to the HTML.

CSS selectors (also referred to as CSS query or CSS selector query) are defined patterns used by CSS to select HTML elements, using the element name or global attributes (`ID`, and `Class`). CSS selectors, as the name suggests, select or provide the option to select HTML elements in various ways.

In the following example code, we can visualize a few elements found in `<body>`:

- `<h1>` is an element and a selector.
- The `<p>` element or selector has the `class` attribute with the `header` style type. When it comes to selecting, `<p>` we can use either the element name, the attribute name, or just the type name.
- Multiple `<a>` are found inside `<div>`, but they differ with their `class` attribute, `id`, and value for the `href` property:

```
<html>
<head>
    <title>CSS Selectors: Testing</title>
```

```
        <style>
            h1{color:black;}
            .header,.links{color: blue;}
            .plan{color: black;}
            #link{color: blue;}
        </style>
    </head>
    <body>
        <h1>Main Title</h1>
        <p class="header">Page Header</p>
        <div class="links">
            <a class="plan" href="*.pdf">Document Places</a>
            <a id="link" href="mailto:xyz@domain.com">Email Link1!</a>
            <a href="mailto:abc@domain.com">Email Link2!</a>
        </div>
    </body>
</html>
```

The distinguishable patterns we have identified in the preceding code can be used to select those particular elements individually or in groups. Numbers of DOM parsers are available online, which provide a CSS query-related facility. One of them, as shown in the following screenshot, is `https://try.jsoup.org/`:

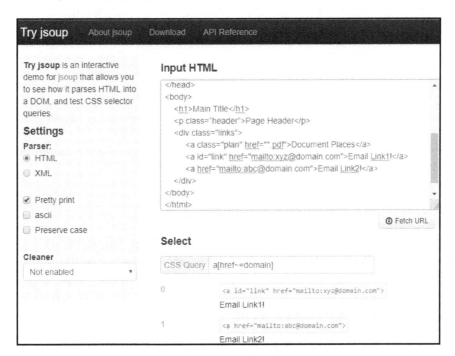

Evaluating CSS query from https://try.jsoup.org/

The DOM parser converts provided XML or HTML into a DOM object or tree type of structure, which facilitates accessing and manipulating element or tree nodes. For more detail information on the DOM, please visit `https://dom.spec.whatwg.org/`.

In a CSS query, various symbols, as listed in the following code text, represent certain characteristics and can be used inside a CSS query:

- The global `id` attribute and `class` are represented by `#` and `.`, respectively, as seen in this query:
  - `a#link`: `<a id="link" href="mailto:xyz@domain.com">Email Link1!</a>`
  - `a.plan`: `<a class="plan" href="*.pdf">Document Places</a>`
- Combinators (showing the relationship between elements) are also used, such as `+`, `>`, `~`, and the space character, as seen in the query here:
  - `h1 + p`: `<p class="header">Page Header</p>`
  - `div.links a.plan`: `<a class="plan" href="*.pdf">Document Places</a>`
- Operators, such as `^`, `*`, `$` are used for positioning and selecting, as seen in this query:
  - `a[href$="pdf"]`: `<a class="plan" href="*.pdf">Document Places</a>`
  - `a[href^="mailto"]`: `<a id="link" href="mailto:xyz@domain.com">Email Link1!</a><a href="mailto:abc@domain.com">Email Link2!</a>`

These symbols are used and explained side-by-side, referring to the preceding HTML code with various types of selectors, in the following sections.

Element selectors

Element selectors are basic selectors that choose elements from HTML. Most often, these elements are the basic tags of HTML. The following table lists some of the selectors and their usage for this category:

CSS query	Description
h1	Selects `<h1>` elements
a	Selects all of the `<a>` elements

*	Selects all elements in the HTML code
body *	Selects all \<h1\>, \<p\>, \<div\>, and \<a\> elements inside \<body\>
div a	Selects all \<a\> inside \<div\> (using space character in between)
h1 + p	Selects immediate \<p\> elements after \<h1\>
h1 ~ p	Selects every \<p\> elements preceded by \<h1\>
h1,p	Selects all \<h1\> and \<p\> elements
div > a	Selects all \<a\> elements that are a direct child of \<div\>

ID and class selectors

ID and class selectors are additional features available with element selectors. We can find HTML tags with the class and id attributes. These are also known as global attributes. These attributes are mostly preferred over other attributes as they define the tags for structure and with identification.

For more details on global attributes, please refer to Chapter 1, *Web Scraping Fundamentals*, the *Global attributes* section. The following table lists the usage of this category of selectors:

CSS query	Description
.header	Selects an element with class=header
.plan	Selects \<a\> with class=plan
div.links	Selects \<div\> with class=plan
#link	Selects an element with id=link
a#link	Selects \<a\> elements with id=link
a.plan	Selects \<a\> elements with class=plan

Attribute selectors

Attribute selectors are used to define selectors with the available attributes. HTML tags contain an attribute that helps to identify a particular element with the attribute and the value that it carries.

The following table lists a few ways to show the usage of attribute selectors:

CSS query	Description
`a[href*="domain"]`	Selects `<a>` elements that contain the domain substring in its href: `<a id="link" href="mailto:xyz@domain.com">Email Link1!</a>` `<a href="mailto:abc@domain.com">Email Link2!</a>`
`a[href^="mailto"]`	Selects `<a>` elements that start with the mailto substring of the href attributes: `<a id="link" href="mailto:xyz@domain.com">Email Link1!</a>` `<a href="mailto:abc@domain.com">Email Link2!</a>`
`a[href$="pdf"]`	Selects `<a>` elements that have a pdf substring at the end of its href attribute: `<a class="plan" href="*.pdf"> Document Places </a>`
`[href~=do]`	Selects all elements with the href attribute and matches do in values. The two `<a>` elements listed in the following both contain do inside of their href value: `<a id="link" href="mailto:xyz@domain.com">Email Link1!</a>` `<a href="mailto:abc@domain.com">Email Link2!</a>`
`[class]`	Selects all elements or `<p>`, `<div>`, and `<a>` with the class attribute: `<p class='header'>Page Header</p>` `<div class="links">` `<a class="plan" href="*.pdf"> Document Places </a>`
`[class=plan]`	Selects `<a>` with class=plan: `<a class="plan" href="*.pdf"> Document Places </a>`

Pseudo selectors

Pseudo selectors are a set of handy choices when it comes to identifying or selecting the elements based on their position.

The following table lists some of the ways these types of selectors might be used, with a brief description:

CSS query	Description

a:gt(0)	Selects all \<a> elements except those indexed at a 0 position:
	`<a id="link" href="mailto:xyz@domain.com">Email Link1!</a>`
	`<a href="mailto:abc@domain.com">Email Link2!</a>`

a:eq(2)	Selects \<a> element which are indexed at 2: `<a href="mailto:abc@domain.com">`
a:first-child	Selects every \<a> element that is the first child of its parent: `<a class="plan" href="*.pdf">Document Places</a>`
a:last-child	Selects every \<a> element that is the last child of its parent: `<a href="mailto:abc@domain.com">Email Link2!</a>`
a:last-of-type	Selects the last element \<a> of its parent: `<a href="mailto:abc@domain.com">Email Link2!</a>`
:not(p)	Selects all elements except \<p>.
a:nth-child(1)	Selects every \<a> from the first child of its parent: `<a class="plan" href="*.pdf">Document Places</a>`
a:nth-last-child(3)	Selects every third \<a> from the last child of its parent: `<a class="plan" href="*.pdf">Document Places</a>`
a:nth-of-type(3)	Selects every third \<a> element of its parent: `<a href="mailto:abc@domain.com">Email Link2!</a>`
a:nth-last-of-type(3)	Selects every \<a> element, at the third position from last, of its parent: `<a class="plan" href="*.pdf">Document Places</a>`

CSS selectors are used as a convenient alternative to XPath expressions for selecting elements, as they are shorter in length compared to absolute XPath and use simple patterns in expressions that are easy to read and manage. CSS selectors can be converted into XPath expressions, but not vice versa.

There are also a number of tools available online, which allow the conversion of a CSS selector query into an XPath expression; one of these is `https://css-selector-to-xpath.appspot.com/`, as seen in the following screenshot; we shouldn't always trust the tools available and results should be tested before applying them in code:

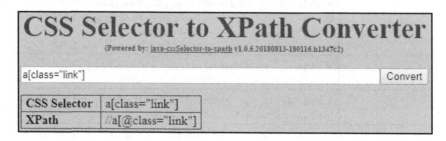

CSS selector to XPath converter

As described in the preceding screenshot, CSS selectors are used to select elements from a data extraction perspective and can be used in `Scraper` codes or even while applying styles to selected elements from a styling perspective.

In this section, we learned about the most popular web-related pattern-finding techniques of XPath and CSS selectors. In the next section, we will explore browser-based developer tools (DevTools) and learn to use the features inside DevTools. DevTools can be used to search, analyze, identify, and select elements and obtain XPath expressions and CSS selectors.

Using web browser developer tools for accessing web content

In Chapter 1, *Web Scraping Fundamentals*, under the *Data finding techniques (seeking data from the web)* section and inside *Developer tools (DevTools)*, we introduced browser-based DevTools to locate content and explore the various panels found. DevTools offers various functional panels, which provide us with supportive tools to manage related resources.

In this particular section, our motive will be specific to identifying the particular elements that hold the content we are looking for. This identification-based information, such as XPath expression, CSS query, or even DOM-based navigation flow will be beneficial while coding `Scraper`.

We will explore web pages using Google Chrome. Chrome has a built-in developer tool with plenty of features (available for element identification, selection, DOM navigation, and so on). In the following sections, we will explore and use these features.

HTML elements and DOM navigation

We will be using `http://books.toscrape.com/` from `http://toscrape.com/`. `toscrape` provides resources related to web scraping for beginners and developers to learn and implement `Scraper`.

Let's open the `http://books.toscrape.com` URL using the web browser, Google Chrome, as shown here:

Inspect view of books.toscrape.com

As the page content is successfully loaded, we can load DevTools with a right-click on the page and press the option **Inspect** or by pressing *Ctrl + Shift + I*. If accessing through the Chrome menu, click **More Tools** and **Developer Tools**. The browser should look similar to the content in the preceding screenshot.

As you can see in the preceding screenshot, in inspect mode, the following is loaded:

- Panel elements are default on the left-hand side.
- CSS styles-based content is on the right-hand side.
- We notice the DOM navigation or elements path in the bottom left-hand corner, for example, `html.no-js body .... div.page_inner div.row`.

We have covered a basic overview of such panels in Chapter 1, *Web Scraping Fundamentals*, in the *Developer Tools* section. As developer tools get loaded, we can find a pointer-icon listed, at first, from the left; this is used for selecting elements from the page, as shown in the following screenshot; this element selector (inspector) can be turned ON/OFF using *Ctrl + Shift + C*:

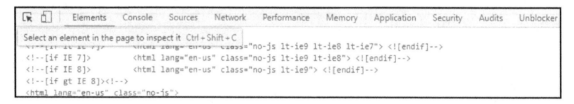

Element selector (inspector) on inspect bar

We can move the mouse on the page loaded after turning ON the element selector. Basically, we are searching for the exact HTML element that we are pointing to using the mouse:

Using element selector on the book image

As seen in the preceding screenshot, the element has been selected and, as we move the mouse over the first book picture available, this action results in the following:

- The `div.image_container` element is displayed and selected in the page itself.
- Inside the elements panel source, we can find the particular HTML code, `<div class="image_container">`, being highlighted too. This information (where the book picture is located) can also be found using right-click + page source or *Ctrl + U* and searching for the specific content.

The same action can be repeated for various sections of HTML content that we wish to scrape, as in the following examples:

- The price for a listed book is found inside the `div.product_price` element.
- The star-rating is found inside `p.star-rating`.
- The book title is found inside `<h3>`, found before `div.product_price` or after `p.star-rating`.
- The book detail link is found inside `<a>`, which exists inside `<h3>`.

- From the following screenshot, it's also clear that the previously listed elements are all found inside `article.product_prod`. Also, at the bottom of the following screenshot, we can identify the DOM path as `article.product_prod`:

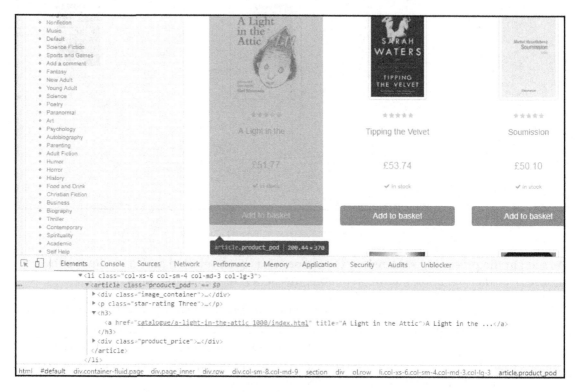

Element selection under inspect mode

DOM navigation, as found in the preceding screenshots, can be beneficial while dealing with XPath expressions, and can verify the content using the page source, if the path or element displayed by the element inspector actually exists (inside the obtained page source).

 DOM elements, navigation paths, and elements found using the elements inspector or selectors should be cross-verified for their existence in page sources or inside resources that are found in **Network** panels, to be sure.

XPath and CSS selectors using DevTools

In this section, we will be collecting XPath expressions and CSS queries for the required element. In a similar way to how we explored the **Page Inspector** and **Elements** panel in the preceding section, let's proceed with the following steps to obtain an XPath expression and CSS query for the selected element:

1. Choose the **Element Selector** and obtain the element code
2. Right-click the mouse on the element code obtained
3. Choose the **Copy** option from the menu
4. From the sub-menu options, choose **Copy XPath** for XPath expression for chosen element
5. Or choose **Copy selector** for the CSS selector (query)

As seen in the following screenshot, we select various sections of a single book item and obtain respective CSS selectors or XPath expressions, accessing the menu options:

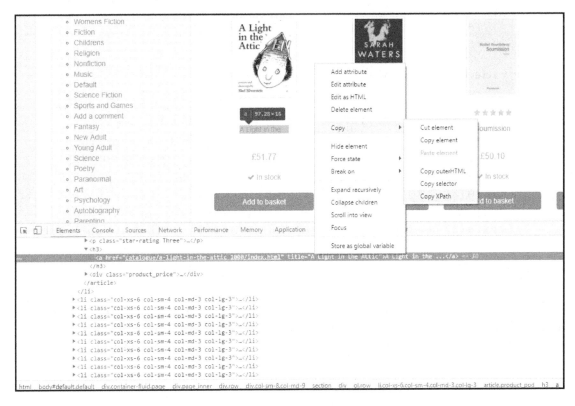

Copying XPath and CSS selector using page inspect

The following are some XPath and CSS selectors collected using DevTools for items available with products such as book title and price.

XPath selectors using DevTools:

- Book title:
  ```
  //*[@id="default"]/div/div/div/div/section/div[2]/ol/li[1]/arti
  cle/h3/a
  ```
- Price:
  ```
  //*[@id="default"]/div/div/div/div/section/div[2]/ol/li[1]/arti
  cle/div[2]
  ```
- Image:
  ```
  //*[@id="default"]/div/div/div/div/section/div[2]/ol/li[1]/arti
  cle/div[1]
  ```
- Stock information:
  ```
  //*[@id="default"]/div/div/div/div/section/div[2]/ol/li[1]/arti
  cle/div[2]/p[2]
  ```
- Star rating:
  ```
  //*[@id="default"]/div/div/div/div/section/div[2]/ol/li[1]/arti
  cle/p
  ```

CSS query selectors using DevTools:

- Book title: `#default > div > div > div > div > section > div:nth-child(2) > ol > li:nth-child(1) > article > h3 > a`
- Price: `#default > div > div > div > div > section > div:nth-child(2) > ol > li:nth-child(1) > article > div.product_price`
- Image: `#default > div > div > div > div > section > div:nth-child(2) > ol > li:nth-child(1) > article > div.image_container`
- Stock info: `#default > div > div > div > div > section > div:nth-child(2) > ol > li:nth-child(1) > article > div.product_price > p.instock.availability`
- Star rating: `#default > div > div > div > div > section > div:nth-child(2) > ol > li:nth-child(1) > article > p.star-rating`

Similarly other essential XPath or CSS selectors will also be collected as required. After collection and verification or cleaning (shortening) of these expressions and queries, scraping logic is applied using Python programming to automate the data collection.

Again, there's no particular way out of following the steps as discussed in the previous section. The XPath or CSS selector can also be determined or formed revealing the HTML source or page source; there are also lots of browser-based extensions that support similar tasks. It's the developer's choice to be comfortable with any way out that we have discussed to deal with the XPath and CSS selectors.

 One of the recently listed browser-based extensions to generate XPath and CSS selectors for Google Chrome is ChroPath (`https://autonomiq.io/ chropath/`). Writing customized expressions and queries is advised for self-practice and knowledge. Extensions and other similar applications should be used while processing a large information source.

In this section, we inspected and explored the **Elements** panel for element identification and DOM navigation: modifying, removing elements, altering scripts, and so on. Related options also exist in the **Elements** panel. In the following section, we will be using the Python library, `lxml`, to code `Scraper` and collect data from the chosen website using XPath and CSS selector.

Scraping using lxml, a Python library

lxml is a XML toolkit, with a rich library set to process XML and HTML. lxml is preferred over other XML-based libraries in Python for its high speed and effective memory management. It also contains various other features to handle both small or large XML files. Python programmers use lxml to process XML and HTML documents. For more detailed information on lxml and its library support, please visit `https://lxml.de/`.

lxml provides native support to XPath and XSLT and is built on powerful C libraries: `libxml2` and `libxslt`. Its library set is used normally with XML or HTML to access XPath, parsing, validating, serializing, transforming, and extending features from ElementTree (`http://effbot.org/zone/element-index.htm#documentation`). Parsing, traversing ElementTree, XPath, and CSS selector-like features from lxml makes it handy enough for a task such as web scraping. lxml is also used as a parser engine in Python Beautiful Soup (`https://www.crummy.com/software/BeautifulSoup/bs4/doc/`) and pandas (`https://pandas.pydata.org/`).

Elements of a markup language such as XML and HTML have start and close tags; tags can also have attributes and contain other elements. ElementTree is a wrapper that loads XML files as trees of elements. The Python built-in library, ElementTree (etree), is used to search, parse elements, and build a document tree. Element objects also exhibit various accessible properties related to Python lists and dictionaries.

XSLT is a language to transform an XML document into HTML, XHML, text, and so on. XSLT uses XPath to navigate in XML documents. XSLT is a template type of structure that is used to transform XML document into new documents.

The lxml library contains important modules, as listed here:

- `lxml.etree` (https://lxml.de/api/lxml.etree-module.html): Parsing and implementing ElementTree; supports XPath, iterations, and more
- `lxml.html` (https://lxml.de/api/lxml.html-module.html): Parses HTML, supports XPath, CSSSelect, HTML form, and form submission
- `lxml.cssselect` (https://lxml.de/api/lxml.cssselect-module.html): Converts CSS selectors into XPath expressions; accepts a CSS selector or CSS Query as an expression

lxml by examples

lxml has a large module set, and, in this section, we will learn to explore lxml using most of its features with examples before moving into scraping tasks. The examples are geared toward extraction activity rather than development.

Example 1 – reading XML from file and traversing through its elements

In this example, we will be reading the XML content available from the `food.xml` file. We will use XML content:

```
from lxml import etree
xml = open("food.xml","rb").read() #open and read XML file
```

The XML response obtained from the preceding code needs to be parsed and traversed using `lxml.etree.XML()`. The `XML()` function parses the XML document and returns the `menus` root node, in this case. Please refer to https://lxml.de/api/lxml.etree-module.html for more detailed information on `lxml.etree`:

```
tree = etree.XML(xml)
#tree = etree.fromstring(xml)
#tree = etree.parse(xml)
```

The functions `fromstring()` and `parse()` functions, found in the preceding code, also provide content to a default or chosen parser used by `lxml.etree`.

 A number of parsers are provided by lxml (XMLParser and HTMLParser) and the default one used in code can be found using >>> `etree.get_default_parser()`. In the preceding case, it results in `<lxml.etree.XMLParser>`.

Let's verify `tree` received after parsing:

```
print(tree)
print(type(tree))

<Element menus at 0x3aa1548>
<class 'lxml.etree._Element'>
```

The preceding two statements confirm that `tree` is an XML root element of the `lxml.etree._Element` type. For traversing through all elements inside a tree, tree iteration can be used, which results in elements in their found order.

Tree iteration is performed using the `iter()` function. The elements' tag name can be accessed using the element property, `tag`; similarly, elements' text can be accessed by the `text` property, as shown in the following:

```
for element in tree.iter():
    print("%s - %s" % (element.tag, element.text))
```

The preceding tree iteration will result in the following output:

```
menus -
food -

name - Butter Milk with Vanilla
price - $3.99
description - Rich tangy buttermilk with vanilla essence
rating - 5.0
feedback - 6
```

```
. . . . . . . . . . . . . . .
food -

name - Orange Juice
price - $2.99
description - Fresh Orange juice served
rating - 4.9
feedback - 10
```

We, too, can pass child elements as an argument to the tree iterator (price and name) to obtain selected element-based responses. After passing the child element to tree.iter(), we can obtain Tag and Text or Content child elements using element.tag and element.text, respectively, as shown in the following code:

```
#iter through selected elements found in Tree
for element in tree.iter('price','name'):
 print("%s - %s" % (element.tag, element.text))

name - Butter Milk with Vanilla
price - $3.99
name - Fish and Chips
price - $4.99
. . . . . . . . . . .
name - Eggs and Bacon
price - $5.50
name - Orange Juice
price - $2.99
```

Also to be noted is that the food.xml file has been opened in rb mode and not in r mode. While dealing with local file-based content and files having encoding declarations, such as <?xml version="1.0" encoding="UTF-8"?>, there's a possibility of encountering the error as ValueError: Unicode strings with encoding declaration are not supported. Please use bytes input or XML fragments without declaration. Encoding/decoding the content might solve the issue mentioned, which is also based on the file mode.

To deal with the preceding condition or reading the content from file, HTTP URL, or FTP, parse() is a really effective approach. It uses the default parser unless specified; one is supplied to it as an extra argument. The following code demonstrates the use of the parse() function, which is being iterated for the element name to obtain its text:

```
from lxml import etree

#read and parse the file
tree = etree.parse("food.xml")
```

```
#iterate through 'name' and print text content
for element in tree.iter('name'):
    print(element.text)
```

The preceding code results in the following output: `Butter Milk with Vanilla`, `Fish and Chips`, and so on, which are obtained from the `name` element and from the `food.xml` file:

```
Butter Milk with Vanilla
Fish and Chips
Egg Roll
Pineapple Cake
Eggs and Bacon
Orange Juice
```

A multiple-tree element can also be iterated, as seen here:

```
for element in tree.iter('name','rating','feedback'):
    print("{} - {}".format(element.tag, element.text))

name - Butter Milk with Vanilla
rating - 5.0
feedback - 6
name - Fish and Chips
rating - 5.0
..........
feedback - 4
name - Orange Juice
rating - 4.9
feedback - 10
```

Example 2 – reading HTML documents using lxml.html

In this example, we will be using the `lxml.html` module to traverse through the elements from `http://httpbin.org/forms/post`:

```
from lxml import html
from urllib.request import urlopen

root = html.parse(urlopen('http://httpbin.org/forms/post')).getroot()
tree = html.parse(urlopen('http://httpbin.org/forms/post'))

print(type(root)) #<class 'lxml.html.HtmlElement'>
print(type(tree)) #<class 'lxml.etree._ElementTree'>
```

We are using `parse()` from `lxml.html` to load the given URL content. `parse()` acts similarly to `lxml.etree` but, in this case, `root` obtained is of the HTML type. The `getroot()` method returns the document root. The object type can be compared for `root` and `tree`, as shown in the preceding code. We are interested in `root` or HTMLElement for this example. The content parsed as `root` is shown in the following screenshot:

```
1   <!DOCTYPE html>
2   <html>
3     <head>
4     </head>
5     <body>
6     <!-- Example form from HTML5 spec http://www.w3.org/TR/html5/forms.html#writing-a-form's-user-interface -->
7     <form method="post" action="/post">
8      <p><label>Customer name: <input name="custname"></label></p>
9      <p><label>Telephone: <input type=tel name="custtel"></label></p>
10     <p><label>E-mail address: <input type=email name="custemail"></label></p>
11     <fieldset>
12      <legend> Pizza Size </legend>
13      <p><label> <input type=radio name=size value="small"> Small </label></p>
14      <p><label> <input type=radio name=size value="medium"> Medium </label></p>
15      <p><label> <input type=radio name=size value="large"> Large </label></p>
16     </fieldset>
17     <fieldset>
18      <legend> Pizza Toppings </legend>
19      <p><label> <input type=checkbox name="topping" value="bacon"> Bacon </label></p>
20      <p><label> <input type=checkbox name="topping" value="cheese"> Extra Cheese </label></p>
21      <p><label> <input type=checkbox name="topping" value="onion"> Onion </label></p>
22      <p><label> <input type=checkbox name="topping" value="mushroom"> Mushroom </label></p>
23     </fieldset>
24     <p><label>Preferred delivery time: <input type=time min="11:00" max="21:00" step="900" name="delivery"></label></p>
25     <p><label>Delivery instructions: <textarea name="comments"></textarea></label></p>
26     <p><button>Submit order</button></p>
27     </form>
28    </body>
29  </html>
```

Page source: http://httpbin.org/forms/post

HTMLElement `root` has various properties, as listed here:

```
print(dir(root))

[...'addnext', 'addprevious', 'append', 'attrib', 'base', 'base_url',
'body', 'clear', 'cssselect', 'drop_tag', 'drop_tree', 'extend', 'find',
'find_class', 'find_rel_links', 'findall', 'findtext', 'forms', 'get',
'get_element_by_id', 'getchildren', 'getiterator', 'getnext', 'getparent',
'getprevious', 'getroottree', 'head', 'index', 'insert', 'items', 'iter',
'iterancestors', 'iterchildren', 'iterdescendants', 'iterfind',
'iterlinks', 'itersiblings', 'itertext', 'keys', 'label',
'make_links_absolute', 'makeelement', 'nsmap', 'prefix', 'remove',
'replace', 'resolve_base_href', 'rewrite_links', 'set', 'sourceline',
'tag', 'tail', 'text', 'text_content', 'values', 'xpath']
```

Let's find <p> from `root`; `find()` can be used to locate the first element by the path. Text can be retrieved using the `text_content()` function. The `findtext()` function can also be used for similar cases, as shown here:

```
p = root.find('.//p') #find first <p> from root

print(p.text_content())  # Customer name:
print(root.findtext('.//p/label')) #Customer name:
```

As we can see in the following code, `findall()` is used to find and iterate through all of the elements in `root`:

```
elemP = root.findall('.//p') #find all <p> element from root
for p in elemP :
    print(p.text_content())
```

The preceding code lists the text from finding all `p` tags, as seen here:

```
Customer name:
Telephone:
E-mail address:
 Small
 Medium
 Large
 Bacon
 Extra Cheese
 Onion
 Mushroom
Preferred delivery time:
Delivery instructions:
Submit order
```

The HTMLElement `root` also supports XPath and CSSSelect:

```
print(root.xpath('//p/label/input/@value'))
print(root.xpath('//legend/text()'))
```

This will result in the output seen here:

```
['small','medium','large','bacon','cheese','onion','mushroom']
['Pizza Size', 'Pizza Toppings']
```

CSSSelect translates CSS selectors into XPath expressions and is used with a related object:

```
#print text_content() for label inside <p>
for e in root.cssselect('p label'):
    print(e.text_content())
```

```
Customer name:
Telephone:
E-mail address:
 Small
 ......
 Mushroom
Preferred delivery time:
Delivery instructions:

#print text_content for element <p> inside <form>
for e in root.cssselect('form > p'):
    print(e.text_content())

Customer name:
Telephone:
E-mail address:
Preferred delivery time:
Delivery instructions:
Submit order
```

The following code demonstrates the HTML `<form>` element being explored for its attributes and properties. We are targeting the `<form>` element first, which is found in `root`, **that is,** `<form method="post" action="/post">`:

```
print(root.forms[0].action)  #http://httpbin.org/post
print(root.forms[0].keys())  #['method', 'action']
print(root.forms[0].items()) #[('method', 'post'), ('action', '/post')]
print(root.forms[0].method)  # POST
```

As we can see from the preceding code, outputs are displayed as in-line comments:

- `action` returns the URL value for the `key` attribute, `action`. The URL obtained is actually a link that will process the information submitted or options chosen.
- `items()` returns the list of tuples containing the element's key and value.
- `keys()` returns the list of element keys.
- `method` returns the value for the attribute method, that is, HTTP request or HTTP methods. For more information on HTTP methods, please refer to `Chapter 1`, *Web Scraping Fundamentals*, the *Understanding web development and technologies* section.

Example 3 – reading and parsing HTML for retrieving HTML form type element attributes

In this example, we will be reading HTML from the `http://httpbin.org/forms/post` URL, which contains HTML-based form elements. Form elements have various predefined attributes such as type, value, and name and can exist with manual attributes. In the preceding examples, we tried to implement various functions—XPath and CSSSelect—to retrieve content from the desired element.

Here, we will try to collect the attributes and their values found in HTML-form elements:

```
from lxml import html
import requests
response = requests.get('http://httpbin.org/forms/post')

# build the DOM Tree
tree = html.fromstring(response.text)

for element in tree.iter('input'):
    print("Element: %s \n\tvalues(): %s \n\tattrib: %s \n\titems(): %s
\n\tkeys(): %s"%
    (element.tag,
element.values(),element.attrib,element.items(),element.keys()))
    print("\n")
```

In the preceding code, the `response.text` and a `str` type object is obtained for the given URL. The `fromstring()` function parses the provided string object and returns the root node or the HTMLElement `tree` type.

In this example, we are iterating the `input` element or `<input...>` and are looking to identify the attributes each input possesses.

The preceding code results in the output shown here:

```
Element: input
    values(): ['custname']
    attrib: {'name': 'custname'}
    items(): [('name', 'custname')]
    keys(): ['name']
Element: input
    values(): ['tel', 'custtel']
    attrib: {'name': 'custtel', 'type': 'tel'}
    items(): [('type', 'tel'), ('name', 'custtel')]
    keys(): ['type', 'name']
.......
.......
```

```
Element: input
    values(): ['checkbox', 'topping', 'mushroom']
    attrib: {'name': 'topping', 'type': 'checkbox', 'value': 'mushroom'}
    items(): [('type', 'checkbox'), ('name', 'topping'), ('value',
'mushroom')]
    keys(): ['type', 'name', 'value']
Element: input
    values(): ['time', '11:00', '21:00', '900', 'delivery']
    attrib: {'max': '21:00', 'type': 'time', 'step': '900', 'min':
'11:00', 'name': 'delivery'}
    items(): [('type', 'time'), ('min', '11:00'), ('max', '21:00'),
('step', '900'), ('name',      'delivery')]
    keys(): ['type', 'min', 'max', 'step', 'name']
```

There are a number of functions and properties used with the `<input>` element in the code resulting from the output. Listed in the following in some of the code used in the example with an explanation:

- `element.tag`: This r
    - eturns the element `tag` name (for example, `input`).
    - `element.values()`: The attributes of HTML form element exist as a `key:value` pair. The `value` attribute holds the exact data for the particular element. `values()` returns the `value` attribute for the chosen element in the `List` object.
    - `element.attrib`: `attrib` returns a `Dict` type object (dictionary) with a `key:value` pair.
    - `element.items()`: `items()` returns a `List` object with a tuple possessing a key and value.
    - `element.keys()`: Similar to
- `items()`, `keys()` returns the attributes `key` in the `List` object.

With a general overview on lxml and its features explained through the preceding examples, we will now perform a few web scraping tasks.

Web scraping using lxml

In this section, we will utilize most of the techniques and concepts learned throughout the chapters so far and implement some scraping tasks.

For the task ahead, we will first select the URLs required. In this case, it will be `http://books.toscrape.com/`, but by targeting a music category, which is `http://books.toscrape.com/catalogue/category/books/music_14/index.html`. With the chosen target URL, its time now to explore the web page and identify the content that we are willing to extract.

We are willing to collect certain information such as the title, price, availability, `imageUrl`, and rating found for each individual item (that is, the `Article` element) listed in the page. We will attempt different techniques using lxml and XPath to scrape data from single and multiple pages, plus the use of CSS selectors.

 Regarding element identification, XPath, CSS selectors and using DevTools, please refer to the *Using web browser developer tools for accessing web content* section.

Example 1 – extracting selected data from a single page using lxml.html.xpath

In this example, we will use XPath to collect information from the provided URL and use lxml features.

In the following code, a `musicUrl` string object contains a link to the page. `musicUrl` is parsed using the `parse()` function, which results in the `doc` and `lxml.etree.ElementTree` objects:

```
import lxml.html
musicUrl=
"http://books.toscrape.com/catalogue/category/books/music_14/index.html"
doc = lxml.html.parse(musicUrl)
```

We now have an ElementTree `doc` available; we will be collecting the XPath expressions for the chosen fields such as title and price, found on the `musicUrl` page. For generating XPath expressions, please refer to the *XPath and CSS selectors using DevTools* section:

```
#base element
articles =
doc.xpath("//*[@id='default']/div/div/div/div/section/div[2]/ol/li[1]/article")[0]

#individual element inside base
title = articles.xpath("//h3/a/text()")
price = articles.xpath("//div[2]/p[contains(@class,'price_color')]/text()")
```

```
availability =
articles.xpath("//div[2]/p[2][contains(@class,'availability')]/text()[norma
lize-space()]")
imageUrl =
articles.xpath("//div[1][contains(@class,'image_container')]/a/img/@src")
starRating = articles.xpath("//p[contains(@class,'star-rating')]/@class")
```

The XPath for the preceding `articles` posseses all of the fields that are available inside `<article>`, such as `title`, `price`, `availability`, `imageUrl`, and `starRating`. The `articles` field is an expression of a type of parent element with child elements. Also, individual XPath expressions for child elements are also declared, such as the `title` field, that is, `title = articles.xpath("//h3/a/text()")`. We can notice the use of `articles` in the expression.

It is also to be noticed in child expressions that element attributes or key names such as `class` or `src` can also be used as `@class` and `@src`, respectively.

Now that the individual expressions have been set up, we can print the items that collect all of the found information for available expressions and return those in the Python list. The cleaning and formatting for data received has also been done with the `map()`, `replace()`, and `strip()` Python functions and Lambda operator, as seen in the following code:

```
#cleaning and formatting
stock = list(map(lambda stock:stock.strip(),availability))
images = list(map(lambda
img:img.replace('../../../..','http://books.toscrape.com'),imageUrl))
rating = list(map(lambda rating:rating.replace('star-rating
',''),starRating))

print(title)
print(price)
print(stock)
print(images)
print(rating)
```

Collected or extracted data might require the additional task of cleaning, that is, removing unwanted characters, white spaces, and so on. It might also require formatting or transforming data into the desired format such as converting string date and time into numerical values, and so on. These two actions help to maintain some predefined or same-structured data.

The final output for the preceding code is shown in the following screenshot:

```
['Rip it Up and ...', 'Our Band Could Be ...', 'How Music Works', 'Love Is a Mix ...
', 'Please Kill Me: The ...', "Kill 'Em and Leave: ...", 'Chronicles, Vol. 1', 'This
Is Your Brain ...', 'Orchestra of Exiles: The ...', 'No One Here Gets ...', 'Life',
'Old Records Never Die: ...', 'Forever Rockers (The Rocker ...']

['£35.02', '£57.25', '£37.32', '£18.03', '£31.19', '£45.05', '£52.60', '£38.40', '£1
2.36', '£20.02', '£31.58', '£55.66', '£28.80']

['In stock', 'In stock', 'In stock', 'In stock', 'In stock', 'In stock', 'In stock',
'In stock', 'In stock', 'In stock', 'In stock', 'In stock', 'In stock']

['http://books.toscrape.com/media/cache/81/c4/81c4a973364e17d01f217e1188253d5e.jpg',
'http://books.toscrape.com/media/cache/54/60/54607fe8945897cdcced0044103b10b6.jpg',
'http://books.toscrape.com/media/cache/5c/c8/5cc8e107246cb478960d4f0aba1e1c8e.jpg',
'http://books.toscrape.com/media/cache/a2/6d/a26d8449abb3381e09126eda5f4e8151.jpg',
'http://books.toscrape.com/media/cache/06/f1/06f185c0be2ad6e2fe059464c03f1b47.jpg',
'http://books.toscrape.com/media/cache/85/42/8542841f5644a6daf433504f1e106e97.jpg',
'http://books.toscrape.com/media/cache/11/fc/11fc94453c4dc0d68543971d7843afb0.jpg',
'http://books.toscrape.com/media/cache/35/a4/35a4a7c6c76c4e82186753078e441654.jpg',
'http://books.toscrape.com/media/cache/15/de/15de75548ee9a4c6be1420ee309c03e0.jpg',
'http://books.toscrape.com/media/cache/7a/7e/7a7eb52e7075a5305522948375c1316e.jpg',
'http://books.toscrape.com/media/cache/99/97/9997eda658c2fe50e724171f9c2a2b0b.jpg',
'http://books.toscrape.com/media/cache/7e/94/7e947f3dd04f178175b85123829467a9.jpg',
'http://books.toscrape.com/media/cache/7f/b0/7fb03a053c270000667a50dd8d594843.jpg']

['Five', 'Three', 'Two', 'One', 'Four', 'Five', 'Two', 'One', 'Three', 'Five', 'Five
', 'Two', 'Three']
```

Python lists with various data from the selected page

As we can see from the preceding screenshot, there is an individual collection of targeted data. Data collected in such a way can be merged into a single Python object as shown in the following code or can be written into external files such as CSV or JSON for further processing:

```
#Merging all
dataSet = zip(title,price,stock,images,rating)
print(list(dataSet))

[('Rip it Up and ...', '£35.02', 'In stock',
'http://books.toscrape.com/media/cache/81/c4/81c4a973364e17d01f217e1188253d
5e.jpg', 'Five'),
('Our Band Could Be ...', '£57.25', 'In stock',
'http://books.toscrape.com/media/cache/54/60/54607fe8945897cdcced0044103b10
b6.jpg', 'Three'),
.........
.........
('Old Records Never Die: ...', '£55.66', 'In stock',
'http://books.toscrape.com/media/cache/7e/94/7e947f3dd04f178175b85123829467
```

```
a9.jpg', 'Two'),
('Forever Rockers (The Rocker ...', '£28.80', 'In stock',
'http://books.toscrape.com/media/cache/7f/b0/7fb03a053c270000667a50dd8d5948
43.jpg', 'Three')]
```

dataSet in the preceding code is generated using the zip() Python function. zip()
collects individual indexes from all provided list objects and appends them as a tuple. The
final output from dataSet has particular values for each <article>, as shown in the
previous code.

Example 2 – looping with XPath and scraping data from multiple pages

In example 1, we tried the simple XPath-based technique for a URL with a limited number
of results on a single page. In this case, we will be targeting a *food and drink* category, that is,
http://books.toscrape.com/catalogue/category/books/food-and-drink_33/index.
html, which has its content across pages. An XPath-based looping operation will be used in
this example, which supports a more effective collection of data.

As we will be dealing with multiple pages, it's good practice to check for a few individual
page URLs that can be found in the browser while moving through the listed pages. Most
of the time, it might contain some patterns that can solve the puzzle easily, as used in the
following code:

```
import lxml.html
from lxml.etree import XPath

baseUrl = "http://books.toscrape.com/"

#Main URL
bookUrl =
"http://books.toscrape.com/catalogue/category/books/food-and-drink_33/index
.html"

#Page URL Pattern obtained (eg: page-1.html, page-2.html...)
pageUrl =
"http://books.toscrape.com/catalogue/category/books/food-and-drink_33/page-
"
```

bookUrl is the main URL we are interested in; it also contains the page link for the next
page, which contains a pattern, as found in pageUrl, for example, page-2.html:

```
dataSet = []
page=1
```

```
totalPages=1
while(page<=totalPages):
    print("Rows in Dataset: "+str(len(dataSet)))
    if(page==1):
        doc = lxml.html.parse(pageUrl+str(page)+".html").getroot()
        perPageArticles =
doc.xpath("//*[@id=\"default\"]//form/strong[3]/text()")
        totalArticles =
doc.xpath("//*[@id=\"default\"]//form/strong[1]/text()")
        totalPages = round(int(totalArticles[0])/int(perPageArticles[0]))
        print(str(totalArticles[0])+" Results, showing
"+str(perPageArticles[0])+" Articles per page")
    else:
        doc = lxml.html.parse(pageUrl+str(page)+".html").getroot()

    #used to find page URL pattern
    nextPage =
doc.xpath("//*[@id=\"default\"]//ul[contains(@class,'pager')]/li[2]/a/@href
")
    if len(nextPage)>0:
        print("Scraping Page "+str(page)+" of "+str(totalPages)+". NextPage
> "+str(nextPage[0]))
    else:
        print("Scraping Page "+str(page)+" of "+str(totalPages))
```

An empty `dataSet` list is defined to hold data found from each article across pages.

An individual page URL is obtained by concatenating `pageUrl` with a page number, and `.html`. `totalPages` is found after calculating `totalArticles` and `perPageArticles` as traced from the page itself. `totalPages` obtained will give an exact loop count and is more manageable to apply in the loop (the `while` loop is found in the code):

```
articles = XPath("//*[@id='default']//ol/li[position()>0]")

titlePath = XPath(".//article[contains(@class,'product_pod')]/h3/a/text()")
pricePath =
XPath(".//article/div[2]/p[contains(@class,'price_color')]/text()")
stockPath =
XPath(".//article/div[2]/p[2][contains(@class,'availability')]/text()[norma
lize-space()]")
imagePath =
XPath(".//article/div[1][contains(@class,'image_container')]/a/img/@src")
starRating = XPath(".//article/p[contains(@class,'star-rating')]/@class")
```

As we can see in the previous code, `articles` is the major XPath expression used to loop for finding individual elements inside the `<article>` field. The expression should contain a certain condition that can be fulfilled to preform a loop; in this case, we identified that the `<article>` field exists inside of the `<ol><li>` element.

So, we can perform a loop with `li[position()>0]` that identifies each `<article>` field found inside `<li>` until it exists in `<ol>` with its traced position, that is, `articles = XPath("//*[@id='default']//ol/li[position()>0]")`:

```
#looping through 'articles' found in 'doc' i.e each <li><article> found in
Page Source
for row in articles(doc):
    title = titlePath(row)[0]
    price = pricePath(row)[0]
    availability = stockPath(row)[0].strip()
    image = imagePath(row)[0]
    rating = starRating(row)[0]
    #cleaning and formatting applied to image and rating
dataSet.append([title,price,availability,image.replace('../../../..',baseUr
l),rating.replace('star-rating','')])

page+=1 #updating Page Count for While loop

#Final Dataset with data from all pages.
print(dataSet)
```

Individual elements of the XPath expression are defined as the `titlePath` element, the `imagePath` element, and so on, targeting particular elements whose data is to be obtained. Finally, the expression set for articles is looped into the HTMLElement obtained for each page, that is, the `doc` element and collects the first occurrence of each `title` and `image` element and the other elements found. These collected data are appended to the `dataSet` field as a list with the cleaning and formatting done, which results in the output shown in the following screenshot:

```
Rows in Dataset: 0
30 Results, showing 20 Articles per page
Scraping Page 1 of 2. NextPage > page-2.html
Rows in Dataset: 20
Scraping Page 2 of 2


[['Foolproof Preserving: A Guide ...', '£30.52', 'In stock', 'http://books.toscrape.com//media/cache/9f/59/9f59f01fa916a7bb8f0b28a4012179a4.jpg', 'Three'], ['T
he Pioneer Woman Cooks: ...', '£56.41', 'In stock', 'http://books.toscrape.com//media/cache/b7/f4/b7f4843dbe062d44be1ffcfa16b2faa4.jpg', 'One'], ['My Paris Kit
chen: Recipes ...', '£33.37', 'In stock', 'http://books.toscrape.com//media/cache/f5/65/f565af3d9dd20a1ad72a1e7c4157387d.jpg', 'Two'], ['Mama Tried: Traditiona
l Italian ...', '£14.02', 'In stock', 'http://books.toscrape.com//media/cache/10/c6/10c61053002db1fec4089d8076678624.jpg', 'Four'], ['Layered: Baking, Building
, and ...', '£40.11', 'In stock', 'http://books.toscrape.com//media/cache/98/d1/98d1c979c4bac9e147a6718546578b0f.jpg', 'One'], ['The Nerdy Nummies Cookbook: ..
.', '£37.34', 'In stock', 'http://books.toscrape.com//media/cache/61/bd/61bdfe3950643c47d70c37c4123530f3.jpg', 'Five'], ['The Love and Lemons ...', '£37.60', '
In stock', 'http://books.toscrape.com//media/cache/0d/1f/0d1f3f934960f5a50aaa8c366641234c.jpg', 'Two'], ['The Cookies & Cups ...', '£41.25', 'In stock', 'http:
//books.toscrape.com//media/cache/54/59/54899b4584e94lceced511d81092c88a.jpg', 'One'], ['Deliciously Ella Every Day: ...', '£42.16', 'In stock', 'http://books.
toscrape.com//media/cache/20/f2/20f28657b49f8cb24ed2ec6448bb6df3.jpg', 'Three'], ['It's All Easy: Healthy, ...', '£19.55', 'In stock', 'http://books.toscrape.com//med
ia/cache/fe/67/fe67c381d6a0c4c00a7c191d16939554.jpg', 'One'], ['Barefoot Contessa Back to ...', '£28.01', 'In stock', 'http://books.toscrape.com//media/cache/b
8/38/b838b65e0e1ac3a9b498dfb1bf004420.jpg', 'One'], ['Barefoot Contessa at Home: ...', '£50.62', 'In stock', 'http://books.toscrape.com//media/cache/74/aa/74aa
29b1ba4147eaf5b4667lbf235861.jpg', 'Five'], ['My Kitchen Year: 136 ...', '£11.53', 'In stock', 'http://books.toscrape.com//media/cache/76/a1/76a1516c8d9c3e6206
26f30840013a85.jpg', 'Two'], ['Everyday Italian: 125 Simple ...', '£20.10', 'In stock', 'http://books.toscrape.com//media/cache/5a/64/5a6499d4lccaad4c4f7eeaa90
e16345a.jpg', 'Five'], ['A la Mode: 120 ...', '£38.77', 'In stock', 'http://books.toscrape.com//media/cache/98/19/9819ff3a8290dc6ab8797d00de5ec554.jpg', 'One']
, ['Cravings: Recipes for What ...', '£20.50', 'In stock', 'http://books.toscrape.com//media/cache/ae/5c/ae5ca435fb095e374d2c2aa9f7b6f380.jpg', 'Three'], ['The
Moosewood Cookbook: Recipes ...', '£12.34', 'In stock', 'http://books.toscrape.com//media/cache/d4/53/d453cfb6c08dbf76d200ffa858bc9979.jpg', 'Four'], ['32 Yolk
s', '£53.63', 'In stock', 'http://books.toscrape.com//media/cache/1d/1f/1d1fbd89f0290275b9166877663ee9f3.jpg', 'Two'], ['Naturally Lean: 125 Nourishing ...', '
£11.38', 'In stock', 'http://books.toscrape.com//media/cache/59/2d/592dc2dee11b798780f5ae613b970a34.jpg', 'Four'], ['How to Be a ...', '£28.25', 'In stock', 'http://books.t
oscrape.com//media/cache/e2/5c/e25cbc27ebc12e47cdf3f7adc87cccdc.jpg', 'Two'], ['The Barefoot Contessa Cookbook', '£59.92', 'In stock', 'http://books.toscrape.c
om//media/cache/dd/07/dd07bd0c443756b9dc260813c1949b4f.jpg', 'Five'], ['Better Homes and Gardens ...', '£39.61', 'In stock', 'http://books.toscrape.com//media/
cache/75/82/7582e20b84f603358a6d55cd6a0a50f4.jpg', 'Three'], ['The Power Greens Cookbook ...', '£11.05', 'In stock', 'http://books.toscrape.com//media/cache/8
2/1d/821d2c02dcd0a10fc9d533917482746e.jpg', 'Five'], ['Mexican Today: New and ...', '£24.91', 'In stock', 'http://books.toscrape.com//media/cache/5d/02/5d029bf
f295cdb777e06f35800faa628.jpg', 'Five'], ['Vegan Vegetarian Omnivore: Dinner ...', '£13.66', 'In stock', 'http://books.toscrape.com//media/cache/80/63/8063lf8b
ca03f361343fdce528725654.jpg', 'Two'], ['The Smitten Kitchen Cookbook', '£23.59', 'In stock', 'http://books.toscrape.com//media/cache/8e/09/3e09faaea71886048b2
7959e607e6c7b.jpg', 'One'], ['The Art of Simple ...', '£34.32', 'In stock', 'http://books.toscrape.com//media/cache/96/57/9657c6d89024e343879a7b5512474fle.jpg'
, 'Three'], ['Hungry Girl Clean & ...', '£33.14', 'In stock', 'http://books.toscrape.com//media/cache/6f/c4/6fc450625cd672e871a6176f74909be2.jpg', 'Three']]
```

Output with paging information and dataSet contents

Example 3 – using lxml.cssselect to scrape content from a page

CSS selectors have a broad range of query options as described in the *Introduction to XPath and CSS selector* section, and is often used as an easy alternative to XPath. In the two preceding examples, we explored the XPath to collect the desired information. In this example, we will be using cssselect from lxml to collect relevant data from a single page available on https://developer.ibm.com/announcements/category/data-science/?fa=date%3ADESCfb=.

To identify a CSS query, we can browse through the page source or use the DevTools. For more detail on using DevTools, refer to the *XPath and CSS selectors using DevTools* section. In this case, we are identifying and collecting CSS Query using DevTools, as shown in the following screenshot:

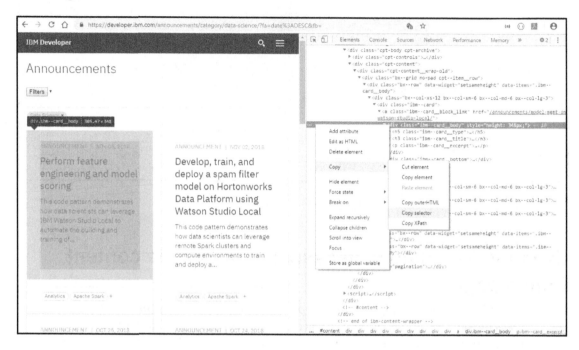

Using DevTools and selecting selector from https://developer.ibm.com/announcements

From the preceding screenshot, we can see that the individual announcements are a block identified by `a.ibm--card__block_link` found inside `div.ibm--card`, which possesses HTML elements with classes, such as `ibm--card__body`, and `ibm--card__type`. The CSS selector is copied using the described process and will result in the following list for `a.ibm--card__block_link` and `div.ibm--card__body`, respectively:

- `#content > div > div.code_main > div > div.cpt-content > div > div.bx--grid.no-pad.cpt--item__row > div:nth-child(1) > div:nth-child(1) > div > a`

- `#content > div > div.code_main > div > div.cpt-content > div > div.bx--grid.no-pad.cpt--item__row > div:nth-child(1) > div:nth-child(1) > div > a > div.ibm--card__body`

Let's deploy the preceding concept using Python code, as shown in the following snippet:

```
from lxml import html
import requests
from lxml.cssselect import CSSSelector
url =
'https://developer.ibm.com/announcements/category/data-science/?fa=date%3AD
ESC&fb='
url_get = requests.get(url)
tree = html.document_fromstring(url_get.content)
```

The required Python library and URLs are declared and the page content `url_get` is parsed with `lxml.html`. With `lxml.html.HTMLElement` obtained, we can now select and navigate to the desired element in the tree with the XPath or CSS selector:

```
announcements=[]
articles = tree.cssselect('.ibm--card > a.ibm--card__block_link')

for article in articles:
    link = article.get('href')
    atype = article.cssselect('div.ibm--card__body > h5')[0].text.strip()
    adate = article.cssselect('div.ibm--card__body > h5 > .ibm--
card__date')[0].text
    title = article.cssselect('div.ibm--card__body > h3.ibm--
card__title')[0].text_content()
    excerpt= article.cssselect(' div.ibm--card__body > p.ibm--
card__excerpt')[0].text
    category= article.cssselect('div.ibm--card__bottom > p.cpt-
byline__categories span')
    #only two available on block: except '+'
#announcements.append([link,atype,adate,title,excerpt,[category[0].text,cat
egory[1].text]])
    announcements.append([link,atype,adate,title,excerpt,[span.text for
span in category if     span.text!='+']])

print(announcements)
```

`articles` is a defined main CSS query and is looped for all available `articles` found in the page as `article`. Each article has different elements for type, date, title, category, and so on. Element data or attributes are collected using `text`, `text_content()`, and `get()`. `cssselect` returns the Python list objects, hence, indexing, such as `[0]`, is used to collect particular element content.

`category` in the preceding code doesn't have any indexing, as it contains a multiple `<span>` element whose value is being extracted using a list comprehension technique, while appending or using indexing as shown in the comments. Output obtained for the code is shown in the following screenshot. Minor cleaning of data has been attempted, but the final list still contains the obtained raw data:

```
[['/announcements/model-mgmt-on-watson-studio-local/', 'Announcement', 'Nov 05, 2018', 'Perform feature engineering and model scoring'
, 'This code pattern demonstrates how data scientists can leverage IBM Watson Studio Local to automate the building and training of...',
['Analytics', 'Apache Spark']], ['/announcements/develop-and-deploy-a-sms-spam-filter-with-hortonworks-data-platform/', 'Announcement'
, 'Nov 02, 2018', 'Develop, train, and deploy a spam filter model on Hortonworks Data Platform using Watson Studio Local', 'This code
pattern demonstrates how data scientists can leverage remote Spark clusters and compute environments to train and deploy a...', ['Analyt
ics', 'Apache Spark']], ['/announcements/max-image-segmenter-magic-cropping-tool-web-app/', 'Announcement', 'Oct 25, 2018', 'Taking se
lfies (and more) to the next level with open source deep learning models', 'Use an open source image segmentation deep learning model
to detect different types of objects from within submitted images, then...', ['Artificial Intelligence', 'Data Science']], ['/announceme
nts/training-machine-learning-models-in-watson-studio/', 'Announcement', 'Oct 24, 2018', 'Train your data no matter where it lives', '
Easily and securely connect to your data source for initial model training and continuous learning, no matter where your data...', ['Ana
lytics', 'Artificial Intelligence']], ['/announcements/generate-insights-from-multiple-data-formats-using-watson-services/', 'Announce
ment', 'Oct 10, 2018', 'Get recommendations by linking structured and unstructured data', 'End-to-end process of integrating structure
d and unstructured data to generate recommendations using a custom algorithm that is configurable and scalable', ['Artificial Intellig
ence', 'Data Science']], ['/announcements/build-a-cognitive-moderator-microservice/', 'Announcement', 'Oct 03, 2018', 'Build a chatbot
moderator for anger detection, natural language understanding, and removal of explicit images', 'Process messages and images exchanged
in a chat channel using Watson services to moderate the discussions.', ['Artificial Intelligence', 'Data Science']], ['/announcements/
build-a-product-recommendation-engine-with-watson-machine-learning/', 'Announcement', 'Sep 24, 2018', 'Build an interactive product re
commender with Spark and PixieDust', 'Use Jupyter Notebooks with IBM Watson Studio to build an interactive recommendation engine Pixie
App.', ['Apache Spark', 'Artificial Intelligence']], ['/announcements/predict-phishing-attempts-in-email-with-nlc/', 'Announcement', '
Sep 18, 2018', 'Spam email classification with Watson Natural Language Classifier', "Build an app that classifies email, either labeli
ng it as 'Phishing,' 'Spam,' or 'Ham' if it does not appear suspicious.", ['Artificial Intelligence', 'Data Science']]]
```

Output from list announcements obtained using lxml.cssselect

It's also to be noted that CSS selector queries copied or obtained using DevTools and used in the example code seem to be different in expression and length. DevTools-provided queries contain details and linked expressions from the parent element found for all chosen elements. In code, we have used the CSS query for only the particular elements identified.

Summary

Element identification, DOM-based navigation, using browser-based developer tools, deploying data-extraction techniques, and an overview on XPath and CSS selectors, plus the use of lxml in a Python library, were the main topics explored in this chapter.

We have also explored various examples using lxml, implementing different techniques plus library features to deal with the element and ElementTree. Finally, web Scraping techniques were explored through examples focusing on different situations that might arise in real cases.

In the next chapter, we will learn more about web scraping techniques and some new Python libraries deploying these techniques.

Further reading

- The DOM: `https://dom.spec.whatwg.org/`
- XPath: `https://www.w3.org/TR/xpath/`, `https://www.w3.org/TR/2017/REC-xpath-31-20170321/`
- XML DOM: `https://www.w3schools.com/xml/dom_intro.asp`
- XPath introduction: `https://www.w3schools.com/xml/xpath_intro.asp`
- XPath tester: `https://freeformatter.com/xpath-tester.html`, `http://www.xpathtester.com/xslt`, `https://codebeautify.org/Xpath-Tester`
- XPath tutorial: `https://doc.scrapy.org/en/xpath-tutorial/topics/xpath-tutorial.html`
- CSS Selector reference: `https://www.w3schools.com/cssref/css_selectors.asp`
- CSS pseudo class and elements: `https://www.w3schools.com/css/css_pseudo_elements.asp`
- CSS information: `http://www.css3.info/`, `https://developer.mozilla.org/en-US/docs/Web/CSS`
- CSS query parser: `https://try.jsoup.org/`
- CSS Selector to XPath: `https://css-selector-to-xpath.appspot.com`
- ElementTree overview: `http://effbot.org/zone/element-index.htm`

4
Scraping Using pyquery – a Python Library

Starting from this chapter, we will be exploring scraping-related tools and techniques, as we will also be deploying some scraping code. Features related to web exploration, Python libraries, element identification, and traversing are the major concepts we have learned about so far.

Web scraping is often a challenging and long process that requires an understanding of how the website is performing. A basic ability to understand and identify the backends or tools that are used to build a website will assist in any scraping task. This is also related to a process known as reverse engineering. For more information on such tools, please refer to Chapter 3, *Using LXML, XPath, and CSS Selectors*, and the *using web browser developer tools for accessing web content* section. In addition to this, identifying the tools for traversing and manipulating elements such as HTML tags is also required, and pyquery is one of them.

In the previous chapters, we explored XPath, CSS Selectors, and LXML. In this chapter, we will look into using pyquery, which has a jQuery-like ability that seems to be more efficient and, hence, easier to deal with when it comes to web scraping procedures.

In this chapter, you will learn about the following topics:

- Introduction to pyquery
- Exploring pyquery (major methods and attributes)
- Using pyquery for web scraping

Technical requirements

A web browser (Google Chrome or Mozilla Firefox) is required for this chapter. We will be using the following Python libraries:

- pyquery
- urllib
- requests

If these libraries don't exist in your current Python setup, refer to Chapter 2, *Python and the Web – Using urllib and Requests*, and the *Setting things up* section, for installation and setup help.

The code files for this chapter are available in this book's GitHub repository: https://github.com/PacktPublishing/Hands-On-Web-Scraping-with-Python/tree/master/Chapter04.

Introduction to pyquery

pyquery is a jQuery-like library for Python that uses the lxml library. This provides an easy and interactive environment for dealing with markup elements in terms of manipulation and traversal purposes.

 pyquery expressions are also similar to jquery, and users with jquery knowledge will find it more convenient to use in Python.

The pyquery Python library, as its name suggests, enhances query writing procedures related to elements found in XML and HTML. pyquery shortens element processing and provides a more insightful scripting approach that is fit for scraping and DOM-based traversal and manipulation tasks.

pyquery expressions use CSS selectors to perform queries, alongside additional features that it implements. For example, the following expression is used by pyquery:

```
page.find('a').attr('href')     -- (pyquery expression)
```

The following expression is used by cssselect:

```
cssselect('a').get('href')      -- (cssselect expression)
```

jQuery (write less, do more) is one of the most admired JavaScript libraries and is small, quick, and has lots of features that support DOM/HTML/CSS, and more. Web document-based traversing, manipulation, event handling, animation, AJAX, and more are some of its main features. Please visit `https://jquery.com/` for more information.

For more information on `pyquery` and its documentation, please visit `https://pythonhosted.org/pyquery/` or `https://github.com/gawel/pyquery/`.

Exploring pyquery

Before we move on and explore `pyquery` and its features, let's start by installing it by using `pip`:

```
C:\> pip install pyquery
```

For more information on using `pip` and library installation, please refer to the *Setting things up* section in `Chapter 2`, *Python and the Web – Using urllib and Requests*.

The following libraries are installed on a successful installation of `pyquery` using `pip`:

- `cssselect-1.0.3`
- `lxml-4.3.1`
- `pyquery-1.4.0`

`>>>` in the code represents the use of the Python IDE; it accepts the code or instructions and displays the output on the next line.

Once the installation is completed and successful, we can use `pyquery`, as shown in the following code, to confirm the setup. We can explore the properties it contains by using the `dir()` function:

```
>>> from pyquery import PyQuery as pq

>>> print(dir(pq))
```

```
['Fn', '__add__', '__call__', '__class__', '__contains__', '__delattr__',
'__delitem__', '__dict__', '__dir__', '__doc__', '__eq__', '__format__',
'__ge__', '__getattribute__', '__getitem__', '__gt__', '_filter_only',
'_get_root', '_next_all', '_prev_all', '_translator_class',
'_traverse','addClass', 'add_class', 'after', 'append', 'appendTo',
'append_to','attr','base_url','before','children', 'clear', 'clone',
'closest', 'contents', 'copy', 'count', 'css','each','empty',
'encoding','end','eq', 'extend', 'filter',
'find','fn','hasClass','has_class','height','hide', 'html',
'index','insert', 'insertAfter', 'insertBefore',
'insert_after','insert_before', 'is_', 'items',
'length','make_links_absolute',
'map','next','nextAll','next_all','not_','outerHtml','outer_html','parent',
'parents', 'pop', 'prepend', 'prependTo', 'prepend_to','prev', 'prevAll',
'prev_all', 'remove', 'removeAttr', 'removeClass', 'remove_attr',
'remove_class','remove_namespaces', 'replaceAll', 'replaceWith',
'replace_all', 'replace_with', 'reverse', 'root','show',
siblings','size','sort','text', 'toggleClass', 'toggle_class', 'val',
'width', 'wrap', 'wrapAll','wrap_all','xhtml_to_html']
```

Now we will explore certain features from `pyquery` that are relevant to scraping concepts. For this purpose, we will be using a page source available from `https://www.python.org` that has been saved locally as `test.html` to provide real-world usability:

```
    <title>Welcome to Python.org</title>

    <meta name="description" content="The official home of the Python Programming Language">
    <meta name="keywords" content="Python programming language object oriented web free open source software license documentation download community">


    <meta property="og:type" content="website">
    <meta property="og:site_name" content="Python.org">
    <meta property="og:title" content="Welcome to Python.org">
    <meta property="og:description" content="The official home of the Python Programming Language">

    <meta property="og:image" content="https://www.python.org/static/opengraph-icon-200x200.png">
    <meta property="og:image:secure_url" content="https://www.python.org/static/opengraph-icon-200x200.png">

    <meta property="og:url" content="https://www.python.org/">

    <link rel="author" href="/static/humans.txt">
```

Page source obtained from https://www.python.org

In Google Chrome, you can right-click on the web page and choose the **View page source** menu option or press *Ctrl + U* to obtain the page source.

Obtaining the page source or HTML code only is not enough, though, as we need to load this content into the library to gain more tools to explore with. We'll be doing this in the upcoming section.

While testing or following the code, you might find or require changes to be done on the `pyquery` code expressions in order to obtain the real output. Page sources that are obtained now might be updated or changed. You are suggested to obtain the latest page source from the source URL (`https://www.python.org`).

Loading documents

In most cases, a document's content is obtained by using `requests` or `urllib` and is provided to `pyquery` as follows:

```
>>> from pyquery import PyQuery as pq
>>> import requests
>>> response = requests.get('http://www.example.com').text #content

>>> from urllib.request import urlopen
>>> response = urlopen('http://www.example.com').read()
>>> docTree = pq(response)
```

`pyquery` can also load URLs using the Python library, `urllib` (default), or requests. It also supports requests-based parameters:

```
>>> pq("https://www.python.org")
[<html.no-js>]

>>> site=pq("https://www.python.org")
>>> print(type(site))
<class 'pyquery.pyquery.PyQuery'>

>>> pq("https://www.samsclub.com")
[<html>]
```

The `pq` object we obtained from the preceding code is being parsed using the XML parser (default) that's available from `lxml`, which can also be updated with the extra `parser` argument being passed to it:

```
>>> doc = pq('http://www.exaple.com', parser = 'xml')  #using parser xml

>>> doc = pq('http://www.exaple.com', parser = 'html') #using parser html
```

Normally, HTML code from a page source or other sources, such as files, is provided as a string to `pyquery` for further processing, as shown in the following code:

```
>>> doc = pq('<div><p>Testing block</p><p>Second block</p></div>')
>>> print(type(doc))
```

```
<class 'pyquery.pyquery.PyQuery'>

>>> pagesource = open('test.html','r').read() #reading locally saved HTML
>>> print(type(pagesource))
<class 'str'>

>>> page = pq(pagesource)
>>> print(type(page))
<class 'pyquery.pyquery.PyQuery'>
```

With the `PyQuery` object or `pq` that was received from the document or URL that was loaded, we can proceed and explore the features that are available from `pyquery`.

Element traversing, attributes, and pseudo-classes

`pyquery` has a large set of attributes and methods that can be deployed to obtain the desired content. In the following examples, we'll identify the implementation from the code that's found in this section:

```
>>> page('title') #find element <title>
[<title>]

>>> page.find('title').text() #find element <title> and return text content
'Welcome to Python.org'

>>> page.find('meta[name="description"]').attr('content')
'The official home of the Python Programming Language'

>>> page.find('meta[name="keywords"]').attr('content')
'Python programming language object oriented web free open source software
license documentation download community'

>>> buttons = page('a.button').html() #return HTML content for element <a>
with class='button'
>>> buttons
'>_\n <span class="message">Launch Interactive Shell</span>\n '
```

The following are a few of their functions, along with a description, that can be seen in the preceding code:

- `find()`: Searches the provided element or evaluates the query expression build using CSS selectors
- `text()`: Returns the element content as a string

- `attr()`: Identifies the attribute and returns its content
- `html()`: Returns the HTML content of the evaluated expression

> The `class` and `id` CSS attributes are represented with `.` and `#`, respectively, and are prefixed to the attribute's value. For example, `<a class="main" id="mainLink">` will be identified as `a.main` and `a#mainLink`.

In the following code, we are listing all the identified `<ul>` elements with the `class` attribute and the `menu` value:

```
>>> page('ul.menu') #<ul> element with attribute class='menu'
[<ul.menu>, <ul.navigation.menu>, <ul.subnav.menu>, <ul.navigation.menu>,
<ul.subnav.menu>, <ul.navigation.menu>,..............,<ul.subnav.menu>,
<ul.footer-links.navigation.menu.do-not-print>]
```

The expression was passed to a PyQuery object, which generated a list of evaluated elements. These elements are iterated for their exact values or their content.

PyQuery also contains pseudo classes or `:pseudo element`, and are used for indexing and obtaining predefined expression results. `:pseudo element` can also be appended to an existing selector query. The following code implements some of the pseudo elements that are common while traversing:

```
>>> page('nav:first') #first <nav> element
[<nav.meta-navigation.container>]

>>> page('a:first') #first <a> element
[<a>]

>>> page('ul:first') #first <ul> element
[<ul.menu>]

>>> page('ul:last') #last <ul> element
[<ul.footer-links.navigation.menu.do-not-print>]
```

Let's go over the pseudo elements that were used in the preceding code:

- `:first`: Returns the first occurrence of an element from the content provided
- `:last`: Returns the last occurrence of an element from the content provided

Let's look at a general implementation of a few more :pseudo element to list the HTML elements:

```
>>> page(':header') #header elements found
[<h1.site-headline>, <h1>, <h1>, <h1>, <h1>, <h1>, <h2.widget-title>,
<h2.widget-title>..........,<h2.widget-title>, <h2.widget-title>,
<h2.widget-title>]

>>> page(':input') #input elements found
[<input#id-search-field.search-field>, <button#submit.search-button>]

>>> page(':empty') #empty elements found
[<meta>, <meta>, <link>, <meta>, <meta>, <meta>, <meta>,<script>, <link>,
<link>,........,<img.python-logo>, <span.icon-search>,<span.icon-facebook>,
<span.icon-twitter>, <span.icon-freenode>, ...........,<span.icon-feed>,
<div.python-logo>, <span#python-status-indicator.python
-status-indicator-default>, <script>, <script>, <script>]

>>> page(':empty:odd') #empty elements, only Odd ones are listed
[<meta>, <meta>, <meta>, <meta>, <meta>, <meta>, <script>, <link>, <link>,
<link>, <link>, <meta>, .......,<img.python-logo>, <span.icon-google-plus>,
<span.icon-twitter>, <span.breaker>, <span.icon-download>, <span.icon-
jobs>, <span.icon-calendar>, <span.icon-python>, <div.python-logo>,
<script>,<script>]
```

The following are the :pseudo element that we used in the preceding code:

- :header: Returns the header elements (*h1, h2,..., h5, h6*) found in the page.

- :input: Returns all the input elements. Large numbers of HTML <form>-based pseudo elements exist. Please refer to https://pythonhosted.org/pyquery/ for more information.

- :empty: Returns all the elements that don't have any child element.

- :odd: Returns elements indexed as odd numbers. They can be used with other :pseudo element as :empty:odd.

- :even: Similar to :odd, but returns evenly indexed elements.

The following code demonstrates an expression for traversing, `:pseudo element`, and element attributes together:

```
>>> page.find('ul:first').attr('class') #class name of first <ul> element
'menu'

>>> page.find('a:first').attr('href') #href value of first <a> element
'#content'

>>> page.find('a:last').attr('href') #href value of last <a> element
'/psf/sponsorship/sponsors/'

>>> page.find('a:eq(0)').attr('href') #href value of first <a> element
using Index!
'#content'

>>> page.find('a:eq(0)').text() #text from first <a> element
'Skip to content'
```

The following are a few more `:pseudo element`. We can use these to address the `index` of the elements:

- `:eq`: Selects the particular index number; evaluates to `equals to`.
- `:lt`: Evaluates to `less than` for the provided index number. For example, `page('a:lt(2)')`.
- `:gt`: Evaluates to `greater than` for the provided index numbers. For example, `page('a:gt(0)')`.

Apart from the general features that are used to identify the index and find elements, `:pseudo element` can also be used to search the element with the provided text, as shown in the following code:

```
>>> page('p:contains("Python")') #return elements <p> with text 'Python'
[<p>, <p>, <p>, <p>, <p>, <p>, <p>, <p>, <p>, <p>, <p>, <p>, <p>, <p>]

>>> page('p:contains("python.org")') #return elements <p> with text
"python.org"
[<p>, <p>]

#return text from second <p> element containing text "python.org"
>>> page('p:contains("python.org")').eq(1).text()
'jobs.python.org'
```

The following list describe simple definitions of `:contains` and `eq()`, as used in the previous code:

- `:contains`: Matches all elements that contain the provided text.
- `eq()`: Returns the element that was found for a particular index number. Evaluates as `equals to` and is similar to `:eq`.

`pyquery` has a few functions that return a Boolean answer, which is quite effective in circumstances where you need to search for an element with attributes and also confirm the attribute's value:

```
#check if class is 'python-logo'
>>> page('h1.site-headline:first a img').is_('.python-logo')
True

#check if <img> has class 'python-logo'
>>> page('h1.site-headline:first a img').has_class('python-logo')
True
```

The following are the functions that were used in the previous code, along with their definitions:

- `is_()`: Accepts a selector as an argument and returns `True` if the selector matches elements, otherwise, it returns `False`.
- `has_class()`: Returns `True` if the selector matches the class that's provided. It is useful for identifying elements with the `class` attribute.

We have used a few important functions and tools with `pyquery` that enhance element identification and traversal-related properties. In the next section, we will learn about and demonstrate iteration.

Iterating

In this section, we will be demonstrating the iterating (perform repeatedly) facility that's available with `pyquery`. It's effective and easy to process in many situations.

In the following code, we are searching for the `name` and `property` attributes that are found in the `<meta>` tags that contain the word `Python.org`. We are also using Python's `List Comprehension` technique to demonstrate the one-line coding feature:

```
#Find <meta> with attribute 'content' containing '..Python.org..'
#and list the attribute 'name' that satisfies the find()

>>> meta=page.find('meta[content*="Python.org"]')
>>> [item.attr('name') for item in meta.items() if item.attr('name') is not
None]
['application-name', 'apple-mobile-web-app-title']

#Continuing from code above list value for attribute 'property'

>>> [item.attr('property') for item in meta.items() if
item.attr('property') is not None]
['og:site_name', 'og:title']
```

As we can see in the preceding code, we are using the `items()` function in a loop with the element meta to iterate for the provided option. An expression resulting in iterable objects can be explored using `items()`. Results that return `None` are excluded from the list:

```
>>> social = page.find('a:contains("Socialize") + ul.subnav li a')
>>> [item.text() for item in social.items() if item.text() is not None]
['Google+', 'Facebook', 'Twitter', 'Chat on IRC']

>>> [item.attr('href') for item in social.items() if item.attr('href') is
not None]
['https://plus.google.com/+Python',
'https://www.facebook.com/pythonlang?fref=ts',
'https://twitter.com/ThePSF', '/community/irc/']

>>> webdevs = page.find('div.applications-widget:first ul.menu
li:contains("Web Development") a')
>>> [item.text() for item in webdevs.items() if item.text() is not None]
['Django', 'Pyramid', 'Bottle', 'Tornado', 'Flask', 'web2py']
```

In the preceding code, the `pyquery` object collects the names and links that are available from the social and web development section. These can be found under **Use Python for...** in the following screenshot. The object is iterated using the Python list comprehension technique:

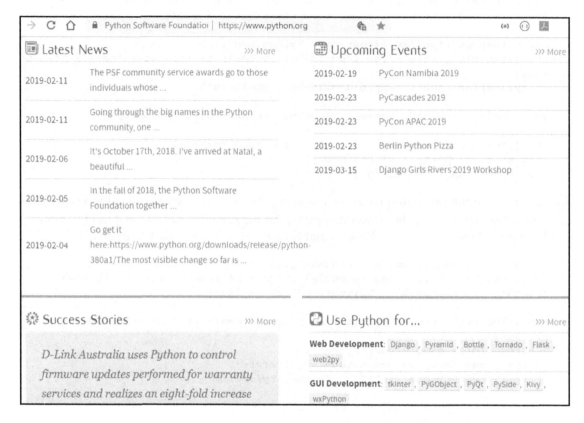

Upcoming events to be extracted using pyquery

In the following code, we will be exploring a few more details that were retrieved from the `upcomingevents` iteration:

```
>>> eventsList = []
>>> upcomingevents = page.find('div.event-widget ul.menu li')
>>> for event in upcomingevents.items():
...       time = event.find('time').text()
...       url = event.find('a[href*="events/python"]').attr('href')
...       title = event.find('a[href*="events/python"]').text()
...       eventsList.append([time,title,url])
...
>>> eventsList
```

eventsList contains extracted details from **Upcoming Events**, as shown in the preceding screenshot. The output from eventsList is provided here:

```
[['2019-02-19', 'PyCon Namibia 2019', '/events/python-events/790/'],
['2019-02-23', 'PyCascades 2019', '/events/python-events/757/'],
['2019-02-23', 'PyCon APAC 2019', '/events/python-events/807/'],
['2019-02-23', 'Berlin Python Pizza', '/events/python-events/798/'],
['2019-03-15', 'Django Girls Rivers 2019 Workshop', '/events/python-user-group/816/']]
```

DevTools can be used to identify a CSS selector for the particular section and can be further processed with the looping facility. For more information regarding the CSS Selector, please refer to Chapter 3, *Using LXML, XPath, and CSS Selectors, and the XPath and CSS selectors using DevTools* section.

The following code illustrates a few more examples of the pyquery iterating process via the use of find() and items():

```
>>> buttons = page.find('a.button')
>>> for item in buttons.items():
...     print(item.text(),' :: ',item.attr('href'))
...

>_ Launch Interactive Shell  ::  /shell/
Become a Member  ::  /users/membership/
Donate to the PSF  ::  /psf/donations/

>>> buttons = page.find('a.button:odd')
>>> for item in buttons.items():
...     print(item.text(),' :: ',item.attr('href'))
...

Become a Member  ::  /users/membership/

>>> buttons = page.find('a.button:even')
>>> for item in buttons.items():
...     print(item.text(),' :: ',item.attr('href'))
...

>_ Launch Interactive Shell  ::  /shell/
Donate to the PSF  ::  /psf/donations/
```

For more information on features, attributes, and methods from pyquery, please refer to the https://pythonhosted.org/pyquery/index.html.

Web scraping using pyquery

In the previous section, we learned about using some important features that are available from pyquery and traversing or identifying elements using those features. In this section, we will be using most of these features from pyquery and we will be using them to scrape data from the web by providing examples with various use cases.

Example 1 – scraping data science announcements

In this example, we will be scraping announcements-related details that are found within the data science category from
`https://developer.ibm.com/announcements/category/data-science/.`

The same URL from `https://developer.ibm.com/` has also been used to collect data using `lxml.cssselect` under *Example 3*, in the *Web scraping using LXML* section from Chapter 3, *Using LXML, XPath, and CSS Selectors*. It is suggested that you explore both examples and compare the features that were used.

To begin with, let's import pyquery and requests:

```
from pyquery import PyQuery as pq
import requests
dataSet = list()
```

Create `dataSet` so that you have an empty list to collect data that we will find from various pages, along with the libraries to be used. We have declared `read_url()`, which will be used to read the provided URL and return a `PyQuery` object. In this example, we will be using `sourceUrl`, that is, `https://developer.ibm.com/announcements/`:

```
sourceUrl='https://developer.ibm.com/announcements/'

def read_url(url):
  """Read given Url , Returns pyquery object for page content"""
  pageSource = requests.get(url).content
  return pq(pageSource)
```

The information to be collected can be retrieved from `https://developer.ibm.com/announcements/category/data-science/?fa=date:DESCfb=` or obtained using `sourceUrl+"category/data-science/?fa=date:DESC&fb="`. Here, we will be looping through `pageUrls`.

`pageUrls` results in the following page URLs. These were obtained by using list comprehension and `range()`:

- `https://developer.ibm.com/announcements/category/data-science/page/1?f a=date:DESC&fb=`
- `https://developer.ibm.com/announcements/category/data-science/page/2? fa=date:DESCfb=`

As shown in the following code, `pageUrls` generates a list of page-based URLs that can be processed further via the use of the `get_details()` function. This is used to retrieve articles:

```
if __name__ == '__main__':
    mainUrl = sourceUrl+"category/data-science/?fa=date:DESC&fb="
    pageUrls = [sourceUrl+"category/data-
science/page/%(page)s?fa=date:DESC&fb=" % {'page': page} for page in
range(1, 3)]

    for pages in pageUrls:
        get_details(pages)

    print("\nTotal articles collected: ", len(dataSet))
    print(dataSet)
```

As we can see from the preceding code, the following URLs were listed:

- `https://developer.ibm.com/announcements/category/data-science/page/1? fa=date:DESCfb=`
- `https://developer.ibm.com/announcements/category/data-science/page/2? fa=date:DESCfb=`

The URLs from `pageUrls` are iterated and passed to `get_details()` for further processing, as shown in the following code:

```
def get_details(page):
    """read 'page' url and append list of queried items to dataSet"""
    response = read_url(page)

    articles = response.find('.ibm--card > a.ibm--card__block_link')
    print("\nTotal articles found :", articles.__len__(), ' in Page: ',
page)

    for article in articles.items():
        link = article.attr('href')
        articlebody = article.find('div.ibm--card__body')
```

```
        adate = articlebody.find('h5 > .ibm--card__date').text()
        articlebody.find('h5 > .ibm--card__date').remove()
        atype = articlebody.find('h5').text().strip()
        title = articlebody.find('h3.ibm--
card__title').text().encode('utf-8')
        excerpt = articlebody.find('p.ibm--
card__excerpt').text().encode('utf-8')
        category = article.find('div.ibm--card__bottom > p.cpt-
byline__categories span')

    if link:
        link = str(link).replace('/announcements/', mainUrl)
        categories = [span.text for span in category if span.text !=
'+']
        dataSet.append([link, atype, adate, title,
excerpt,",".join(categories)])
```

The page URL that's passed to `get_details()` is read by `read_url()` and `response` from a `PyQuery` object is obtained. Information that contains blocks are identified as articles using CSS selectors. Since there's more than one `articles` iteration available, we use `items()`. Individual data elements are then processed with the help of cleaning, replacing, and merging activities before they are appended to the main dataset, which in this case is `dataSet`. PyQuery expressions can also be shortened via the use of `articlebody`.

Also, the `remove()` PyQuery (manipulation) method is used to remove `.ibm--card__date`, which is found inside `<h5>`, in order to obtain `atype`. The `atype` content would also contain additional `.ibm--card__date` details if used without removing with the following code:

```
articlebody.find('h5 > .ibm--card__date').remove())
```

The final output that's obtained from the preceding code is as follows:

```
Total articles found : 8 in Page:
https://developer.ibm.com/announcements/category/data-science/page/1?fa=dat
e:DESC&fb=

Total articles found : 2 in Page:
https://developer.ibm.com/announcements/category/data-science/page/2?fa=dat
e:DESC&fb=

Total articles collected: 10

[['https://developer.ibm.com/announcements/model-mgmt-on-watson-studio-loca
l/', 'Announcement', 'Nov 05, 2018', b'Perform feature engineering and
```

```
model scoring', b'This code pattern demonstrates how data scientists can
leverage IBM Watson Studio Local to automate the building and training
of\xe2\x80\xa6', 'Analytics,Apache Spark'], ..........................,
['https://developer.ibm.com/announcements/algorithm-that-gives-you-answer-t
o-any-particular-question-based-on-mining-documents/', 'Announcement', 'Sep
17, 2018', b'Query a knowledge base to get insights about data', b'Learn a
strategy to query a knowledge graph with a question and find the right
answer.', 'Artificial Intelligence,Data Science'],
['https://developer.ibm.com/announcements/build-a-domain-specific-knowledge
-graph-from-given-set-of-documents/', 'Announcement', 'Sep 14, 2018',
b'Walk through the process of building a knowledge base by mining
information stored in the documents', b'Take a look at all of the aspects
of building a domain-specific knowledge graph.', 'Artificial
Intelligence,Data Science']]
```

Example 2 – scraping information from nested links

In this example, we will be scraping details for quotes found in **books** from `http://quotes.toscrape.com/tag/books/`. Each individual quote contains certain information, plus a link to the author's detail page, which will also be processed so that we can obtain information regarding the author:

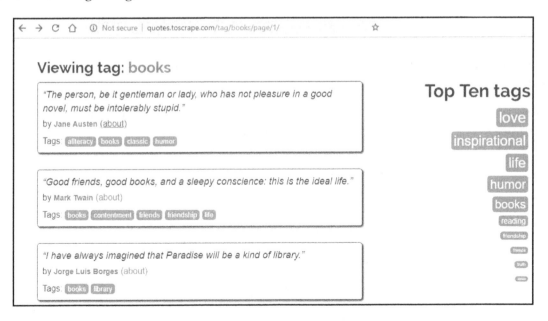

Main page from http://quotes.toscrape.com/tag/books/

In the following code, the elements in `keys` will be used as keys for output and will contain the Python dictionary. Basically, we will be collecting data for elements in keys:

```
from pyquery import PyQuery as pq
sourceUrl = 'http://quotes.toscrape.com/tag/books/'
dataSet = list()
keys =
['quote_tags','author_url','author_name','born_date','born_location','quote
_title']

def read_url(url):
    """Read given Url , Returns pyquery object for page content"""
    pageSource = pq(url)
    return pq(pageSource)
```

`read_url()` from the preceding code is also updated and is different in comparison to the libraries we used in the *Example 1 – scraping data science announcements* section. In this example, it returns the PyQuery object for the provided URL:

```
if __name__ == '__main__':
    get_details(sourceUrl)

    print("\nTotal Quotes collected: ", len(dataSet))
    print(dataSet)

    for info in dataSet:
        print(info['author_name'],' born on ',info['born_date'], ' in
',info['born_location'])
```

There is an additional iteration being done with `dataSet` for certain values from the `info` dictionary, which is found inside `dataSet`.

As shown in the following code, `get_details()` uses a `while` loop for pagination purposes, and is controlled by the `nextPage` value:

```
def get_details(page):
    """read 'page' url and append list of queried items to dataSet"""
    nextPage = True
    pageNo = 1
    while (nextPage):
        response = read_url(page + 'page/' + str(pageNo))
        if response.find("ul.pager:has('li.next')"):
            nextPage = True
        else:
            nextPage = False

        quotes = response.find('.quote')
```

```
        print("\nTotal Quotes found :", quotes.__len__(), ' in Page: ',
pageNo)
        for quote in quotes.items():
            title = quote.find('[itemprop="text"]:first').text()
            author = quote.find('[itemprop="author"]:first').text()
            authorLink =
quote.find('a[href*="/author/"]:first').attr('href')
            tags = quote.find('.tags
[itemprop="keywords"]').attr('content')

            if authorLink:
                authorLink = 'http://quotes.toscrape.com' + authorLink
                linkDetail = read_url(authorLink)
                born_date = linkDetail.find('.author-born-date').text()
                born_location = linkDetail.find('.author-born-
location').text()
                if born_location.startswith('in'):
                    born_location = born_location.replace('in ','')
        dataSet.append(dict(zip(keys,[tags,authorLink,author,born_date,born_locatio
n,title[0:50]])))
        pageNo += 1
```

`:has()` returns the element that matches the selector that's passed to it. In this example, we are confirming whether the `pager` class has an `<li>` element with the `next` class, that is, `ul.pager:has('li.next')`. If the expression is `true`, then a page link exists for another page, and `else` terminates the loop.

`quotes` that are obtained are iterated using `items()` to obtain `title`, `author`, `tags`, and `authorLink`. The `authorLink` URL is further processed using the `read_url()` function in order to obtain author-related, specific information from the `.author-born-date` and `.author-born-location` classes for `born_date` and `born_location`, respectively.

The elements classes we used in the preceding code can be found in **Page Source**, as shown in the following screenshot:

Quotes to Scrape

Jane Austen

Born: December 16, 1775 in Steventon Rectory, Hampshire, The United Kingdom

Description:

Jane Austen was an English novelist whose works of romantic fiction, set among the landed gentry, earned her a place as one of the most widely read writers in English literature, her realism and biting social commentary cementing her historical importance among scholars and critics.Austen lived her entire life as part of a close-knit family located on the lower fringes of the English landed gentry. She was educated primarily by her father and older brothers as well as through her own reading. The steadfast support of her family was critical to her development as a professional writer. Her artistic apprenticeship

Inner page with author details

The `zip()` Python function is used with *keys* and quotes fields, which is appended to `dataSet` as a Python Dictionary.

The output for the preceding code is as follows:

```
Total Quotes found : 10 in Page: 1
Total Quotes found : 1 in Page: 2
Total Quotes collected: 11

[{'author_name': 'Jane Austen', 'born_location': 'Steventon Rectory,
Hampshire, The United Kingdom', 'quote_tags':
'aliteracy,books,classic,humor', 'author_url':
'http://quotes.toscrape.com/author/Jane-Austen', 'quote_title':
'"............................. ', 'born_date': 'December 16, 1775'},
{'author_name': 'Mark Twain', 'born_location': 'Florida, Missouri, The
United States', 'quote_tags': 'books,contentment,friends,friendship,life',
'author_url': 'http://quotes.toscrape.com/author/Mark-Twain',
'quote_title': '".......................................', 'born_date':
'November 30, 1835'}
,.............................................................................
```

```
.........................,
{'author_name': 'George R.R. Martin', 'born_location': 'Bayonne, New
Jersey, The United States', 'quote_tags': 'books,mind', 'author_url':
'http://quotes.toscrape.com/author/George-R-R-Martin', 'quote_title': '"...
...............................', 'born_date': 'September 20, 1948'}]
```

An additional loop was run for the obtained `dataSet`, which results in a string, as shown here:

```
Jane Austen born on December 16, 1775 in Steventon Rectory, Hampshire, The
United Kingdom
Mark Twain born on November 30, 1835 in Florida, Missouri, The United
States
............................
............................
George R.R. Martin born on September 20, 1948 in Bayonne, New Jersey, The
United States
```

Example 3 – extracting AHL Playoff results

In this example, we will be extracting data from **American Hockey League (AHL)** Playoff results, which are available from `http://www.flyershistory.com/cgi-bin/ml-poffs.cgi`:

2001-02					
Win Western Conference Qualifier vs Rochester 2-0					
9-Apr-01	Rch	2	at Phil	4	W
11-Apr-01	Rch	2	at Phil	3	W
Lost Western Conference Quarterfinals vs Syracuse 0-3					
13-Apr-01	Phil	3	at Syr	5	2002P L
17-Apr-01	Phil	1	at Syr	4	L
21-Apr-01	Syr	3	at Phil	1	L
2002-03					

AHL Playoff results

The preceding URL contains the Playoff results for the AHL. This page presents information about the results in tabular format. The portion of the page source that shows relevant information is shown in the following screenshot:

```
<CENTER><h1><font color=white>AHL Playoff Results</font></h1><TABLE BORDER=0 CELLPADDING=2
BGCOLOR=white>
<TR ALIGN=CENTER>
<TD COLSPAN=8 BGCOLOR=black><B><FONT COLOR=white><FONT SIZE=+2>1967-68</FONT></FONT></B></TD>
</TR><tr><td colspan=8 BGCOLOR="FF6600"><center><b><font color=white>Won Quarterfinal Over Buffalo 3-
2</font></b></center></td></tr>
<tr><td>3-Apr-68</td><td>Buff</td><td>2</td><td>at</td><td>Que</td><td>4</td><td>W</td><td></td></tr>
<tr><td>5-Apr-68</td><td>Buff</td><td>1</td><td>at</td><td>Que</td><td>3</td><td>W</td><td></td></tr>
<tr><td>9-Apr-68</td><td>Que</td><td>7</td><td>at</td><td>Buff</td><td>10</td><td>L</td><td></td></tr>
<tr><td>10-Apr-68</td><td>Que</td><td>4</td><td>at</td><td>Buff</td><td>7</td><td>L</td><td></td></tr>
<tr><td>12-Apr-68</td><td>Buff</td><td>1</td><td>at</td><td>Que</td><td>3</td><td>W</td><td></td></tr>

<TR ALIGN=CENTER>
<TD COLSPAN=8 BGCOLOR=black><B><FONT COLOR=white><FONT SIZE=+2>2008-09</FONT></FONT></B></TD>
</TR><tr><td colspan=8 BGCOLOR="FF6600"><center><b><font color=white>Lost Conference Quarterfinals vs Hershey 0-
4</font></b></center></td></tr>
<tr><td>16-Apr-09</td><td>Phantoms</td><td>2</td><td>at</td><td>Hershey</td><td>4</td><td>2009P</td><td>L</td></tr>
<tr><td>18-Apr-09</td><td>Phantoms</td><td>2</td><td>at</td><td>Hershey</td><td>6</td><td>2009P</td><td>L</td></tr>
<tr><td>22-Apr-09</td><td>Hershey</td><td>2</td><td>at</td><td>Phantoms</td><td>3</td><td>2009P</td><td>L</td></tr>
<tr><td>24-Apr-09</td><td>Hershey</td><td>0</td><td>at</td><td>Phantoms</td><td>1</td><td>2009P</td><td>L</td></tr>
```

Page source from http://www.flyershistory.com/cgi-bin/ml-poffs.cgi

The preceding screenshot contains the top and bottom part of the tabular information from the source URL and presents two different formats of `<tr>` that are available in the page source. The number of `<td>` that are available in `<tr>` have different, extra information.

With the source format analyzed, it's also necessary to point out that `<td>` containing the desired values has no attributes that can be used to identify particular table cells. In this case, we can target the position of `<td>` or cell with data by using CSS selectors, that is, *pseudo selectors* such as `td:eq(0)` or `td:eq(1)`.

For more information on CSS selectors, please visit `Chapter 3`, *Using LXML, XPath, and CSS Selectors*, the *Introduction to XPath and CSS selector* section, in the *CSS Selectors* and *Pseudo Selectors* sub-section.

Since we will be using `pyquery` for this example, we will use the `eq()` method, which accepts the index and returns the element. For example, we could use `tr.find('td').eq(1).text()` for the chosen PyQuery object, `tr`, search for the element `td`, that is, `<td>`, with the index equal to `1`, and return the text of the element.

Here, we are interested in collecting data for the columns that are listed in `keys`:

```
keys = ['year','month','day','game_date','team1', 'team1_score', 'team2',
'team2_score', 'game_status']
```

Now, let's import the code with `pyquery` and `re`. Regex will be used to separate the date that was obtained from the page source:

```
from pyquery import PyQuery as pq
import re

sourceUrl = 'http://www.flyershistory.com/cgi-bin/ml-poffs.cgi'
dataSet = list()
keys = ['year','month','day','game_date','team1', 'team1_score', 'team2',
'team2_score', 'game_status']

def read_url(url):
    """Read given Url , Returns pyquery object for page content"""
    pageSource = pq(url)
    return pq(pageSource)

if __name__ == '__main__':
    page = read_url(sourceUrl)
```

Here, `read_url()` accepts one argument, that is, the link to the page, and returns the PyQuery object of the page source or `pageSource`. PyQuery automatically returns the page source for the provided URL. The page source can also be obtained by using other libraries, such as `urllib`, `urllib3`, `requests`, and LXML, and passed to create a PyQuery object:

```
tableRows = page.find("h1:contains('AHL Playoff Results') + table tr")
print("\nTotal rows found :", tableRows.__len__())
```

`tableRows` is a PyQuery object that will be used to traverse `<tr>` that exists inside `<table>`, which is located after `<h1>`. It contains the `AHL Playoff Results` text, which is obtained by using the `find()` function. As we can see in the following output, a total of `463` `<tr>` elements exist, but the actual number of records that were obtained might be lower, in terms of the number of available `<td>` with the actual data:

```
Total rows found : 463
```

Let's do some more processing. Each `<tr>` or `tr` element is an item of `tableRows` and is traversed with the help of the `items()` method to find the exact `<td>` or `td` by using their index and retrieving the data it contains:

```
for tr in tableRows.items():
    #few <tr> contains single <td> and is omitted using the condition
    team1 = tr.find('td').eq(1).text()

    if team1 != '':
        game_date = tr.find('td').eq(0).text()
        dates = re.search(r'(.*)-(.*)-(.*)',game_date)
        team1_score = tr.find('td').eq(2).text()
        team2 = tr.find('td').eq(4).text()
        team2_score = tr.find('td').eq(5).text()

        #check Game Status should be either 'W' or 'L'
        game_status = tr.find('td').eq(6).text()
        if not re.match(r'[WL]',game_status):
            game_status = tr.find('td').eq(7).text()

        #breaking down date in year,month and day
        year = dates.group(3)
        month = dates.group(2)
        day = dates.group(1)

        #preparing exact year value
        if len(year)==2 and int(year)>=68:
            year = '19'+year
        elif len(year)==2 and int(year) <68:
            year = '20'+year
        else:
            pass
```

So far, the desired data from the targeted `<td>` has been collected and also formatted in the case of `year`. Regex has also been applied in the code and used with `dates` and `game_status`. Finally, the collected objects are appended as a list to `dataSet`:

```
#appending individual data list to the dataSet
dataSet.append([year,month,day,game_date,team1,team1_score,team2,team2_scor
e,game_status])

print("\nTotal Game Status, found :", len(dataSet))
print(dataSet)
```

The output regarding the total record count and `dataSet` is as follows:

```
Total Game Status, found : 341

[['1968', 'Apr', '3', '3-Apr-68', 'Buff', '2', 'Que', '4', 'W'],
 ['1968', 'Apr', '5', '5-Apr-68', 'Buff', '1', 'Que', '3', 'W'],
 ['1968', 'Apr', '9', '9-Apr-68', 'Que', '7', 'Buff', '10', 'L'],
 ['1968', 'Apr', '10', '10-Apr-68', 'Que', '4', 'Buff', '7', 'L'],
 ['1968', 'Apr', '12', '12-Apr-68', 'Buff', '1', 'Que', '3', 'W'],
 ...............
 ['2008', 'May', '9', '9-May-2008', 'Phantoms', '3', 'Wilkes-Barre', '1',
'L'],
 ['2009', 'Apr', '16', '16-Apr-09', 'Phantoms', '2', 'Hershey', '4', 'L'],
 ['2009', 'Apr', '18', '18-Apr-09', 'Phantoms', '2', 'Hershey', '6', 'L'],
 ['2009', 'Apr', '22', '22-Apr-09', 'Hershey', '2', 'Phantoms', '3', 'L'],
 ['2009', 'Apr', '24', '24-Apr-09', 'Hershey', '0', 'Phantoms', '1', 'L']]
```

Example 4 – collecting URLs from sitemap.xml

In this example, we will be extracting URLs that have been found for blogs in the `sitemap.xml` file from `https://webscraping.com/sitemap.xml`.

In the preceding examples, we used HTML content, but PyQuery can also be used to traverse XML file content. By default, `pyquery` uses an LXML-based `xml` parser, which can be provided while creating a PyQuery object. We will be using both `lxml.html` and `xml` in the file's content.

 For more information on `pyquery` and `parser`, please visit the *Exploring pyquery* section of this chapter. For information regarding the site map, please visit `Chapter 1`, *Web Scraping Fundamentals*, the *Data finding techniques (seeking data from the web)* section, in the *Sitemaps* subsection.

The following screenshot shows the content that's available in the `sitemap.xml` file:

```
▼<urlset xmlns="https://www.sitemaps.org/schemas/sitemap/0.9">
  ▼<url>
      <loc>https://webscraping.com</loc>
    </url>
  ▼<url>
      <loc>https://webscraping.com/about</loc>
    </url>
  ▼<url>
      <loc>https://webscraping.com/blog</loc>
    </url>
  ▼<url>
      <loc>https://webscraping.com/blog/10/</loc>
    </url>
  ▼<url>
      <loc>https://webscraping.com/blog/11/</loc>
    </url>
  ▼<url>
      <loc>https://webscraping.com/blog/12/</loc>
    </url>
  ▼<url>
```

sitemap.xml file from https://webscraping.com

To begin with, let's import `pyquery` and read the file's content as `xmlFile`:

```
from pyquery import PyQuery as pq

if __name__ == '__main__':
    # reading file
    xmlFile = open('sitemap.xml', 'r').read()
```

Case 1 – using the HTML parser

Here, we will be using the `lxml.html` parser to parse `xmlFile` by passing an argument parser, `parser='html'`, to PyQuery:

```
# creating PyQuery object using parser 'html'
 urlHTML = pq(xmlFile, parser='html')

print("Children Length: ",urlHTML.children().__len__())
print("First Children: ",urlHTML.children().eq(0))
print("Inner Child/First Children: ",urlHTML.children().children().eq(0))
```

Using PyQuery's `urlHTML` object allows us to check the count and the child elements that were obtained from the data, as shown in the following output:

```
Children Length: 137

First Children:
<url>
<loc>https://webscraping.com</loc>
</url>

Inner Child/First Children: <loc>https://webscraping.com</loc>
```

As we can see, `urlHTML.children()` contains the required elements to look for the URL. We can process this data with the `items()` method, which traverses through each element that's obtained. Let's create `dataSet` (Python `list()`) that will be appended with the URLs that are extracted.

Element-based iteration can be performed with `urlHTML.children().find('loc:contains("blog")').items()` by using a selector that contains the `blog` string:

```
dataSet=list()
for url in urlHTML.children().find('loc:contains("blog")').items():
    dataSet.append(url.text())

print("Length of dataSet: ", len(dataSet))
print(dataSet)
```

Finally, we will receive the following output:

```
Length of dataSet: 131

['https://webscraping.com/blog', 'https://webscraping.com/blog/10/',
'https://webscraping.com/blog/11/', 'https://webscraping.com/blog/12/',
'https://webscraping.com/blog/13/', 'https://webscraping.com/blog/2/'
,.............................................................
........,
'https://webscraping.com/blog/Reverse-Geocode/',
'https://webscraping.com/blog/Scraping-Flash-based-websites/',
'https://webscraping.com/blog/Scraping-JavaScript-based-web-pages-with-Chic
kenfoot/', 'https://webscraping.com/blog/category/web2py',
'https://webscraping.com/blog/category/webkit',
'https://webscraping.com/blog/category/website/',
'https://webscraping.com/blog/category/xpath']
```

Case 2 – using the XML parser

In this case, we will be processing XML content with the PyQuery urlXML object, which uses parser='xml':

```
#creating PyQuery object using parser 'xml'
urlXML = pq(xmlFile, parser='xml')

print("Children Length: ",urlXML.children().__len__())
```

The preceding code returns the length of the children's count, that is, 137 total URLs:

```
Children Length: 137
```

As shown in the following code, the first and inner children elements return the required URL content we are willing to extract:

```
print("First Children: ", urlXML.children().eq(0))
print("Inner Child/First Children: ", urlXML.children().children().eq(0))

First Children:
<url xmlns="https://www.sitemaps.org/schemas/sitemap/0.9">
<loc>https://webscraping.com</loc>
</url>

Inner Child/First Children:
<loc
xmlns="https://www.sitemaps.org/schemas/sitemap/0.9">https://webscraping.co
m</loc>
```

Let's proceed with the child elements by using a selector similar to the one we used in the *Case 1 – using the HTML parser* section:

```
dataSet=list()
for url in urlXML.children().find('loc:contains("blog")').items():
    dataSet.append(url.text())

print("Length of dataSet: ", len(dataSet))
print(dataSet)
```

Here, we have received no output in dataSet, and it looks like the selector isn't working like it did in *Case 1 – using the HTML parser*:

```
Length of dataSet: 0
[]
```

Let's verify this case by using the following code:

```
for url in urlXML.children().children().items():
    print(url)
    break

<loc
xmlns="https://www.sitemaps.org/schemas/sitemap/0.9">https://webscraping.co
m</loc>
```

The node that we received belongs to `https://www.sitemaps.org/schemas/sitemap/0.9`. Without removing the namespace selectors, it will not work.

The `remove_namespace()` function can be used on a PyQuery object and processed for its final output, as shown in the following code:

```
for url in
urlXML.remove_namespaces().children().find('loc:contains("blog")').items():
    dataSet.append(url.text())

print("Length of dataSet: ", len(dataSet))
print(dataSet)
```

We receive the following output:

```
Length of dataSet: 131

['https://webscraping.com/blog', 'https://webscraping.com/blog/10/',
'https://webscraping.com/blog/11/', 'https://webscraping.com/blog/12/',
'https://webscraping.com/blog/13/', 'https://webscraping.com/blog/2/',
'https://webscraping.com/blog/3/', 'https://webscraping.com/blog/4/',
'https://webscraping.com/blog/5/', 'https://webscraping.com/blog/6/',
'https://webscraping.com/blog/7/', 'https://webscraping.com/blog/8/',
. . . . . . . . . . . . . . . . . . . . . . . . . . . . . . . . . . . . . . . . . . . . . . . . . . . . . . . . .
'https://webscraping.com/blog/category/screenshot',
'https://webscraping.com/blog/category/sitescraper',
'https://webscraping.com/blog/category/sqlite',
'https://webscraping.com/blog/category/user-agent',
'https://webscraping.com/blog/category/web2py',
'https://webscraping.com/blog/category/webkit',
'https://webscraping.com/blog/category/website/',
'https://webscraping.com/blog/category/xpath']
```

The PyQuery `remove_namespace()` and `xhtml_to_html()` methods remove the namespaces from XML and XHTML, respectively. Use of these two methods allows us to work with elements that use HTML-related properties.

We can also process the same content with a different approach; that is, by using a regular expression and obtaining the output as required. Let's proceed with the following code:

```
print("URLs using Children: ",urlXML.children().text())
#print("URLs using Children: ",urlXML.children().children().text())
#print("URLs using Children: ",urlXML.text())
```

The PyQuery `children()` object method returns all the child nodes, and `text()` will extract the text content, as shown here:

```
URLs using Children: https://webscraping.com https://webscraping.com/about
https://webscraping.com/blog
............https://webscraping.com/blog/Converting-UK-Easting-Northing-co
ordinates/ https://webscraping.com/blog/Crawling-with-threads/
https://webscraping.com/blog/Discount-coupons-for-data-store/
https://webscraping.com/blog/Extracting-article-summaries/
https://webscraping.com/blog/10/ https://webscraping.com/feedback.........
```

As shown in the preceding output, all the links from the child nodes are returned as a single string:

```
blogXML = re.split(r'\s',urlXML .children().text())
print("Length of blogXML: ",len(blogXML))

#filter(), filters URLs from blogXML that matches string 'blog'
dataSet= list(filter(lambda blogXML:re.findall(r'blog',blogXML),blogXML))
print("Length of dataSet: ",len(dataSet))
print("Blog Urls: ",dataSet)
```

Here, `re.split()` is used to split the string of URLs received with the space character, `\s`. This returns a total of 139 elements. Finally, `blogXML` is filtered using `re.findall()`, which finds the `blog` string in the `blogXML` elements and results in the following:

```
Length of blogXML: 139
Length of dataSet: 131

Blog Urls: ['https://webscraping.com/blog',
'https://webscraping.com/blog/10/', 'https://webscraping.com/blog/11/',
'https://webscraping.com/blog/12/', 'https://webscraping.com/blog/13/',
'https://webscraping.com/blog/2/', 'https://webscraping.com/blog/3/',
'https://webscraping.com/blog/4/', 'https://webscraping.com/blog/5/',
'https://webscraping.com/blog/6/', 'https://webscraping.com/blog/7/',
```

```
'https://webscraping.com/blog/8/', ..................................
......
'https://webscraping.com/blog/category/web2py',
'https://webscraping.com/blog/category/webkit',
'https://webscraping.com/blog/category/website/',
'https://webscraping.com/blog/category/xpath']
```

In this section, we have used a few scraping techniques to extract the desired content from files and websites. Content identification and the requirement to scrape is pretty dynamic and is also based on the structure of the website. With libraries such as `pyquery`, we can obtain and deploy the necessary tools and techniques for scraping in an effective and efficient manner.

Summary

`pyquery` seems to be more efficient in dealing with CSS selectors and provides a lot of features related to LXML. Simple and readable code is always in demand, and `pyquery` provides these features for scraping purposes. In this chapter, we explored various cases that you may encounter while performing scraping tasks and successfully managed to get the desired outcome.

In the next chapter, we will be exploring a few more libraries related to web scraping.

Further reading

- PyQuery complete API: `https://pyquery.readthedocs.io/en/latest/api.html`
- pyquery: a jquery-like library for Python: `https://pythonhosted.org/pyquery/`
- CSS Selector Reference: `https://www.w3schools.com/cssref/css_selectors.asp`
- CSS Pseudo Class and Elements: `https://www.w3schools.com/css/css_pseudo_elements.asp`
- CSS information: `http://www.css3.info/` and `https://developer.mozilla.org/en-US/docs/Web/CSS`
- Sitemaps: `https://www.sitemaps.org/`
- XML: `https://www.w3schools.com/xml/` and `https://www.w3.org/XML/`

5
Web Scraping Using Scrapy and Beautiful Soup

So far, we have learned about web-development technologies, data-finding techniques, and accessing various Python libraries to scrape data from the web.

In this chapter, we will be learning about and exploring two Python libraries that are popular for document parsing and scraping activities: Scrapy and Beautiful Soup.

Beautiful Soup deals with document parsing. Parsing a document is done for element traversing and extracting its content. Scrapy is a web crawling framework written in Python. It provides a project-oriented scope for web scraping. Scrapy provides plenty of built-in resources for email, selectors, items, and so on, and can be used from simple to API-based content extraction.

In this chapter, we will learn about the following:

- Web scraping using Beautiful Soup
- Web scraping using Scrapy
- Deploying a web crawler (learning how to deploy scraping code using `https://www.scrapinghub.com`

Technical requirements

A web browser (Google Chrome or Mozilla Firefox) is required and we will be using the application and Python libraries listed here:

- Latest Python 3.7* or Python 3.0* (installed)
- The Python libraries required are the following:
    - `lxml`
    - `requests, urllib`

- bs4 or beautifulsoup4
- scrapy

For setting up or installation refer to Chapter 2, *Python and the Web – Using urllib and Requests, Setting things up* section.

Code files are available online at GitHub: https://github.com/PacktPublishing/Hands-On-Web-Scraping-with-Python/tree/master/Chapter05.

Web scraping using Beautiful Soup

Web scraping is a procedure for extracting data from web documents. For data collection or extracting data from web documents, identifying and traversing through elements (of HTML, XML) is the basic requirement. Web documents are built with various types of elements that can exist either individually or nested together.

Parsing is an activity of breaking down, exposing, or identifying the components with contents from any given web content. Such activity enhances features such as searching and collecting content from the desired element or elements. Web documents obtained, parsed, and traversed through looking for required data or content is the basic scraping task.

In Chapter 3, *Using LXML, XPath, and CSS Selectors*, we explored lxml for a similar task and used XPath and CSS Selectors for data-extraction purposes. lxml is also used for scraping and parsing because of its memory-efficient features and extensible libraries.

In the next subsection, we will learn and explore features of the Python bs4 library (for Beautiful Soup).

Introduction to Beautiful Soup

Beautiful Soup is generally identified as a parsing library, and is also known as an HTML parser that is used to parse web documents either in HTML or XML. It generates a parsed tree similar to lxml (ElementTree), which is used to identify and traverse through elements to extract data and perform web scraping.

Beautiful Soup provides complete parsing-related features that are available using lxml and htmllib. Collections of simple and easy-to-use methods, plus properties to deal with navigation, searching, and parsing-related activity, make Beautiful Soup a favorite among other Python libraries.

Document encoding can be handled manually using the Beautiful Soup constructor, but Beautiful Soup handles encoding-related tasks automatically unless specified by the constructor.

One of the distinguishing features of Beautiful Soup, over other libraries and parsers, is that it can also be used to parse broken HTML or files with incomplete or missing tags. For more information on Beautiful Soup, please visit `https://www.crummy.com/software/BeautifulSoup`.

Let's now explore and learn some of the major tools and methods relevant to the data-extraction process using Beautiful Soup.

Exploring Beautiful Soup

The Python `bs4` library contains a `BeautifulSoup` class, which is used for parsing. For more details on Beautiful Soup and installing the library, please refer to the official documentation on installing Beautiful Soup at `https://www.crummy.com/software/BeautifulSoup/`. On successful installation of the library, we can obtain the details as shown in the following screenshot, using Python IDE:

```
>>> import bs4
>>> bs4.__version__
'4.7.1'
>>> dir(bs4)
['BeautifulSoup', 'BeautifulStoneSoup', 'CData', 'Comment', 'DEFAULT_OUTPUT_ENCODING', 'Declaration', 'Doctype', 'F
eatureNotFound', 'NavigableString', 'PageElement', 'ParserRejectedMarkup', 'ProcessingInstruction', 'ResultSet', 'S
oupStrainer', 'StopParsing', 'Tag', 'UnicodeDammit', '__all__', '__author__', '__builtins__', '__cached__', '__copy
right__', '__doc__', '__file__', '__license__', '__loader__', '__name__', '__package__', '__path__', '__spec__', '__
version__', '_s', '_soup', 'builder', 'builder_registry', 'dammit', 'element', 'os', 're', 'sys', 'traceback', 'wa
rnings']
>>> dir(bs4.BeautifulSoup)
['ASCII_SPACES', 'DEFAULT_BUILDER_FEATURES', 'HTML_FORMATTERS', 'NO_PARSER_SPECIFIED_WARNING', 'ROOT_TAG_NAME', 'XM
L_FORMATTERS', '__bool__', '__call__', '__class__', '__contains__', '__copy__', '__delattr__', '__delitem__', '__di
ct__', '__dir__', '__doc__', '__eq__', '__format__', '__ge__', '__getattr__', '__getattribute__', '__getitem__', '__
getstate__', '__gt__', '__hash__', '__init__', '__init_subclass__', '__iter__', '__le__', '__len__', '__lt__', '__
module__', '__ne__', '__new__', '__reduce__', '__reduce_ex__', '__repr__', '__setattr__', '__setitem__', '__sizeof_
_', '__str__', '__subclasshook__', '__unicode__', '__weakref__', '_all_strings', '_check_markup_is_url', '_feed', '
_find_all', '_find_one', '_formatter_for_name', '_is_xml', '_lastRecursiveChild', '_last_descendant', '_linkage_fix
er', '_popToTag', '_should_pretty_print', 'append', 'childGenerator', 'children', 'clear', 'decode', 'decode_conten
ts', 'decompose', 'descendants', 'encode', 'encode_contents', 'endData', 'extend', 'extract', 'fetchNextSiblings',
'fetchParents', 'fetchPrevious', 'fetchPreviousSiblings', 'find', 'findAll', 'findAllNext', 'findAllPrevious', 'fin
dChild', 'findChildren', 'findNext', 'findNextSibling', 'findNextSiblings', 'findParent', 'findParents', 'findPrevi
ous', 'findPreviousSibling', 'findPreviousSiblings', 'find_all', 'find_all_next', 'find_all_previous', 'find_next',
'find_next_sibling', 'find_next_siblings', 'find_parent', 'find_parents', 'find_previous', 'find_previous_sibling',
'find_previous_siblings', 'format_string', 'get', 'getText', 'get_attribute_list', 'get_text', 'handle_data', 'hand
le_endtag', 'handle_starttag', 'has_attr', 'has_key', 'index', 'insert', 'insert_after', 'insert_before', 'isSelfCl
osing', 'is_empty_element', 'new_string', 'new_tag', 'next', 'nextGenerator', 'nextSibling', 'nextSiblingGenerator'
, 'next_elements', 'next_siblings', 'object_was_parsed', 'parentGenerator', 'parents', 'parserClass', 'popTag', 'pr
ettify', 'previous', 'previousGenerator', 'previousSibling', 'previousSiblingGenerator', 'previous_elements', 'prev
ious_siblings', 'pushTag', 'recursiveChildGenerator', 'renderContents', 'replaceWith', 'replaceWithChildren', 'repl
ace_with', 'replace_with_children', 'reset', 'select', 'select_one', 'setup', 'string', 'strings', 'stripped_string
s', 'text', 'unwrap', 'wrap']
```

Successful installation of bs4 with details

Also, the collection of simple (named) and explainable methods available as seen in the preceding screenshot and encoding support makes it more popular among developers.

Let's import `BeautifulSoup` and `SoupStrainer` from `bs4`, as seen in the following code:

```
from bs4 import BeautifulSoup
from bs4 import SoupStrainer #,BeautifulSoup
```

We will be using the HTML as shown in the following snippet or `html_doc` as a sample to explore some of the fundamental features of Beautiful Soup. The response obtained for any chosen URL, using `requests` or `urllib`, can also be used for content in real scraping cases:

```
html_doc="""<html><head><title>The Dormouse's story</title></head>
<body>
<p class="title"><b>The Dormouse's story</b></p>
<p class="story">Once upon a time there were three little sisters; and
their names were
<a href="http://example.com/elsie" class="sister" id="link1">Elsie</a>,
<a href="http://example.com/lacie" class="sister" id="link2">Lacie</a> and
<a href="http://example.com/tillie" class="sister" id="link3">Tillie</a>;
and they lived at the bottom of a well.</p>
<p class="story">...</p>
<h1>Secret agents</h1>
<ul>
    <li data-id="10784">Jason Walters, 003: Found dead in "A View to a
Kill".</li>
    <li data-id="97865">Alex Trevelyan, 006: Agent turned terrorist leader;
James' nemesis in "Goldeneye".</li>
    <li data-id="45732">James Bond, 007: The main man; shaken but not
stirred.</li>
</ul>
</body>
</html>"""
```

To proceed with parsing and accessing Beautiful Soup methods and properties, a Beautiful Soup object, generally known as a soup object, must be created. Regarding the type of string or markup content provided in the constructor, a few examples of creating Beautiful Soup objects, along with the parameters mentioned earlier, are listed next:

- `soup = Beautifulsoup(html_markup)`
- `soup = Beautifulsoup(html_markup, 'lxml')`
- `soup = Beautifulsoup(html_markup, 'lxml',`
  `parse_from=SoupStrainer("a"))`
- `soup = Beautifulsoup(html_markup, 'html.parser')`
- `soup = Beautifulsoup(html_markup, 'html5lib')`

- `soup = Beautifulsoup(xml_markup, 'xml')`
- `soup = Beautifulsoup(some_markup, from_encoding='ISO-8859-8')`
- `soup = Beautifulsoup(some_markup,`
  `exclude_encodings=['ISO-8859-7'])`

The Beautiful Soup constructor plays an important part and we will explore some of the important parameters here:

- `markup`: The first parameter passed to the constructor accepts a string or objects to be parsed.
- `features`: The name of the parser or type of markup to be used for `markup`. The parser can be `lxml`, `lxml-xml`, `html.parser`, or `html5lib`. Similarly, markup types that can be used are `html`, `html5`, and `xml`. Different types of supported parsers can be used with Beautiful Soup. If we just want to parse some HTML, we can simply pass the markup to Beautiful Soup and it will use the appropriate parser installed accordingly. For more information on parsers and their installation, please visit installing a parser at `https://www.crummy.com/software/BeautifulSoup/bs4/doc/#installing-a-parser`.
- `parse_only`: Accepts a `bs4.SoupStrainer` object, that is, only parts of the document matching the `SoupStrainer` object will be used to parse. It's pretty useful for scraping when only part of the document is to be parsed considering the effectiveness of the code and memory-related issues. For more information on `SoupStrainer`, please visit parsing only part of a document at `https://www.crummy.com/software/BeautifulSoup/bs4/doc/#parsing-only-part-of-a-document`.
- `from_encoding`: Strings indicating the proper encoding are used to parse the markup. This is usually provided if Beautiful Soup is using the wrong encoding.
- `exclude_encodings`: A list of strings indicating the wrong encodings if used by Beautiful Soup.

Response time is a considerable factor when using Beautiful Soup. As Beautiful Soup uses the parsers (`lxml`, `html.parser`, and `html5lib`), there is always a concern regarding the extra time consumption.

Using a parser is always recommended to obtain similar results across platforms and systems. Also, for speeding up, it is recommended to use `lxml` as the parser with Beautiful Soup.

For this particular case, we will be creating the soupA object using lxml as a parser, along with the SoupStrainer object tagsA (parsing only <a>, that is, the elements or anchor tag of HTML). We can obtain partial content to parse using SoupStrainer, which is very useful when dealing with heavy content.

soupA, an object of Beautiful Soup, presents all of the <a> elements found for the SoupStrainer object tagsA as used in the following code; as seen in the output, only the <a> tag has been collected, or the parsed document is the SoupStrainer object parsed using lxml:

```
tagsA = SoupStrainer("a")
soupA = BeautifulSoup(html_doc,'lxml',parse_only=tagsA)

print(type(soupA))
<class 'bs4.BeautifulSoup'>

print(soupA)
<a class="sister" href="http://example.com/elsie" id="link1">Elsie</a><a
class="sister" href="http://example.com/lacie" id="link2">Lacie</a><a
class="sister" href="http://example.com/tillie" id="link3">Tillie</a>
```

HTML content, available from the website, might not always be formatted in a clean string. It would be difficult and time-consuming to read page content that is presented as paragraphs rather than as a line-by-line code.

The Beautiful Soup prettify() function returns a Unicode string, presents the string in a clean, formatted structure that is easy to read, and identifies the elements in a tree structure as seen in the following code; the prettify() function also accepts the parameter encoding:

```
print(soupA.prettify())

<a class="sister" href="http://example.com/elsie" id="link1">
 Elsie
</a>
<a class="sister" href="http://example.com/lacie" id="link2">
 Lacie
</a>
<a class="sister" href="http://example.com/tillie" id="link3">
 Tillie
</a>
```

Document-based elements (such as HTML tags) in a parsed tree can have various attributes with predefined values. Element attributes are important resources as they provide identification and content together within the element. Verifying whether the element contains certain attributes can be handy when traversing through the tree.

For example, as seen in the following code, the HTML <a> element contains the class, href, and id attributes, each carrying predefined values, as seen in the following snippet:

```
<a class="sister" href="http://example.com/lacie" id="link2">
```

The has_attr() function from Beautiful Soup returns a Boolean response to the searched attribute name for the chosen element, as seen in the following code element a:

- Returns False for the name attribute
- Returns True for the class attribute

We can use the has_attr() function to confirm the attribute keys by name, if it exists inside the parsed document as follows:

```
print(soupA.a.has_attr('class'))
True

print(soupA.a.has_attr('name'))
False
```

With a basic introduction to Beautiful Soup and a few methods explored in this section, we will now move forward for searching, traversing, and iterating through the parsed tree looking for elements and their content in the upcoming section.

Searching, traversing, and iterating

Beautiful Soup provides a lot of methods and properties to traverse and search elements in the parsed tree. These methods are often named in a similar way to their implementation, describing the task they perform. There are also a number of properties and methods that can be linked together and used to obtain a similar result.

The `find()` function returns the first child that is matched for the searched criteria or parsed element. It's pretty useful in scraping context for finding elements and extracting details, but only for the single result. Additional parameters can also be passed to the `find()` function to identify the exact element, as listed:

- `attrs`: A dictionary with a key-value pair
- `text`: With element text
- `name`: HTML tag name

Let's implement the `find()` function with different, allowed parameters in the code:

```
print(soupA.find("a")) #print(soupA.find(name="a"))
<a class="sister" href="http://example.com/elsie" id="link1">Elsie</a>

print(soupA.find("a",attrs={'class':'sister'}))
<a class="sister" href="http://example.com/elsie" id="link1">Elsie</a>

print(soupA.find("a",attrs={'class':'sister'},text="Lacie"))
<a class="sister" href="http://example.com/lacie" id="link2">Lacie</a>

print(soupA.find("a",attrs={'id':'link3'}))
<a class="sister" href="http://example.com/tillie" id="link3">Tillie</a>

print(soupA.find('a',id="link2"))
<a class="sister" href="http://example.com/lacie" id="link2">Lacie</a>
```

Here is a list of short descriptions of codes implemented in the preceding example:

- `find("a")` or `find(name="a")`: Search the HTML `<a>` element or tag name provided that a returns the first existence of `<a>` found in `soupA`
- `find("a",attrs={'class':'sister'})`: Search element `<a>`, with attribute key as class and value as sister
- `find("a",attrs={'class':'sister'}, text="Lacie")`: Search the `<a>` element with the `class` attribute key and the `sister` value and text with the `Lacie` value
- `find("a",attrs={'id':'link3'})`: Search the `<a>` element with the `id` attribute key and the `link3` value
- `find("a",id="link2")`: Search the `<a>` element for the `id` attribute with the `link2` value

The find_all() function works in a similar way to the find() function with the additional attrs and text as a parameters and returns a list of matched (multiple) elements for the provided criteria or name attribute as follows:

```
#find all <a> can also be written as #print(soupA.find_all(name="a"))
print(soupA.find_all("a"))

[<a class="sister" href="http://example.com/elsie" id="link1">Elsie</a>, <a
class="sister" href="http://example.com/lacie" id="link2">Lacie</a>, <a
class="sister" href="http://example.com/tillie" id="link3">Tillie</a>]

#find all <a>, but return only 2 of them
print(soupA.find_all("a",limit=2)) #attrs, text

[<a class="sister" href="http://example.com/elsie" id="link1">Elsie</a>, <a
class="sister" href="http://example.com/lacie" id="link2">Lacie</a>]
```

The additional limit parameter, which accepts numeric values, controls the total count of the elements to be returned using the find_all() function.

The string, list of strings, regular expression objects, or any of these, can be provided to the name and text attributes as a value for attrs parameters, as seen in the code used in the following snippet:

```
print(soupA.find("a",text=re.compile(r'cie'))) #import re
<a class="sister" href="http://example.com/lacie" id="link2">Lacie</a>

print(soupA.find_all("a",attrs={'id':re.compile(r'3')}))
[<a class="sister" href="http://example.com/tillie" id="link3">Tillie</a>]

print(soupA.find_all(re.compile(r'a')))
[<a class="sister" href="http://example.com/elsie" id="link1">Elsie</a>, <a
class="sister" href="http://example.com/lacie" id="link2">Lacie</a>, <a
class="sister" href="http://example.com/tillie" id="link3">Tillie</a>]
```

The find_all() function has in-built support for global attributes such as class name along with a name as seen in the following:

```
soup = BeautifulSoup(html_doc,'lxml')

print(soup.find_all("p","story")) #class=story
[<p class="story">Once upon a time there were three little sisters; and
their names were
<a class="sister" href="http://example.com/elsie" id="link1">Elsie</a>,
<a class="sister" href="http://example.com/lacie" id="link2">Lacie</a> and
<a class="sister" href="http://example.com/tillie" id="link3">Tillie</a>;
and they lived at the bottom of a well.</p>, <p class="story">...</p>]
```

```
print(soup.find_all("p","title"))
#soup.find_all("p",attrs={'class':"title"})
[<p class="title"><b>The Dormouse's story</b></p>]
```

Multiple `name` and `attrs` values can also be passed through a list as shown in the following syntax:

- `soup.find_all("p",attrs={'class':["title","story"]})`: Finding all the <p> elements with the class attribute `title` and `story` values
- `soup.find_all(["p","li"])`: Finding all the <p> and <li> elements from the soup object

The preceding syntax can be observed in the following code:

```
print(soup.find_all("p",attrs={'class':["title","story"]}))
[<p class="title"><b>The Dormouse's story</b></p>,
<p class="story">Once upon a...
<a class="sister" href="http://example.com/elsie" id="link1">Elsie</a>,....
<a class="sister" href="http://example.com/tillie" id="link3">Tillie</a>;
and they lived at the bottom of a well.</p>, <p class="story">...</p>]

print(soup.find_all(["p","li"]))
[<p class="title"><b>The Dormouse's story</b></p>,
<p class="story">Once...<a class="sister"
href="http://example.com/elsie"....,
<p class="story">...</p>,
<li data-id="10784">Jason Walters, 003:....</li>,<li.....,
<li data-id="45732">James Bond, 007: The main man; shaken but not
stirred.</li>]
```

We can also use element text to search and list the content. A `string` parameter, similar to a `text` parameter, is used for such cases; it can also be used with, or without, any tag names as in the following code:

```
print(soup.find_all(string="Elsie")) #text="Elsie"
['Elsie']

print(soup.find_all(text=re.compile(r'Elsie'))) #import re
['Elsie']

print(soup.find_all("a",string="Lacie")) #text="Lacie"
[<a class="sister" href="http://example.com/elsie" id="link2">Lacie</a>]
```

Iteration through elements can also be achieved using the `find_all()` function. As can be seen in the following code, we are retrieving all of the `<li>` elements found inside the `<ul>` element and printing their tag name, attribute data, ID, and text:

```
for li in soup.ul.find_all('li'):
    print(li.name, ' > ',li.get('data-id'),' > ', li.text)
li > 10784 > Jason Walters, 003: Found dead in "A View to a Kill".
li > 97865 > Alex Trevelyan, 006: Agent turned terrorist leader; James'
nemesis in "Goldeneye".
li > 45732 > James Bond, 007: The main man; shaken but not stirred.
```

> The elements `value` attribute can be retrieved using the `get()` function as seen in the preceding code. Also, the presence of attributes can be checked using the `has_attr()` function.

Element traversing can also be done with just a tag name, and with, or without, using the `find()` or `find_all()` functions as seen in the following code:

```
print(soupA.a) #tag a
<a class="sister" href="http://example.com/elsie" id="link1">Elsie</a>

print(soup.li) #tag li
<li data-id="10784">Jason Walters, 003: Found dead in "A View to a
Kill".</li>

print(soup.p)
<p class="title"><b>The Dormouse's story</b></p>

print(soup.p.b) #tag p and b
<b>The Dormouse's story</b>

print(soup.ul.find('li',attrs={'data-id':'45732'}))
<li data-id="45732">James Bond, 007: The main man; shaken but not
stirred.</li>
```

The `text` and `string` attributes or the `get_text()` method can be used with the elements to extract their text while traversing through the elements used in the following code. There's also a parameter `text` and `string` in the `find()` or `find_all()` functions, which are used to search the content as shown in the following code:

```
print(soup.ul.find('li',attrs={'data-id':'45732'}).text)
James Bond, 007: The main man; shaken but not stirred.

print(soup.p.text) #get_text()
The Dormouse's story
```

```
print(soup.li.text)
Jason Walters, 003: Found dead in "A View to a Kill".

print(soup.p.string)
The Dormouse's story
```

In this section, we explored searching and traversing using elements and by implementing important functions such as the `find()` and `find_all()` functions alongside their appropriate parameters and criteria.

In the next sections, we will explore elements based on their positions in the parsed tree.

Using children and parents

For parsed documents, traversing through children or child elements can be achieved using the `contents`, `children`, and `descendants` elements:

- `contents` collect children for the provided criteria in a list.
- `children` are used for iteration that has direct children.
- `descendants` work slightly differently to the `contents` and `children` elements. It allows iteration over all children, not just the direct ones, that is, the element tag and the contents inside the tag are actually two separate children.

The preceding list showed the features that can also be used for iteration. The following code illustrates the use of these features with output:

```
print(list(soup.find('p','story').children))
['Once upon a time there were three little sisters; and their names
were\n', <a class="sister" href="http://example.com/elsie"
id="link1">Elsie</a>, ',\n', <a class="sister"
href="http://example.com/lacie" id="link2">Lacie</a>, ' and\n', <a
class="sister" href="http://example.com/tillie" id="link3">Tillie</a>,
';\nand they lived at the bottom of a well.']

print(list(soup.find('p','story').contents))
['Once upon a time there were three little sisters; and their names
were\n', <a class="sister" href="http://example.com/elsie"
id="link1">Elsie</a>, ',\n', <a class="sister"
href="http://example.com/lacie" id="link2">Lacie</a>, ' and\n', <a
class="sister" href="http://example.com/tillie" id="link3">Tillie</a>,
';\nand they lived at the bottom of a well.']

print(list(soup.find('p','story').descendants))
['Once upon a time there were three little sisters; and their names
```

```
were\n', <a class="sister" href="http://example.com/elsie"
id="link1">Elsie</a>, 'Elsie', ',\n', <a class="sister"
href="http://example.com/lacie" id="link2">Lacie</a>, 'Lacie', ' and\n', <a
class="sister" href="http://example.com/tillie" id="link3">Tillie</a>,
'Tillie', ';\nand they lived at the bottom of a well.']
```

Selected `children` and `descendants` tag names can be obtained using the `name` attribute. Parsed strings and the `\n` function (newline) are returned as `None`, which can be filtered out, as in the following code:

```
#using List Comprehension Technique
print([a.name for a in soup.find('p','story').children])
[None, 'a', None, 'a', None, 'a', None]

print([{'tag':a.name,'text':a.text,'class':a.get('class')} for a in
soup.find('p','story').children if a.name!=None])
[{'tag': 'a', 'text': 'Elsie', 'class': ['sister']}, {'tag': 'a', 'text':
'Lacie', 'class': ['sister']}, {'tag': 'a', 'text': 'Tillie', 'class':
['sister']}]

print([a.name for a in soup.find('p','story').descendants])
[None, 'a', None, None, 'a', None, None, 'a', None, None]

print(list(filter(None,[a.name for a in
soup.find('p','story').descendants])))
['a', 'a', 'a']
```

Similar to the `find()` and `find_all()` functions, we can also traverse child elements using the `findChild()` and `findChildren()` functions. The `findChild()` function is used to retrieve the single child and the `findChildren()` function retrieves a list of children as illustrated in the following code:

```
print(soup.find('p','story').findChildren())
[<a class="sister" href="http://example.com/elsie" id="link1">Elsie</a>, <a
class="sister" href="http://example.com/lacie" id="link2">Lacie</a>, <a
class="sister" href="http://example.com/tillie" id="link3">Tillie</a>]

print(soup.find('p','story').findChild()) #soup.find('p','story').find()
<a class="sister" href="http://example.com/elsie" id="link1">Elsie</a>
```

Similar to the `children` element, the `parent` element returns the parent object found for the searched criteria. The main difference here is that the `parent` element returns the single parent object from the tree as seen in the following code:

```
#print parent element of <a> with class=sister
print(soup.find('a','sister').parent)
<p class="story">Once upon a time there were three little sisters; and
```

```
their names were
<a class="sister" href="http://example.com/elsie" id="link1">Elsie</a>,
<a class="sister" href="http://example.com/lacie" id="link2">Lacie</a> and
<a class="sister" href="http://example.com/tillie" id="link3">Tillie</a>;
and they lived at the bottom of a well.</p>

#print parent element name of <a> with class=sister
print(soup.find('a','sister').parent.name)
p

#print text from parent element of <a> with class=sister
print(soup.find('a','sister').parent.text)
Once upon a time there were three little sisters; and their names were
Elsie,
Lacie and
Tillie;
and they lived at the bottom of a well.
```

The limitation of the single parents returned can be overcome by using the `parents` element; this returns multiple existing parent elements and matches the searched criteria provided in the `find()` function as seen in code here, which is normally used for iteration:

```
for element in soup.find('a','sister').parents:
    print(element.name)

p
body
html #complete HTML
[document]  #soup object
```

 As seen in the preceding output, [document] refers to the soup object and html refers to the complete HTML block found in the soup. The Beautiful Soup object that created itself is a parsed element.

Similar to the functions that exist for child traversing, parents can also be traversed and retrieved using the `findParent()` and `findParents()` search functions. The `findParent()` function traverses to the immediate parent, while the `findParents()` function returns all parents found for the criteria provided.

It must also be noted that the children and parent traversing functions are used with the `find()` function where necessary arguments and conditions are provided, as seen in the following code:

```
#find single Parent for selected <a> with class=sister
print(soup.find('a','sister').findParent())

<p class="story">Once upon a time there were three little sisters; and
their names were
<a class="sister" href="http://example.com/elsie" id="link1">Elsie</a>,
<a class="sister" href="http://example.com/lacie" id="link2">Lacie</a> and
<a class="sister" href="http://example.com/tillie" id="link3">Tillie</a>;
and they lived at the bottom of a well.</p>

#find Parents for selected <a> with class=sister
print(soup.find('a','sister').findParents())

[<p class="story">Once upon a time there were three little sisters; and
their names were
<a class="sister".........Tillie</a>;and they lived at the bottom of a
well.</p>,
<body><p class="title"><b>The Dormouse's story</b></p>
<p class="story">Once upon.......... <li data-id="45732">James Bond, 007:
The main man; shaken but not stirred.</li> </ul> </body>,
<html><head><title>The Dormouse's story</title></head><body><p
class="title"><b>The Dormouse's story</b></p> .......... </ul>
</body></html>,
<html><head><title>The Dormouse's story</title></head><body><p
class="title"><b>The Dormouse's story</b></p>..........</body></html>]
```

We explored traversing and searching with the children and parent element using a varied handful of functions. In the next section, we'll explore and use positional elements from the parsed tree.

Using next and previous

Similar to traversing through parsed children and parents in the tree, Beautiful Soup also has the support to traverse and iterate elements located previous to and next to the provided criteria.

The properties `next` and `next_element` return the immediately parsed content for the selected criteria. We can also append the `next` and `next_element` functions to create a chain of code for traversal, as seen in the following code:

```
print(soup.find('p','story').next)
Once upon a time there were three little sisters; and their names were
```

```
print(soup.find('p','story').next.next)
<a class="sister" href="http://example.com/elsie" id="link1">Elsie</a>

print(soup.find('p','story').next_element)
Once upon a time there were three little sisters; and their names were

print(soup.find('p','story').next_element.next_element)
<a class="sister" href="http://example.com/elsie" id="link1">Elsie</a>

print(soup.find('p','story').next_element.next_element.next_element)
Elsie
```

Similar to the `next` and `next_elements` functions, there also exist properties with traversal result that returns results from prior or previous parsed elements, such as the `previous` and `previous_element`, which are opposite to work reversely when compared to the `next` and `next_element` functions.

As seen in the following code, the `previous` and `previous_element` can also be appended to themselves to create a traversal series:

```
print(soup.find('p','story').previous) #returns empty or new-line.
print(soup.find('p','title').next.next.next) #returns empty or newline
similar to code above

print(soup.find('p','story').previous.previous)
The Dormouse's story

print(soup.find('p','story').previous_element) #returns empty or new-line.
print(soup.find('p','story').previous_element.previous_element)
The Dormouse's story

print(soup.find('p','story').previous_element.previous_element.previous_ele
ment)
<b>The Dormouse's story</b>
```

We now combine the `next` or `next_element` and `previous` or `previous_element` elements together to traverse as seen in the following:

```
print(soup.find('p','title').next.next.previous.previous)

<p class="title"><b>The Dormouse's story</b></p>
```

Iterating features for the `next_element` and `previous_element` are obtained using the `next_elements` and `previous_elements`, respectively. These iterators are used to move to the next or previous parsed content as seen in the following:

```
for element in soup.find('ul').next_elements:
    print(element)

<li data-id="10784">Jason Walters, 003: Found dead in "A View to a
Kill".</li>
Jason Walters, 003: Found dead in "A View to a Kill".

<li data-id="97865">Alex Trevelyan, 006: Agent ............
"Goldeneye".</li>
Alex Trevelyan, 006: Agent turned terrorist leader; James' nemesis in
"Goldeneye".

<li data-id="45732">James Bond, 007: The main man; shaken but not
stirred.</li>
James Bond, 007: The main man; shaken but not stirred.
```

The `find_next()` function implements the `next_elements` but returns only a single element that is found after the `next` or `next_element` element. There's also an advantage of using the `find_next()` function over the `next_elements` as we can implement additional search logic for elements.

The following code demonstrates the use of the `find_next()` function, with, and without, search conditions; it also displays the outputs from the `next` element and `next_elements` to compare the actual usage as shown in the following:

```
print(soup.find('p','story').next)
Once upon a time there were three little sisters; and their names were

print(soup.find('p','story').next_element)
Once upon a time there were three little sisters; and their names were

print(soup.find('p','story').find_next()) #element after next_element
<a class="sister" href="http://example.com/elsie" id="link1">Elsie</a>

print(soup.find('p','story').find_next('h1'))
<h1>Secret agents</h1>
```

The `find_all_next()` function works in a similar way to the `find_next()` function, but returns all of the next elements. It's also used as an iterating version of the `find_next()` function. Additional search criteria and arguments such as `limit` can be used to search and control the results returned as used in the following code:

```
print(soup.find('p','story').find_all_next())
[<a class="sister" href="http://example.com/elsie" id="link1">Elsie</a>, <a
class="sister" href="http://example.com/lacie" id="link2">Lacie</a>, <a
class="sister" href="http://example.com/tillie" id="link3">Tillie</a>, <p
class="story">...</p>, <h1>Secret agents</h1>, <ul>
<li data-id="10784">Jason Walters, 003: Found dead in "A View to a
Kill".</li>
<li data-id="97865">Alex Trevelyan, 006: Agent turned terrorist leader;
James' nemesis in "Goldeneye".</li>
<li data-id="45732">James Bond, 007: The main man; shaken but not
stirred.</li>
</ul>, <li data-id="10784">Jason Walters, 003: Found dead in "A View to a
Kill".</li>, <li data-id="97865">Alex Trevelyan, 006: Agent turned
terrorist leader; James' nemesis in "Goldeneye".</li>, <li data-
id="45732">James Bond, 007: The main man; shaken but not stirred.</li>]

print(soup.find('p','story').find_all_next('li',limit=2))
[<li data-id="10784">Jason Walters, 003: Found dead in "A View to a
Kill".</li>, <li data-id="97865">Alex Trevelyan, 006: Agent turned
terrorist leader; James' nemesis in "Goldeneye".</li>]
```

The `find_previous()` function implements `previous_elements` but returns only the single element that was found before the `previous` or `previous_element`. It also has an advantage over the `previous_elements` as we can implement additional search logic for elements. The following code demonstrates the use of the `find_previous()` function and the `previous` function:

```
print(soup.find('ul').previous.previous.previous)
<h1>Secret agents</h1>

print(soup.find('ul').find_previous())
<h1>Secret agents</h1>

print(soup.find('ul').find_previous('p','title'))
<p class="title"><b>The Dormouse's story</b></p>
```

The `find_all_previous()` function is an iterated version of the `find_previous()`; it returns all previous elements satisfied with the available criteria as seen in the following code:

```
print(soup.find('ul').find_all_previous('p'))

[<p class="story">...</p>, <p class="story">Once upon a time there were
three little sisters; and their names were
<a class="sister" href="http://example.com/elsie" id="link1">Elsie</a>,
<a class="sister" href="http://example.com/lacie" id="link2">Lacie</a> and
<a class="sister" href="http://example.com/tillie" id="link3">Tillie</a>;
and they lived at the bottom of a well.</p>, <p class="title"><b>The
Dormouse's story</b></p>]
```

`next_sibling` and `previous_sibling` are yet another way of traversing along the parsed tree looking for next and previous siblings. A sibling or siblings are termed to the element that appears or is found on the same level, in the parsed tree or those elements that share the same parent. The following code illustrates the use of the `next_sibling` and `previous_sibling` elements:

```
print(soup.find('p','title').next_sibling) #returns empty or new-line

print(soup.find('p','title').next_sibling.next_sibling)
#print(soup.find('p','title').next_sibling.next)
<p class="story">Once upon a time there were three little sisters; and
their names were
<a class="sister" href="http://example.com/elsie" id="link1">Elsie</a>,
<a class="sister" href="http://example.com/lacie" id="link2">Lacie</a> and
<a class="sister" href="http://example.com/tillie" id="link3">Tillie</a>;
and they lived at the bottom of a well.</p>

print(soup.find('ul').previous_sibling) #returns empty or new-line

print(soup.find('ul').previous_sibling.previous_sibling)
<h1>Secret agents</h1>
```

Iteration is also possible with siblings, using the `next_siblings` and `previous_siblings` elements as shown in the following code:

```
#using List Comprehension
title = [ele.name for ele in soup.find('p','title').next_siblings]
print(list(filter(None,title)))
['p', 'p', 'h1', 'ul']

ul = [ele.name for ele in soup.find('ul').previous_siblings]
print(list(filter(None,ul)))
['h1', 'p', 'p', 'p']
```

Similar to the `find_next()` and `find_all_next()` functions for the next elements, there's also functions available for siblings, that is, the `find_next_sibling()` and `find_next_siblings()` functions. These functions implement the `next_siblings` function to iterate and search for available siblings. As seen in following code, the `find_next_sibling()` function returns a single element, whereas the `find_next_siblings()` function returns all matched siblings:

```
#find next <p> siblings for selected <p> with class=title
print(soup.find('p','title').find_next_siblings('p'))
[<p class="story">Once upon a time there were three little sisters; and
their names were
<a class="sister" href="http://example.com/elsie" id="link1">Elsie</a>,
<a class="sister" href="http://example.com/lacie" id="link2">Lacie</a> and
<a class="sister" href="http://example.com/tillie" id="link3">Tillie</a>;
and they lived at the bottom of a well.</p>, <p class="story">...</p>]

#find single or next sibling for selected <h1>
print(soup.find('h1').find_next_sibling())
<ul>
<li data-id="10784">Jason Walters, 003: Found dead in "A View to a
Kill".</li>
<li data-id="97865">Alex Trevelyan, 006: ............in "Goldeneye".</li>
<li data-id="45732">James Bond, 007: The main man; shaken but not
stirred.</li>
</ul>

#find single or next sibling <li> for selected <h1>
print(soup.find('h1').find_next_sibling('li'))
None
```

The `find_previous_sibling()` and `find_previous_siblings()` functions work in a similar way to the `find_next_sibling()` and `find_next_siblings()` functions, but result in elements traced through the `previous_siblings` function. Additional search criteria and a result-controlling parameter `limit` can also be applied to the iterating version, such as the `find_previous_siblings()` function.

As seen in the following code, the `find_previous_sibling()` function returns a single sibling element, whereas the `find_previous_siblings()` function returns all siblings available previously to the given criteria:

```
#find first previous sibling to <ul>
print(soup.find('ul').find_previous_sibling())
<h1>Secret agents</h1>

#find all previous siblings to <ul>
print(soup.find('ul').find_previous_siblings())
```

```
[<h1>Secret agents</h1>, <p class="story">...</p>, <p class="story">Once
upon a time there were three little sisters; and their names were
<a class="sister" href="http://example.com/elsie" id="link1">Elsie</a>,
<a class="sister" href="http://example.com/lacie" id="link2">Lacie</a> and
<a class="sister" href="http://example.com/tillie" id="link3">Tillie</a>;
and they lived at the bottom of a well.</p>, <p class="title"><b>The
Dormouse's story</b></p>]
```

We have explored various ways of searching and traversing through the parsed tree with the functions and properties explored in this section.

The following is a list of tips that can be helpful in remembering and planning for search and traversing activities using Beautiful Soup:

- A function name that starts with the `find` function is used to search and iterate for providing criteria and parameters:
    - A plural version of the `find` function works for iteration, such as the `findChildren()` and `findParents()` elements
    - A singular version of the `find` function returns a single element such as the `find()`, `findChild()`, or `findParent()` functions
- A function name that starts with the word `find_all` returns all matched elements and is used to search and iterate with provided criteria and parameters such as the `find_all()`, `find_all_next()`, and `find_all_previous()` functions
- Properties with a plural name are used for iteration purposes such as the `next_elements`, `previous_elements`, `parents`, `children`, `contents`, `descendants`, `next_siblings`, and `previous_siblings` elements
- Properties with a singular name return single elements and can also be appended to form a chain of traversal code such as the `parent`, `next`, `previous`, `next_element`, `previous_element`, `next_sibling`, and `previous_sibling` functions

Using CSS Selectors

We have used plenty of properties and functions in the preceding sections, looking for desired elements and their content. Beautiful Soup also supports CSS Selectors (with library SoupSieve at `https://facelessuser.github.io/soupsieve/selectors/`), which enhances its use and allows developers to write effective and efficient codes to traverse the parsed tree.

CSS Selectors (CSS query or CSS Selector query) are defined patterns used by CSS to select HTML elements, by element name or by using global attributes (ID, Class). For more information on CSS Selectors, please refer to Chapter 3, *Using LXML, XPath and CSS Selectors, Introduction to XPath and CSS Selector* section.

For Beautiful Soup, the select() function is used to execute the CSS Selectors. We can perform the searching, traversing, and iteration of elements by defining CSS Selectors. The select() function is implemented individually, that is, it is not extended with other functions and properties found in Beautiful Soup, creating a chain of codes. The select() function returns a list of elements matched to the CSS Selectors provided. It's also notable that code using CSS Selectors are quite short in length compared to the code used in the preceding sections for a similar purpose.

We will explore a few examples using select() to process CSS Selectors.

Example 1 – listing <li> elements with the data-id attribute

In the following example, we will use the select() function to list the <li> element with the data-id attribute:

```
print(soup.select('li[data-id]'))
[<li data-id="10784">Jason Walters, 003: Found dead in "A View to a
Kill".</li>, <li data-id="97865">Alex Trevelyan, 006: Agent turned
terrorist leader; James' nemesis in "Goldeneye".</li>, <li data-
id="45732">James Bond, 007: The main man; shaken but not stirred.</li>]
```

As seen in the preceding code, the li[data-id] selector queries the <li> element with the attribute key named as data-id. The Value for data-id is empty, which allows traversing through all <li> possessing data-id. The result is obtained as a list of objects, in which indexes can be applied to fetch the exact elements as seen in the following code:

```
print(soup.select('ul li[data-id]')[1]) #fetch index 1 only from resulted
List
<li data-id="97865">Alex Trevelyan, 006: Agent turned terrorist leader;
James' nemesis in "Goldeneye".</li>
```

If we wish to extract the first match that has resulted the from CSS query, we can use either the list index, that is, 0 (zero) or the `select_one()` function in place of the `select()` function as seen in the following code. The `select_one()` function returns the string of objects, not the list:

```
print(soup.select_one('li[data-id]'))
<li data-id="10784">Jason Walters, 003: Found dead in "A View to a
Kill".</li>
```

Example 2 – traversing through elements

CSS Selectors have various combinators such as +, >, a space character, and so on, which show relationships between the elements. A few such combinators are used in the following example code:

```
print(soup.select('p.story > a.sister'))#Selects all <a> with
class='sister' that are direct child to <p> with class="story"
[<a class="sister" href="http://example.com/elsie" id="link1">Elsie</a>, <a
class="sister" href="http://example.com/lacie" id="link2">Lacie</a>, <a
class="sister" href="http://example.com/tillie" id="link3">Tillie</a>]

print(soup.select('p b'))#Selects <b> inside <p>
[<b>The Dormouse's story</b>]

print(soup.select('p + h1'))#Selects immediate <h1> after <p>
[<h1>Secret agents</h1>]

print(soup.select('p.story + h1'))#Selects immediate <h1> after <p> with
class 'story'
[<h1>Secret agents</h1>]

print(soup.select('p.title + h1'))#Selects immediate <h1> after <p> with
class 'title'
[]
```

Example 3 – searching elements based on attribute values

There are various ways of finding elements in Beautiful Soup, such as using functions starting with the word `find` or using attributes in CSS Selectors. Patterns can be searched for attributes keys using `*` in CSS Selectors as illustrated in the following code:

```
print(soup.select('a[href*="example.com"]'))
[<a class="sister" href="http://example.com/elsie" id="link1">Elsie</a>, <a
class="sister" href="http://example.com/lacie" id="link2">Lacie</a>, <a
class="sister" href="http://example.com/tillie" id="link3">Tillie</a>]

print(soup.select('a[id*="link"]'))
[<a class="sister" href="http://example.com/elsie" id="link1">Elsie</a>, <a
class="sister" href="http://example.com/lacie" id="link2">Lacie</a>, <a
class="sister" href="http://example.com/tillie" id="link3">Tillie</a>]
```

We were searching for the `<a>` element with the text `example.com`, which might exist in the value of the `href` attribute. Also, we were searching for the `<a>` element, which contains an attribute ID with a text link.

With basic knowledge of CSS Selectors, we can deploy it with Beautiful Soup for various purposes. Using the `select()` function is quite effective when dealing with elements, but there are also limitations we might face, such as extracting text or content from the obtained element.

We have introduced and explored the elements of Beautiful Soup in the preceding sections. To wrap up the concept, we will create a crawler example in the upcoming section.

Building a web crawler

In this section, we will build a web crawler to demonstrate the real content-based scraping, targeting web content.

We will be scraping quotes from `http://toscrape.com/` and targeting quotes from authors found at `http://quotes.toscrape.com/`. The crawler will collect the quote and author information from the first five listing pages and write the data into a CSV file. We will also explore the individual author page and extract information about the authors.

To begin with the basic planning and identification of the fields that we are willing to collect information from, please refer to Chapter 3, *Using LXML, XPath, and CSS Selectors, Using web browser developer tools for accessing web content* section:

```
'''
Listing Quotes from first 5 or less pages found from
'http://quotes.toscrape.com/'
'''

import requests
import re
from bs4 import BeautifulSoup
import csv

sourceUrl = 'http://quotes.toscrape.com/'
keys =
['quote_tags','author_url','author_name','born_date','born_location','quote
_title']
```

In the preceding code there are a few libraries and objects found as listed and described here:

- sourceUrl: Represents the URL of the main page to be scraped for data for category web scraping
- keys: The Python list contains the columns name that will be used while writing records to an external file
- requests: This library is imported to use for making an HTTP request to page URLs with quote listings and receiving a response
- csv: This library will be used to write scraped data to an external CSV file
- bs4: Library for implementing and using Beautiful Soup

 The first line in a CSV file contains column names. We need to write these columns before appending records with real content in the CSV file.

The read_url() function, as found in the following code, will be used to make a request and receive a response using the requests function. This function will accept a url argument for pages:

```
def read_url(url):
    """Read given Url, Returns requests object for page content"""
    response = requests.get(url)
    return response.text
```

dataSet is a handle defined to manage the external file quotes.csv. csv.writer() file handle is use for accessing CSV-based properties. The writerow() function is passed with keys for writing a row containing the column names from the list keys to the external file as shown in the following:

```
if __name__ == '__main__':
    dataSet = open('quotes.csv', 'w', newline='', encoding='utf-8')
    dataWriter = csv.writer(dataSet)

    # Write a Header or Column_names to CSV
    dataWriter.writerow(keys)

    #load details for provided URL
    get_details(sourceUrl, dataWriter)
    dataSet.close()
```

The implemented get_details() function is being coded for pagination and scraping logic. The read_url() function is supplied with a dynamically generated page URL to manage the pagination as follows:

```
def get_details(page, dataWriter):
    """Get 'response' for first 5 pages, parse it and collect data for
'keys' headers"""
    nextPage = True
    pageNo = 1
    while (nextPage and pageNo <= 5):
        response = read_url(page + 'page/' + str(pageNo))
        soup = BeautifulSoup(response, 'lxml')

        rows = soup.find_all('div', 'quote')
        if (len(rows) > 0):
            print("Page ",pageNo," Total Quotes Found ",len(rows))
            for row in rows:
                if row.find('span',attrs={'itemprop':'text'}):
                    title =
row.find(attrs={'itemprop':'text'}).text.strip()
                    author =
row.find(attrs={'itemprop':'author'}).text.strip()
                    authorLink =
row.find('a',href=re.compile(r'/author/')).get('href')
                    tags =
row.find('div','tags').find(itemprop="keywords").get('content')
                    print(title, ' : ', author,' : ',authorLink, ' :
',tags)

                    if authorLink:
                        authorLink = 'http://quotes.toscrape.com' +
```

```
authorLink
                            linkDetail = read_url(authorLink)
                            soupInner = BeautifulSoup(linkDetail, 'lxml')
                            born_date = soupInner.find('span','author-born-
date').text.strip()
                            born_location = soupInner.find('span','author-born-
location').text.strip()
                            # Write a list of values in file
                            dataWriter.writerow(
[tags,authorLink,author,born_date,born_location.replace('in ',''),title])

                    nextPage = True
                    pageNo += 1
             else:
                 print("Quotes Not Listed!")
```

As used in the following code, the `response` element from the `read_url()` function is parsed using `lxml` to obtain the `soup` element. The rows obtained using the soup list all of the quotes available in a single page (that is, the element block containing the single quote details) found inside the `<div class="quote">` function and will be iterated to scrape data for individual items such as `quote_tags`, `author_url`, and `author_name` traversing through the quote element:

```
<div class="quote" itemscope itemtype="http://schema.org/CreativeWork">
    <span class="text" itemprop="text">"A reader lives a thousand lives before he dies, said Jojen. The man who never reads lives only one."</span>
    <span>by <small class="author" itemprop="author">George R.R. Martin</small>
    <a href="/author/George-R-R-Martin">(about)</a>
    </span>
    <div class="tags">
        Tags:
        <meta class="keywords" itemprop="keywords" content="read,readers,reading,reading-books" /    >

        <a class="tag" href="/tag/read/page/1/">read</a>

        <a class="tag" href="/tag/readers/page/1/">readers</a>

        <a class="tag" href="/tag/reading/page/1/">reading</a>

        <a class="tag" href="/tag/reading-books/page/1/">reading-books</a>

    </div>
</div>
<div class="quote" itemscope itemtype="http://schema.org/CreativeWork">
```

Page source with quote element

The individual items received are scraped, cleaned, and collected in a list maintaining the order of their column names and are written to the file using the `writerow()` function (appends the list of values to the file) accessed through the `csv` library and file handle.

The `quotes.csv` data file will contain scraped data as seen in the following screenshot:

```
quote_tags,author_url,author_name,born_date,born_location,quote_title
"change,deep-thoughts,thinking,world",http://quotes.toscrape.com/author/Albert-Einstein,Albert Einstein,"March 14, 1879","Ulm, Germany","The
"abilities,choices",http://quotes.toscrape.com/author/J-K-Rowling,J.K. Rowling,"July 31, 1965","Yate, South Gloucestershire, England, The Un
"inspirational,life,live,miracle,miracles",http://quotes.toscrape.com/author/Albert-Einstein,Albert Einstein,"March 14, 1879","Ulm, Germany"
"aliteracy,books,classic,humor",http://quotes.toscrape.com/author/Jane-Austen,Jane Austen,"December 16, 1775","Steventon Rectory, Hampshire,
"be-yourself,inspirational",http://quotes.toscrape.com/author/Marilyn-Monroe,Marilyn Monroe,"June 01, 1926",The United States,""Imperfection
"adulthood,success,value",http://quotes.toscrape.com/author/Albert-Einstein,Albert Einstein,"March 14, 1879","Ulm, Germany",""Try not to beco
"life,love",http://quotes.toscrape.com/author/Andre-Gide,André Gide,"November 22, 1869","Paris, France",""It is better to be hated for what y
"edison,failure,inspirational,paraphrased",http://quotes.toscrape.com/author/Thomas-A-Edison,Thomas A. Edison,"February 11, 1847","Milan, Oh
misattributed-eleanor-roosevelt,http://quotes.toscrape.com/author/Eleanor-Roosevelt,Eleanor Roosevelt,"October 11, 1884",The United States,""
"humor,obvious,simile",http://quotes.toscrape.com/author/Steve-Martin,Steve Martin,"August 14, 1945","Waco, Texas, The United States",""A da
```

Rows with scraped data from http://quotes.toscrape.com/

In this section, we explored various ways to traverse and search using Beautiful Soup. In the upcoming section, we will be using Scrapy, a web crawling framework.

Web scraping using Scrapy

We have used and explored various libraries and techniques for web scraping so far in this book. The latest libraries available adapt to new concepts and implement the techniques in a more effective, diverse, and easy way; Scrapy is among one of those libraries.

We will be introducing and using Scrapy (an open source web crawling framework written in Python) in this section. For more detailed information on Scrapy, please visit the official documentation at `http://docs.scrapy.org/en/latest/`.

In this section, we will be implementing scraping features and building a project demonstrating useful concepts.

Introduction to Scrapy

Scrapy is a web crawling framework written in Python used for crawling websites with effective and minimal coding. According to the official website of Scrapy (`https://scrapy.org/`), it is *"An open source and collaborative framework for extracting the data you need from websites. In a fast, simple, yet extensible way."*

Scrapy provides a complete framework that is required to deploy a crawler with built-in tools. Scrapy was originally designed for web scraping; with its popularity and development, it is also used to extract data from APIs. Scrapy-based web crawlers are also easy to manage and maintain because of their structure. In general, Scrapy provides a project-based scope for projects dealing with web scraping.

The following are some of the features and distinguishable points that make Scrapy a favorite among developers:

- Scrapy provides built-in support for document parsing, traversing, and extracting data using XPath, CSS Selectors, and regular expressions.
- The crawler is scheduled and managed asynchronously allowing multiple links to be crawled at the same time.
- It automates HTTP methods and actions, that is, there's no need for importing libraries such as `requests` or `urllib` manually for code. Scrapy handles requests and responses using its built-in libraries.
- There's built-in support for feed export, pipelines (items, files, images, and media), that is, exporting, downloading, and storing data in JSON, CSV, XML, and database.
- The availability of the middleware and the large collection of built-in extensions can handle cookies, sessions, authentication, `robots.txt`, logs, usage statistics, email handling, and so on.
- Scrapy-driven projects are composed of easy-to-use distinguishable components and files, which can be handled with basic Python skills and many more.

Please refer to the official documentation of Scrapy at `https://docs.scrapy.org/en/latest/intro/overview.html` for an in-depth and detailed overview.

With a basic introduction to Scrapy, we now begin setting up a project and exploring the framework in more detail in the next sections.

Setting up a project

We will require a Python library with `scrapy` successfully installed on the system before proceeding with the project setup. For setting up or installation refer to `Chapter 2`, *Python and the Web – Using urllib and Requests, Setting things up* section or, for more details on Scrapy installation, please refer to the official installation guide at `https://docs.scrapy.org/en/latest/intro/overview.html`.

Upon successful installation, we can obtain the details shown in the following screenshot, using Python IDE:

```
>>> import scrapy
>>> dir(scrapy)
['Field', 'FormRequest', 'Item', 'Request', 'Selector', 'Spider', '__all__', '__builtins
__', '__cached__', '__doc__', '__file__', '__loader__', '__name__', '__package__', '__pa
th__', '__spec__', '__version__', '_txv', 'http', 'item', 'link', 'selector', 'spiders',
'twisted_version', 'version_info']
>>> scrapy.__version__
'1.6.0'
```

Successful installation of Scrapy with details

With the successful installation of the `scrapy` library, there's also the availability of the `scrapy` command-line tool. This command-line tool contains a number of commands, which are used at various stages of a project from starting or creating a project through to it being fully up and running.

To begin with creating a project, let's follow the steps:

1. Open Terminal or command-line interface
2. Create a folder (`ScrapyProjects`) as shown in the following screenshot or select a folder in which to place Scrapy projects
3. Inside the selected folder, run or execute the `scrapy` command
4. A list of available commands and their brief details will appear, similar to the following screenshot:

```
C:\>mkdir ScrapyProjects

C:\>cd ScrapyProjects

C:\ScrapyProjects>scrapy
Scrapy 1.0.3 - no active project

Usage:
  scrapy <command> [options] [args]

Available commands:
  bench         Run quick benchmark test
  commands
  fetch         Fetch a URL using the Scrapy downloader
  runspider     Run a self-contained spider (without creating a project)
  settings      Get settings values
  shell         Interactive scraping console
  startproject  Create new project
  version       Print Scrapy version
  view          Open URL in browser, as seen by Scrapy

  [ more ]      More commands available when run from project directory

Use "scrapy <command> -h" to see more info about a command

C:\ScrapyProjects>
```

List of available commands for Scrapy

We will be creating a Quotes project to obtain author quotes related to web scraping from http://toscrape.com/, accessing information from the first five pages or less which exists using the URL http://quotes.toscrape.com/.

We are now going to start the Quotes project. From the Command Prompt, run or execute the scrapy startproject Quotes command as seen in the following screenshot:

```
C:\ScrapyProjects>scrapy startproject Blog
2019-04-12 22:07:49 [scrapy] INFO: Scrapy 1.0.3 started (bot: scrapybot)
2019-04-12 22:07:49 [scrapy] INFO: Optional features available: ssl, http11, boto
2019-04-12 22:07:49 [scrapy] INFO: Overridden settings: {}
New Scrapy project 'Blog' created in:
    C:\ScrapyProjects\Blog

You can start your first spider with:
    cd Blog
    scrapy genspider example example.com

C:\ScrapyProjects>
```

Starting a project (using command: scrapy startproject Quotes)

If successful, the preceding command will be the creation of a new folder named
Quotes (that is, the project root directory) with additional files and subfolders as shown in
the following screenshot:

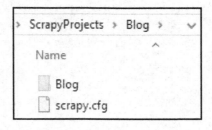

Contents for project folder ScrapyProjects\Quotes

With the project successfully created, let's explore the individual components inside the
project folder:

- scrapy.cfg is a configuration file in which default project-related settings for
  deployment are found and can be added.
- Subfolder will find Quotes named same as project directory, which is actually a
  Python module. We will find additional Python files and other resources in this
  module as follows:

Contents for project folder ScrapyProjects\Quotes\Quotes

As seen in the preceding screenshot, the module is contained in the spiders folder and the items.py, pipelines.py, and settings.py Python files. These content found inside the Quotes module has specific implementation regarding the project scope explored in the following list:

- spiders: This folder will contain Spider classes or Spider writing in Python. Spiders are classes that contain code that is used for scraping. Each individual Spider class is designated to specific scraping activities.
- items.py: This Python file contains item containers, that is, Python class files inheriting scrapy. Items are used to collect the scraped data and use it inside spiders. Items are generally declared to carry values and receive built-in support from other resources in the main project. An item is like a Python dictionary object, where keys are fields or objects of scrapy.item.Field, which will hold certain values.

  Although the default project creates the items.py for the item-related task, it's not compulsory to use it inside the spider. We can use any lists or collect data values and process them in our own way such as writing them into a file, appending them to a list, and so on.

- pipelines.py: This part is executed after the data is scraped. The scraped items are sent to the pipeline to perform certain actions. It also decides whether to process the received scraped items or drop them.
- settings.py: This is the most important file in which settings for the project can be adjusted. According to the preference of the project, we can adjust the settings. Please refer to the official documentation from Scrapy for settings at https://scrapy2.readthedocs.io/en/latest/topics/settings.html

In this section, we have successfully created a project and the required files using Scrapy. These files will be used and updated as described in the following sections.

Generating a Spider

We need to generate a Spider to collect the data. The Spider will perform the crawling activity. An empty default folder named spiders does exist inside the ScrapyProjects\Quotes\Quotes folder.

From the ScrapyProjects\Quotes project folder, run or execute the scrapy genspider quotes quotes.toscrape.com command.

Successful execution of the command will create a `quotes.py` file, that is, a Spider inside the `ScrapyProjects\Quotes\Quotes\spiders\` path. The generated Spider class `QuotesSpider` inherits Scrapy features from `scrapy.Spider`. There's also a few required properties and functions found inside `QuotesSpider` as seen in the following code:

```
import scrapy

class QuotesSpider(scrapy.Spider):
    name = "quotes"
    allowed_domains = ["quotes.toscrape.com"]
    start_urls = (
        'http://www.quotes.toscrape.com/',
    )

    def parse(self, response):
        pass
```

The `QuotesSpider` Spider class contains automatically generated properties that are assigned for specific tasks, as explored in the following list:

- `name`: This variable holds value, that is, the name of the Spider quotes as seen in the preceding code. The name identifies the Spider and can be used to access it. The value of the name is provided through the command-line instructions while issuing `scrapy genspider quotes`, which is the first parameter after `genspider`.
- `allowed_domains`: The created Spiders are allowed to crawl within the listed domains found in the `allowed_domains`. The last parameter passed is the `quotes.toscrape.com` parameter, while generating a Spider is actually a domain name that will be listed inside an `allowed_domains` list.
- A domain name passed to `allowed_domains` will generate URLs for `start_urls`. If there are any chances of URL redirection, such URL domain names need to be mentioned inside the `allowed_domains`.
- `start_urls`: These contain a list of URLs that are actually processed by Spider to crawl. The domain names found or provided to the `allowed_domains` are automatically added to this list and can be manually added or updated. Scrapy generates the URLs for `start_urls` adding HTTP protocols. On a few occasions, we might also need to change or fix the URLs manually, for example, www added to the domain name needs to be removed. `start_urls` after the update will be seen as in the following code:

```
start_urls = ( 'http://quotes.toscrape.com/',)
```

- `parse()`: This function is implemented with the logic relevant to data extraction or processing. `parse()` acts as a main controller and starting point for scraping activity. Spiders created for the main project will begin processing the provided URLs or `start_urls` from, or inside, the `parse()`. XPath-and CSS Selector-related expressions and codes are implemented, and extracted values are also added to the item (that is, the `QuotesItem` from the `item.py` file).

We can also verify the successful creation of Spider by executing these commands:

- `scrapy list`
- `scrapy list spider`

Both of these commands will list the Spider displaying its name, which is found inside the `spiders` folder as seen in the following screenshot:

Listing Spiders from Command Prompt

In this section, we have generated a Spider named `quotes` for our scraping task. In the upcoming section, we will create Item fields that will work with Spider and help with collecting data.

Creating an item

Proceeding with the scraping task and the project folder, we will find a file named `item.py` or item, containing the Python class `QuotesItem`. The item is also automatically generated by Scrapy while issuing the `scrapy startproject Quotes` command. The `QuotesItem` class inherits the `scrapy.Item` for built-in properties and methods such as the `Field`. The `Item` or `QuotesItem` in Scrapy represents a container for collecting values and the `Fields` listed as shown in the following code, including quotes, tags, and so on, which will acts as the keys to the values which we will obtain using the `parse()` function. Values for the same fields will be extracted and collected across the found pages.

The item is accessed as a Python dictionary with the provided fields as keys with their values extracted. It's effective to declare the fields in the item and use them in Spider but is not compulsory to use `item.py` as shown in the following example:

```
class QuotesItem(scrapy.Item):
    # define the fields for your item here like:
    # name = scrapy.Field()

    quote = scrapy.Field()
    tags = scrapy.Field()
    author = scrapy.Field()
    author_link = scrapy.Field()
    pass
```

We need to import the `QuotesItem` when the item is required inside the Spider, as seen in the following code, and process it by creating an object and accessing the declared fields, that is, `quote`, `tags`, `author`, and so on:

```
#inside Spider 'quotes.py'
from Quotes.items import QuotesItem
....
#inside parse()
item = QuotesItem() #create an object 'item' and access the fields
declared.

item['quote'] = .......
item['tags'] = .......
item['author'] = ......
item['author_link'] = ......
......
```

In this section, we declared the `item` fields that we are willing to retrieve data from a website. In the upcoming section, we will explore different methods of data extraction and link them to the item fields.

Extracting data

With Spider generated and the item declared with the fields required, we will now proceed to extract the values or data required for specific item fields. Extraction-related logic can be applied using XPath, CSS Selectors, and regular expressions and we also can implement Python-related libraries such as `bs4` (Beautiful Soup), `pyquery`, and so on.

With proper `start_urls` and item (`QuotesItem`) being set up for the Spider to crawl, we can now proceed with the extraction logic using `parse()` and using selectors at `https://docs.scrapy.org/en/latest/topics/selectors.html`.

Using XPath

The `parse()` function inside Spider is the place to implement all logical processes for scraping data. As seen in the following code, we are using XPath expressions in this Spider to extract the values for the required fields in `QuotesItem`.

 For more information on XPath and obtaining XPath Query, using browser-based developer tools, please refer to Chapter 3, *Using LXML, XPath and CSS Selectors, XPath and CSS Selectors using DevTools* section. Similarly, for more information on the `pyquery` Python library, please refer to Chapter 4, *Scraping Using pyquery – a Python Library*.

As seen in the next code snippet an `item` object from `QuotesItem` is used to collect individual field-related data and it's finally being collected and iterated using the Python keyword `yield`. `parse()` is actually a generator that is returning object `item` from `QuotesItem`.

 Python keyword `yield` is used to return a generator. Generators are functions that return an object that can be iterated. The Python function can be treated as a generator using the yield in place of the return.

`parse()` has an additional argument `response`; this is an object of `scrapy.http.response.html.HtmlResponse` that is returned by Scrapy with the page content of the accessed or crawled URL. The response obtained can be used with XPath and CSS Selectors for further scraping activities:

```
'''
Using XPath
'''
def parse(self, response):
 print("Response Type >>> ", type(response))
 rows = response.xpath("//div[@class='quote']") #root element

 print("Quotes Count >> ", rows.__len__())
 for row in rows:
     item = QuotesItem()

     item['tags'] =
 row.xpath('div[@class="tags"]/meta[@itemprop="keywords"]/@content').extract
```

```
_first().strip()
    item['author'] =
row.xpath('//span/small[@itemprop="author"]/text()').extract_first()
    item['quote'] =
row.xpath('span[@itemprop="text"]/text()').extract_first()
    item['author_link'] =
row.xpath('//a[contains(@href,"/author/")]/@href').extract_first()

    if len(item['author_link'])>0:
        item['author_link'] =
'http://quotes.toscrape.com'+item['author_link']

    yield item
```

As seen in the following code, the XPath expression is being applied to the response using the xpath() expression and is used as a response.xpath(). XPath expressions or queries provided to response.xpath() are parsed as rows, that is, an element block containing the desired elements for fields.

The obtained rows will be iterated for extracting individual element values by providing the XPath query and using additional functions as listed here:

- extract(): Extract all the elements matching the provided expression.
- extract_first(): Extract only the first element that matches the provided expression.
- strip(): Clears the whitespace characters from the beginning and the end of the string. We need to be careful using this function to the extracted content if they result in a type other than string such as NoneType or List, and so on as it can result in an error.

In this section, we have collected quotes listings details using XPath; in the next section, we will cover the same process but using CSS Selectors.

Using CSS Selectors

In this section, we will be using CSS Selectors with their extensions such as ::text and ::attr along with extract() and strip(). Similar to response.xpath(), available to run XPath expressions, CSS Selectors can be run using response.css().
The css() selector matches the elements using the provided expressions:

```
'''
Using CSS Selectors
'''
def parse(self, response):
```

```
print("Response Type >>> ", type(response))
rows = response.css("div.quote") #root element

for row in rows:
    item = QuotesItem()

    item['tags'] = row.css('div.tags >
meta[itemprop="keywords"]::attr("content")').extract_first()
    item['author'] =
row.css('small[itemprop="author"]::text').extract_first()
    item['quote'] =
row.css('span[itemprop="text"]::text').extract_first()
    item['author_link'] =
row.css('a:contains("(about)")::attr(href)').extract_first()

    if len(item['author_link'])>0:
        item['author_link'] =
'http://quotes.toscrape.com'+item['author_link']

    yield item
```

As seen in the preceding code, `rows` represent individual elements with the `post-item` class, iterated for obtaining the `Item` fields.

 For more information on CSS Selectors and obtaining CSS Selectors using browser-based development tools, please refer to Chapter 3, *Using LXML, XPath, and CSS Selectors, CSS Selectors* section and *XPath and CSS Selectors using DevTools* section, respectively.

For more detailed information on selectors and their properties, please refer to the Scrapy official documentation on selectors at `https://docs.scrapy.org/en/latest/topics/selectors.html`. In the upcoming section, we will learn to scrape data from multiple pages.

Data from multiple pages

In the preceding section, we tried scraping data for the URL in `start_urls`, that is, `http://quotes.toscrape.com/`. It's also to be noted that this particular URL results in quotes listings for the first page only.

Quotes listings are found across multiple pages and we need to access each one of those pages to collect the information. A pattern for pagination links is found in the following list:

- `http://quotes.toscrape.com/` (first page)
- `http://quotes.toscrape.com/page/2/`
- `http://quotes.toscrape.com/page/3/`

XPath and CSS Selectors used inside the `parse()`, as found in codes from the preceding section, will be scraping data from the first page or page 1 only. Pagination links found across pages can be requested and extracted by passing the link to `parse()` inside Spider using the `callback` argument from a `scrapy.Request`.

As seen in the following code, a link to page 2 found on page 1 is extracted and passed to `scrapy.Request`, making a request to the `nextPage` processing plus yielding the item fields using `parse()`. Similarly, the iteration takes place until the link to the next page or `nextPage` exists:

```
def parse(self, response):
    print("Response Type >>> ", type(response))
    rows = response.css("div.quote")
    for row in rows:
        item = QuotesItem()
        ......
        ......
        yield item
    #using CSS
    nextPage = response.css("ul.pager > li.next >
a::attr(href)").extract_first()
    #using XPath
    #nextPage =
response.xpath("//ul[@class='pager']//li[@class='next']/a/@href").extract_f
irst()
    if nextPage:
        print("Next Page URL: ",nextPage)
        #nextPage obtained from either XPath or CSS can be used.
        yield
scrapy.Request('http://quotes.toscrape.com'+nextPage,callback=self.parse)

    print('Completed')
```

We can also obtain the pagination-based result by making changes only to `start_urls` as seen in the code next. Using this process doesn't require the use of `nextPage` or `scrapy.Request` as used in the preceding code.

URLs to be crawled can be listed inside `start_url` and are recursively implemented by `parse()` as seen in the following code:

```
'''
To be used for pagination purpose: include the URL to be used by parse()
'''

start_urls = (
    'http://quotes.toscrape.com/',
```

```
        'http://quotes.toscrape.com/page/1/',
        'http://quotes.toscrape.com/page/2/',
)
```

We can also obtain a list of URLs using the Python list comprehension technique. The `range()` function used in the following code accepts the start and end of the argument, that is, 1 and 4, and will result in the numbers 1, 2, and 3 as follows:

```
start_urls = ['http://quotes.toscrape.com/page/%s' % page for page in
xrange(1, 6)]
'''
Results to:
[http://quotes.toscrape.com/page/1,
http://quotes.toscrape.com/page/2,
http://quotes.toscrape.com/page/3,
http://quotes.toscrape.com/page/4,
http://quotes.toscrape.com/page/5,]
'''
```

With extraction logic along with pagination and the item declared, in the next section, we will run the crawler quotes and export the item to the external files.

Running and exporting

We need to run a Spider and look for data for item fields in the provided URLs. We can start running the Spider from the command line by issuing the `scrapy crawl quotes` command or as seen in the following screenshot:

```
C:\ScrapyProjects\Quotes>scrapy crawl quotes
2019-05-20 15:24:46 [scrapy] INFO: Scrapy 1.0.3 started (bot: Quotes)
2019-05-20 15:24:46 [scrapy] INFO: Optional features available: ssl, http11, boto
2019-05-20 15:24:46 [scrapy] INFO: Overridden settings: {'NEWSPIDER_MODULE': 'Quotes.spiders', 'SPIDER_MODULES': ['Quotes.spiders']
2019-05-20 15:24:46 [py.warnings] WARNING: :0: UserWarning: You do not have a working installation of the service_identity module:
   Please install it from <https://pypi.python.org/pypi/service_identity> and make sure all of its dependencies are satisfied. With
```

Running a Spider (scrapy crawl quotes)

The Scrapy argument crawl is provided with a Spider name (`quotes`) in the command. A successful run of the command will result in information about Scrapy, bots, Spider, crawling stats, and HTTP methods, and will list the item data as a dictionary.

While executing a Spider we will receive various forms of information, such as `INFO`/`DEBUG`/`scrapy` statistics and so on, as found in the following code:

```
...[scrapy] INFO: Scrapy 1.0.3 started (bot: Quotes)
...[scrapy] INFO: Optional features available: ssl, http11, boto
...[scrapy] INFO: Overridden settings: {'NEWSPIDER_MODULE':
```

```
'Quotes.spiders', 'SPIDER_MODULES':     ['Quoyes.spiders'], 'BOT_NAME':
'Quotes'}
.......
...[scrapy] INFO: Enabled item pipelines:
...[scrapy] INFO: Spider opened
...[scrapy] INFO: Crawled 0 pages (at 0 pages/min), scraped 0 items (at 0
items/min)
...[scrapy] DEBUG: Telnet console listening on 127.0.0.1:6023
...[scrapy] DEBUG: Redirecting (301) to <GET http://quotes.toscrape.com/>
from <GET http://quotes.toscrape.com/>

[scrapy] DEBUG: Crawled (200) <GET http://quotes.toscrape.com/page/1/>
(referer: None)
('Response Type >>> ', <class
'scrapy.http.response.html.HtmlResponse'>).......
.......
('Response Type >>> ', <class 'scrapy.http.response.html.HtmlResponse'>)
...[scrapy] DEBUG: Scraped from <200 http://quotes.toscrape.com/>
{'author': u'J.K. Rowling',
.......
...[scrapy] DEBUG: Scraped from <200 http://quotes.toscrape.com/page/5/>
{'author': u'James Baldwin',
 'author_link': u'http://quotes.toscrape.com/author/James-Baldwin',
.....
('Next Page URL: ', u'/page/6/')
.......
.......
Completed
...[scrapy] INFO: Closing spider (finished)
```

The Scrapy statistics are as follows:

```
[scrapy] INFO: Dumping Scrapy stats:
{'downloader/request_bytes': 3316,
 'downloader/request_count': 13,
 'downloader/request_method_count/GET': 13,
 'downloader/response_bytes': 28699,
 'downloader/response_count': 13,
 'downloader/response_status_count/200': 11,
 'downloader/response_status_count/301': 2,
 'dupefilter/filtered': 1,
 'finish_reason': 'finished',
 'finish_time': datetime.datetime(.....
 'item_scraped_count': 110,
 'log_count/DEBUG': 126,
 'log_count/ERROR': 2,
 'log_count/INFO': 8,
 'log_count/WARNING': 1,
```

```
'request_depth_max': 8,
'response_received_count': 11,
'scheduler/dequeued': 13,
'scheduler/dequeued/memory': 13,
'scheduler/enqueued': 13,
'scheduler/enqueued/memory': 13,
'start_time': datetime.datetime(....
..... [scrapy] INFO: Spider closed (finished)
```

We can also run the Spider and save the item found or data scraped to the external files. Data is exported or stored in files for easy access, usage, and convenience in sharing and managing.

With Scrapy, we can export scraped data to external files using crawl commands as seen in the following list:

- To extract data to a CSV file we can use the `C:\ScrapyProjects\Quotes> scrapy crawl quotes -o quotes.csv` command as seen in the following screenshot:

```
quote,author_link,tags,author
"The world as we have created it is a process of our thinking. It cannot be changed without changing our thinking.",http://quotes.toscra
""It is our choices, Harry, that show what we truly are, far more than our abilities."",http://quotes.toscrape.com/author/Albert-Einstei
"There are only two ways to live your life. One is as though nothing is a miracle. The other is as though everything is a miracle.",http
""The person, be it gentleman or lady, who has not pleasure in a good novel, must be intolerably stupid."",http://quotes.toscrape.com/au
""Imperfection is beauty, madness is genius and it's better to be absolutely ridiculous than absolutely boring."",http://quotes.toscrape
"Try not to become a man of success. Rather become a man of value.",http://quotes.toscrape.com/author/Albert-Einstein,"adulthood,success
"It is better to be hated for what you are than to be loved for what you are not.",http://quotes.toscrape.com/author/Albert-Einstein,"li
""I have not failed. I've just found 10,000 ways that won't work."",http://quotes.toscrape.com/author/Albert-Einstein,"edison,failure,in
"A woman is like a tea bag; you never know how strong it is until it's in hot water.",http://quotes.toscrape.com/author/Albert-Einstein,
""A day without sunshine is like, you know, night."",http://quotes.toscrape.com/author/Albert-Einstein,"humor,obvious,simile",Albert Ein
""This life is what you make it. No matter what, you're going to mess up sometimes, it's a universal truth. But the good part is you get
```

Contents from file quotes.csv

- To extract data to JSON file format, we can use the `C:\ScrapyProjects\Quotes> scrapy crawl quotes -o quotes.json` command as seen in the following:

```
[{
  "quote": "The world as we have created it is a process of our thinking. It cannot be changed without changing our thinking.",
  "author_link": "http://quotes.toscrape.com/author/Albert-Einstein",
  "tags": "change,deep-thoughts,thinking,world",
  "author": "Albert Einstein"},
{ "quote": "It is our choices, Harry, that show what we truly are, far more than our abilities.",
  "author_link": "http://quotes.toscrape.com/author/J-K-Rowling",
  "tags": "abilities,choices",
  "author": "J.K. Rowling"},
{"quote": "There are only two ways to live your life. One is as though nothing is a miracle. The other is as though everything is a miracle.", "author_link
{"quote": "The person, be it gentleman or lady, who has not pleasure in a good novel, must be intolerably stupid.", "author_link": "http://quotes.toscrape.
{"quote": "Imperfection is beauty, madness is genius and it's better to be absolutely ridiculous than absolutely boring.", "author_link": "http://quotes.to
```

Contents from file quotes.json

The -o parameter followed by a filename will be generated inside the main project folder. Please refer to the official Scrapy documentation about feed exports at `http://docs.scrapy.org/en/latest/topics/feed-exports.html` for more detailed information and file types that can be used to export data.

In this section, we learned about Scrapy and used it to create a Spider to scrape data and export the data scraped to external files. In the next section, we will deploy the crawler on the web.

Deploying a web crawler

Deploying a web crawler online or on a live server will certainly improve the effectiveness of the crawling activity, with its speed, updated technology, web spaces, anytime usage, and so on. Local tests and confirmation are required before deploying online. We need to own or buy web spaces with web-hosting companies or the cloud server.

Scrapy Cloud at `https://scrapinghub.com/scrapy-cloud` from Scrapinghub at `https://scrapinghub.com/` is one of the best platforms to deploy and manage the Scrapy Spider. The Scrapy Cloud provides an easy and interactive interface to deploy Scrapy and is free, with some of the additional features listed here:

- Coding/managing and running Spider
- Deploying Spider to cloud
- Downloading and sharing data
- API access with resource management

The following are the steps performed to deploy projects using Scrapy Cloud:

1. Open the web browser and go to `https://scrapinghub.com/`.
2. From the navigation menu, select **PRODUCTS** and choose **SCRAPY CLOUD** as seen in the following screenshot:

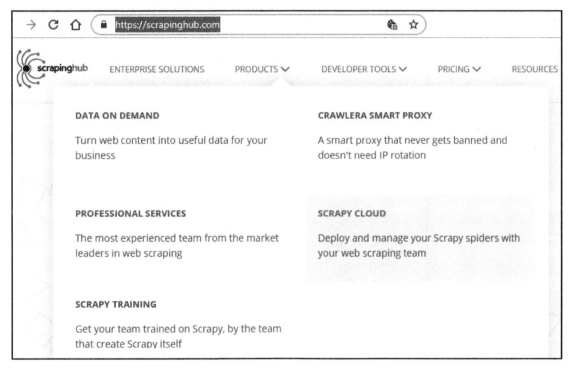

Scrapinghub products

3. Log in or register on the page loaded from `https://scrapinghub.com/scrapy-cloud` (or open the login page: `https://app.scrapinghub.com/account/login/`):

Log in and register page from scraping hub

4. After completing registration and logging in, users are provided with an interactive dashboard and an option to **CREATE A PROJECT,** as seen in the following screenshot:

User dashboard

5. Clicking **CREATE PROJECT** will pop up a window, as seen in the following screenshot:

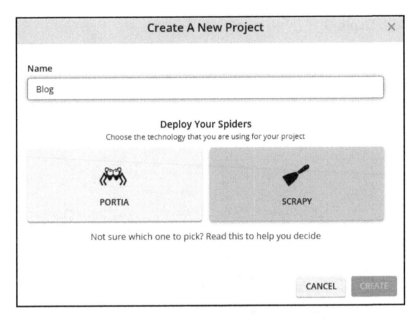

Create a new project from Scrapy Cloud

6. Create a project named as seen in the screenshot and choose technology **SCRAPY** to deploy the spiders; click **CREATE**.

7. A Dashboard with **Scrapy Cloud Projects** will be loaded, listing newly created projects as seen in the following screenshot:

Scrapy Cloud Projects listings with option CREATE PROJECT

8. To deploy the codes for the created project, select the project listed from the **Scrapy Cloud Projects** listings.

9. The project dashboard will be loaded with various options. Choose the option **Code & Deploys**:

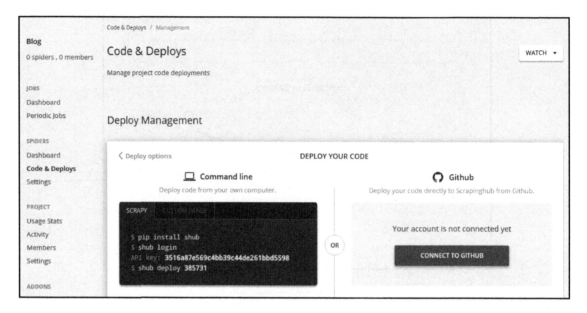

Project dashboard with various options

10. Deploy the code using either the command line or the GitHub.

11. The successful deployment will list the Spider as seen in the following screenshot:

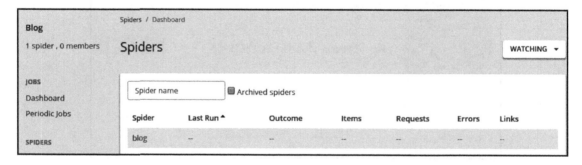

Listing of Spider after code deploy

12. Click the listed Spider, and detailed information and available options will be displayed as shown in the following screenshot:

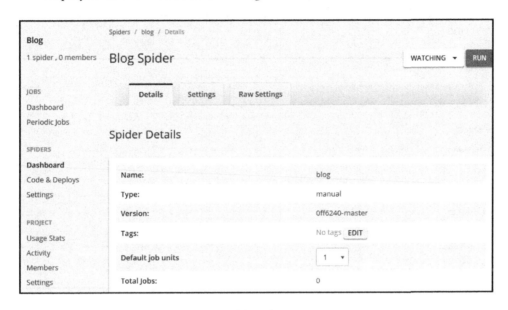

Spider details

13. Click **RUN** to start crawling the chosen Spider as seen here:

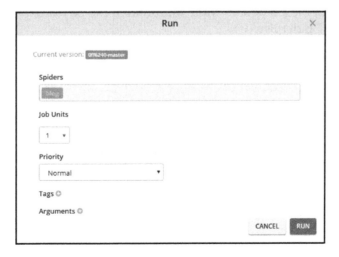

Spider Run window

14. Click **RUN** with the default options.

15. Crawling jobs will be listed as seen in the following screenshot. We can browse through the **Completed jobs** for details on **Items**, **Requests**, **Errors**, **Logs**, and so on:

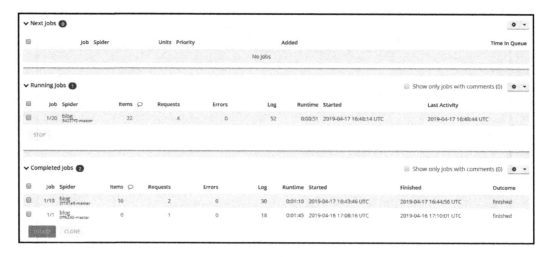

Jobs details for Spider

16. When exploring items for completed jobs, options such as filters, data export, and downloading with crawling job details for requests, logs, stats, and so on are available in the job details. More information can be loaded by clicking a particular Spider listed:

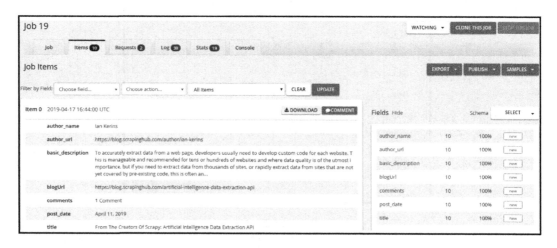

Listing items from Spider

Using the actions listed previously, we can deploy Scrapy Spider successfully using the Scraping hub.

In this section, we used and explored the Scraping hub to deploy the Scrapy Spider.

Summary

Selecting the right libraries and frameworks does depend on the project scope. Users are free to choose libraries and experience the online process.

In this chapter, we have used and explored various aspects of traversing web documents using Beautiful Soup and have explored a framework built for crawling activities using Spiders: Scrapy. Scrapy provides a complete framework to develop a crawler and is effective using XPath and CSS Selectors with support for the data export. Scrapy projects can also be deployed using Scraping hub to experience the live performance of the deployed Spider and enjoy features provided by the Scrapings hub (Scrapy Cloud) at `https://scrapinghub.com/scrapy-cloud`.

In the next chapter, we will explore more information regarding scraping data from the web.

Further reading

- Scrapy: `https://docs.scrapy.org/en/latest/intro/overview.html`
- Learn Scrapy: `https://learn.scrapinghub.com/scrapy/`
- Beautiful Soup: `https://www.crummy.com/software/BeautifulSoup/bs4/doc/`
- SoupSieve: `https://facelessuser.github.io/soupsieve/selectors/`
- XPath tutorial: `https://doc.scrapy.org/en/xpath-tutorial/topics/xpath-tutorial.html`
- CSS Selector reference: `https://www.w3schools.com/cssref/css_selectors.asp`
- Feed exports: `http://docs.scrapy.org/en/latest/topics/feed-exports.html`
- Scraping hub (Scrapy Cloud): `https://scrapinghub.com/`

Section 3: Advanced Concepts 3

In this section, you will learn how to scrape secure websites, and also deal with HTML forms and web cookies. You will also explore web-based APIs for targeted data and use web-based testing frameworks such as Selenium.

This section consists of the following chapters:

Working with Secure Web
6

So far, we have learned about web-development technologies, data-finding techniques, and Python libraries that we can use to access and scrape web content.

Various forms of web-based security measures exist nowadays that protect us against unauthenticated usage and unauthorized access to sensitive web content. A number of tools and technologies exist that are applied by websites; some target user-based actions, while some target a website's contents and their availability.

Secure web (or web-based security-enabled features) is considered to be one of the technologies that's implemented by websites and utilized by end users who want to use or view a website's contents. We will be covering a few basic concepts that deal with such features from a web scraping perspective.

In this chapter, we will learn about the following topics:

- Introduction to secure web
- HTML `<form>` processing
- Handling user authentication
- Working with cookies and sessions

Technical requirements

A web browser (Google Chrome or Mozilla Firefox) is required for this chapter. We will be using the following Python libraries:

- `requests`
- `pyquery`

If these libraries don't exist in your current Python setup, refer to Chapter 2, *Python and the Web – Using urllib and Requests,* the *Setting things up* section for more information on their installation and how to set them up.

The code files for this chapter are available in this book's GitHub repository at `https://github.com/PacktPublishing/Hands-On-Web-Scraping-with-Python/tree/master/Chapter06`.

Introduction to secure web

The implementation of web-based security features (or features that are used to maintain a secure state of access) to access information is rapidly growing, day by day. With ever-growing web-based technologies, websites and web applications deploy secure mechanisms that are basic or highly sophisticated.

Secure web-enabled content is often challenging from a crawling and scraping perspective. In this section, you will be introduced to a few basic security-based concepts. We will explore these concepts, along with their implementation, in the upcoming sections.

The following sections will talk about a few security-enabled concepts or concepts that are vulnerable to security. These concepts can be implemented independently and collaboratively in websites using a number of underlying tools or measures.

Form processing

This is also known as HTML `<form>` processing, form handling, or form submission. This method processes and handles data inside an HTML `<form>`.

HTML `<form>` or elements inside a `<form>` tag, such as `<input>`, `<option>`, `<button>`, `<textarea>`, and so on, with certain specific attributes, are normally used to collect and submit data. Please visit the W3School HTML form (`https://www.w3schools.com/html/html_forms.asp`) for practical examples and detailed information on HTML form.

HTTP methods or request methods, such as GET, POST, PUT, and so on, are used to access or submit data across web pages. For more information on HTTP, please visit https://www. w3.org/Protocols/.

From a security point of view, HTML <form> can contain dynamic and hidden or system-generated values that manage validation, provide value to fields, or perform security-based implementation during form submission. Forms with fields such as <input type="hidden"...> might not be visible to users in pages. The user must get help from the page source or browser-based developer tools in such cases.

A web page with a form might be displaying in certain fields and asking for input, and can contain a few more fields on the backend or in the source, which can contain user-or system-based information. Such information is collected and processed behind the scenes for web-based analysis, marketing, user and system identification, managing security, and more.

For more information on form processing, please refer to Chapter 3, *Using LXML, XPath, and CSS Selectors, Using web browser developer tools for accessing web content* section.

Cookies and sessions

To access cookie and session values that have been set by browsed websites, please refer to Chapter 1, *Web Scraping Fundamentals*, the *Data finding techniques* section of the *Developer tools* section. Now, let's get an idea of what cookies and sessions are.

Cookies

Cookies are data that's generated and stored by websites on your system or computer. Data in cookies helps identify web requests from the user to the website. Data in cookies is stored in key:value pairs. Data that's stored in cookies helps websites access that data and transfer certain saved values in the form of a quick interaction.

Cookies also allow websites to track user profiles, their web habits, and so on, and use such information for indexing, page ads, and marketing activities.

Cookie-based data can last for a session (that is, from the time that a web page is loaded until the browser is closed) forming what are known as a session cookies, or for days, weeks, or months, which are known as permanent or stored cookies. Cookies can also contain expiry values in seconds and are expired or deleted from the system once the period of time expressed in this value elapses.

 For more information on cookies, please refer to `Chapter 1`, *Web Scraping Fundamentals*, the *Understanding Web Development and Technologies* section of the *HTTP* section. You can also visit `https://www.aboutcookies.org/` and `http://www.allaboutcookies.org/` for more information.

Sessions

Sessions are properties that enforce state-based communication between two systems. A session is used to store user information temporarily and is also deleted as soon as the user quits the browser or leaves the website.

A session is used for maintaining security activity. A unique identification number, also known as a session ID or session key, is generated by the website and is used to track their users or security-based features independently. In most cases of session availability, it can be traced using cookies too.

User authentication

User authentication deals with handling and managing user-based identification processes. Websites offer user registration through their registration page and thereby collect user inputs for required or available fields. A user's details are saved in secure places such as the cloud or server-based databases, or any other secure system.

Registered users are verified and are permitted to log in and log out from their system, and are identified by their username, password, and email address.

Form processing, cookies, session management, and other security-based measures can be deployed either individually or collaboratively for this process.

In the previous chapter, we explored and tackled various scenarios based on information availability, accessing web pages, applying various HTTP methods, and so on to extract data. The sections in this chapter deal with various measures and situations that can be implemented or that might be faced during web scraping.

HTML <form> processing

In this section, we will be handling form processing or form submission in order to search for an activity from `http://toscrape.com` (ViewState). ViewState is an AJAX-based filter form.

This particular form submission is performed in multiple steps with the help of AJAX (`https://www.w3schools.com/js/js_ajax_intro.asp`). For more information on AJAX, please visit `W3Schools AJAX`:

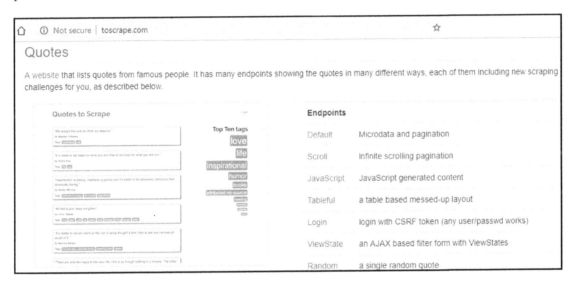

http://toscrape.com with various endpoints in the Quotes section

Let's set up the code. The `pyquery` and `requests` libraries need to be imported and the required URLs need to be collected so that they can be used.
The `processRequests()` function, along with positional and named arguments, is used for processing requests to the provided `url`, with the HTTP `POST` and `GET` methods based on the `params` argument returning a PyQuery object as a response.

We are also interested in iterating `authorTags` and collecting the `quoteAuthor` and `message`, respectively. In a similar way, any information that's obtained from a page can be extracted:

```
from pyquery import PyQuery as pq
import requests
mainurl = "http://toscrape.com/"
```

```
searchurl = "http://quotes.toscrape.com/search.aspx"
filterurl = "http://quotes.toscrape.com/filter.aspx"
quoteurl = "http://quotes.toscrape.com/"
authorTags = [('Albert Einstein', 'success'), ('Thomas A. Edison',
'inspirational')]

def processRequests(url, params={}, customheaders={}):
    if len(params) > 0:
        response = requests.post(url, data=params, headers=customheaders)
    else:
        response = requests.get(url)
    return pq(response.text)

if __name__ == '__main__':
    for authorTag in authorTags:
        authorName,tagName= authorTag
```

The following screenshot displays the content of the `searchurl` page, as defined in the preceding code. Two separate drop-downs exist, each with options for the author and their tags, respectively:

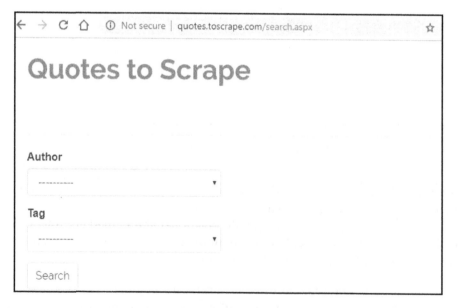

http://quotes.toscrape.com/search.aspx searchurl with author and tag

Let's load `searchurl`, as shown in the following code, and select an author from the **Author** drop-down. The `<option>` tag is generated using AJAX for the selected `<option>` of the **Author**:

> Please refer to `Chapter 3`, *Using LXML, XPath, and CSS Selectors*, the *Using web browser developer tools for accessing web content* section, and `Chapter 1`, *Web Scraping Fundamentals*, the *Data finding techniques* and *Developer tools* sections.

```
#Step 1: load searchURL
searchResponse = processRequests(searchurl)
author = searchResponse.find('select#author option:contains("' + authorName
+ '")').attr('value')
viewstate = searchResponse.find('input#__VIEWSTATE').attr('value')
tag = searchResponse.find('select#tag option').text()

print("Author: ", author)
print("ViewState: ", viewstate)
print("Tag: ", tag)
```

As you can see, the `processRequests()` function is called using an HTTP GET to `searchurl` and will be returning a response as an object of PyQuery. From `searchResponse`, let's collect the necessary form fields. Fields such as `author`, `viewstate`, and `tag` are collected, and the values that were obtained for the fields on each iteration are shown in the following output:

```
Author: Albert Einstein
ViewState:
NTA2MjI4NmE1Y2Q3NGFhMzhjZTgxMzM4ZWU0NjU4MmUsQWxiZXJJOIEVpbnN0ZWluLEouSy4gUm9
3bGluZyxKYW51IEF1c3Rlbi...........BDdW1taW5ncyxLaGFsZWQgSG9zc2Vpbmks SGFycG
VyIElxlZSxlYWRlbGVpbGUgTCdFbmdsZQ==
Tag: ----------

Author: Thomas A. Edison
ViewState:
ZjNhZTUwZDYzY2YyNDZlZmE5ODY0YTI5OWRhNDAyMDYsQWxiZXJJOIEVpbnN0ZWluLEouSy4gUm9
3bGluZyxKYW51IEF1c3Rlbi...........BDdW1taW5ncyxLaGFsZWQgSG9zc2Vpbmks SGFycG
VyIElxlZSxlYWRlbGVpbGUgTCdFbmdsZQ==
Tag: ----------
```

From the preceding output, we can see that `viewstate` (`<input id="__VIEWSTATE"..>`) contains unique values on both iterations for `authorTags`.

ViewState is a unique and random value that's generated by websites to identify individual states of the page, which are often found as a hidden `<input>` value. This `<form>` value exists in most websites that use `<form>` and built-in ASP or ASP.NET technologies. The ViewState value is used on the client side, and it preserves or retains the value of the `<form>` elements, alongside page identity. Use of ViewState is one of the techniques related to state management. For more information, please visit the article from C#Corner found at `https:/ /www.c-sharpcorner.com/article/Asp-Net-state-management- techniques/`.

The value of ViewState is compulsory for obtaining the `<option>` tag for the selected Author. As we can see in the following code, params is created with author, tag, and __VIEWSTATE, and is posted or submitted to filterurl using HTTP POST and customheaders by obtaining filterResponse. The following code shows what happens when filterurl has been loaded with the author and default tag:

```
#Step 2: load filterurl with author and default tag
params = {'author': author, 'tag': tag, '__VIEWSTATE': viewstate}
customheaders = {
    'Accept':
'text/html,application/xhtml+xml,application/xml;q=0.9,image/webp,image/apn
g,*/*;q=0.8',
    'Content-Type': 'application/x-www-form-urlencoded',
    'Referer': searchurl
}

filterResponse = processRequests(filterurl,params,customheaders)
viewstate = filterResponse.find('input#__VIEWSTATE').attr('value')
tagSuccess = filterResponse.find('select#tag option:contains("' + tagName +
'")').attr('value')
submitButton =
filterResponse.find('input[name="submit_button"]').attr('value')

print("Author: ", author)
print("ViewState: ", viewstate)
print("Tag: ", tagSuccess)
print("Submit: ", submitButton)
```

Iterating the preceding code will result in the following output:

- `http://quotes.toscrape.com/filter.aspx` with the selected author (`Thomas A. Edison`) and tag (`inspirational`):

  ```
  Author: Thomas A. Edison
  ViewState:
  ZjNhZTUwZDYzY2YyNDZlZmE5ODY0YTI5OWRhNDAyMDYsQWxiZXJ0OIEVpbnN0ZWluLEo
  uSy4gUm93bGluZychKYW51IEF1c3Rlbi............BDdW1taW5ncyxLaGFsZWQgSG
  9zc2VpbmksSGFycGVyIExlZSxNYWRlbGVpbmUgTCdFbmdsZSwtLS0tLS0tLS0t
  Tag: inspirational
  Submit: Search
  ```

- `http://quotes.toscrape.com/filter.aspx` with the selected author (`Albert Einstein`) and tag (`success`):

  ```
  Author: Albert Einstein
  ViewState:
  NTA2MjI4NmE1Y2Q3NGFhZmhjZTgxMzM4ZWU0NjU4MmUsQWxiZXJ0OIEVpbnN0ZWluLEo
  uSy4gUm93bGluZychKYW51IEF1c3Rlbi............BDdW1taW5ncyxLaGFsZWQgSG
  9zc2VpbmksSGFycGVyIExlZSxNYWRlbGVpbmUgTCdFbmdsZSwtLS0tLS0tLS0t
  Tag: success
  Submit: Search
  ```

Now that we have obtained all the filter `<form>`-based parameters for each `authorTags`, the final step is to submit these parameters—that is, `params` to `filterurl`—using `HTTP POST` and extract the resulting information:

```
#Step 3: load filterurl with author and defined tag
params = {'author': author, 'tag': tagSuccess, 'submit_button':
submitButton, '__VIEWSTATE': viewstate}
customheaders = {
'Accept':
'text/html,application/xhtml+xml,application/xml;q=0.9,image/webp,image/apn
g,*/*;q=0.8',
'Content-Type': 'application/x-www-form-urlencoded',
'Referer': filterurl
}

finalResponse = processRequests(filterurl,params, customheaders)

#Step 4: Extract results
quote = finalResponse.find('div.quote span.content').text()

quoteAuthor = finalResponse.find('div.quote span.author').text()
message = finalResponse.find('div.quote span.tag').text()
print("Author: ", quoteAuthor, "\nMessage: ", message)
```

As we can see, `finalResponse` is a PyQuery object that's returned by
`processRequests()` and is parsed to obtain the `quote`, `quoteAuthor`, and `message`, as
shown in the following screenshot:

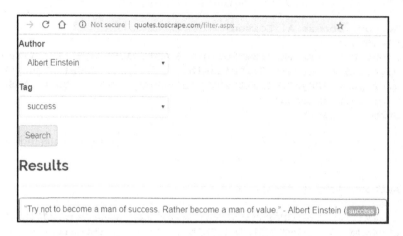

http://quotes.toscrape.com/filter.aspx with results for Author and Tag

The output from iteration number one using the preceding code with `Author` and
`Message` is as follows:

```
Author: Albert Einstein
Message: success
```

The following is a screenshot for iteration number two:

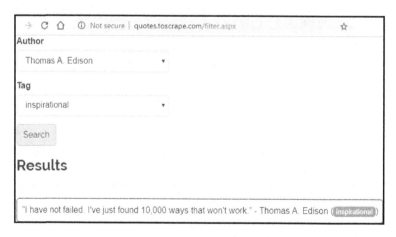

http://quotes.toscrape.com/filter.aspx with results for Author and Tag

The output from iteration number two using the preceding code with `Author` and `Message` is as follows:

Author: Thomas A. Edison
Message: inspirational

Form processing with searching and filtering actions, alongside the use of hidden fields, is shown in the preceding code. The `ViewState` value is used by the system behind the scenes to identify the selected option and filter the tags associated with it, resulting in quotes by the author.

The total number of HTTP `POST` parameters for the final form submission is four, whereas the page only displays or allows you to interact with two options. If any changes are made to a value, such as `viewstate`, or if `viewstate` is missing from `params`, it will result in empty quotes, as shown in the following code:

```
#params={'author':author,'tag':tagSuccess,'submit_button':submitButton,'__V
IEWSTATE':viewstate}
params={'author':author,'tag':tagSuccess,'submit_button':submitButton,'__VI
EWSTATE':viewstate+"TEST"}
#params={'author':author,'tag':tagSuccess,'submit_button':submitButton}
......
finalResponse = processRequests(filterurl,params, customheaders)
......
print("Author: ", quoteAuthor, "\nMessage: ", message)

Quote:
Author:
Message:
```

Form submission is not only dependent on the required parameters that are selected from visible `<form>` elements in the page—there can also be hidden values and dynamically generated state representation that should be processed and handled effectively for successful output.

In the next section, we will be dealing with form submission and user authentication.

Handling user authentication

In this section, we will be exploring a task that's used to process basic user authentication, which is available from `http://testing-ground.scraping.pro/login`. User authentication is often processed with a unique combination of information, such as username, password, email, and so on, to identify the user on the website.

The code in this section deals with logging in and changing the login credentials, as well as with obtaining the respective messages from the page.

As we can see in the following screenshot, the HTML `<form>` exists with two `<input>` boxes that accept the username and password (that is, the login credentials) that are required to login. Login credentials are private and secure information, but for this particular testing site, the values are visible, predefined, and provided—namely, `Username = "admin"` and `Password = "12345"`:

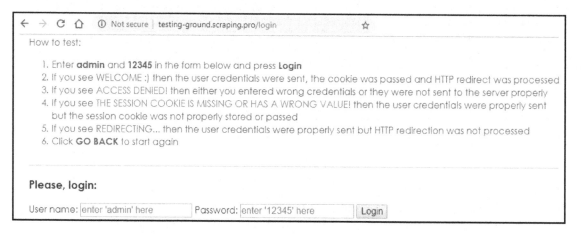

Login page

To process logging in with these credentials on `http://testing-ground.scraping.pro/login`, we need to find the `<form>` attributes—that is, `action` and `method`—that were used on the page to process the entered credentials. As we can see, the HTTP `POST` method will be applied to perform form submission on `http://testing-ground.scraping.pro/login?mode=login`:

Inspecting <form> elements

Let's move on and set up the code. The `pyquery` and `requests` libraries need to be imported and the required URLs need to be collected so that they can be used:

```
from pyquery import PyQuery as pq
import requests
mainUrl = "http://testing-ground.scraping.pro"
loginUrl = "http://testing-ground.scraping.pro/login"
logoutUrl = "http://testing-ground.scraping.pro/login?mode=logout"
postUrl="http://testing-ground.scraping.pro/login?mode=login"
```

As shown in the following code, the `responseCookies()` function will accept response objects that are obtained from `requests.get()` before printing the headers and cookies information. Similarly, the `processParams()` function accepts <form>-based parameters that will be posted and prints the message that's obtained from the page:

```
def responseCookies(response):
    headers = response.headers
    cookies = response.cookies
    print("Headers: ", headers)
    print("Cookies: ", cookies)

def processParams(params):
    response = requests.post(postUrl, data=params)
```

```
        responseB = pq(response.text)
        message = responseB.find('div#case_login h3').text()
        print("Confirm Login : ",message)

if __name__ == '__main__':
    requests.get(logoutUrl)

    response = requests.get(mainUrl)
    responseCookies(response)
    response = requests.get(loginUrl)
    responseCookies(response)
```

Now, let's request `logoutUrl` to clean the cookies and sessions, if they exist. Alternatively, for a completely new process, we can request `mainUrl` and `loginUrl`, respectively, and check the message that was received from `responseCookies()`. Here is the output:

```
Headers:{'Vary':'Accept-Encoding','Content-
Type':'text/html','Connection':'Keep-Alive', ..........., 'Content-
Encoding':'gzip','X-Powered-By':'PHP/5.4.4-14+deb7u12'}
Cookies: <RequestsCookieJar[]>

Headers:{'Vary':'Accept-Encoding','Content-
Type':'text/html','Connection':'Keep-Alive',.............., 'Set-
Cookie':'tdsess=deleted; expires=Thu, 01-Jan-1970 00:00:01 GMT',.........,
'Keep-Alive':'timeout=5, max=100','X-Powered-By':'PHP/5.4.4-14+deb7u12'}
Cookies: <RequestsCookieJar[]>
```

As shown in the preceding output, cookies is empty for both `mainUrl` and `loginUrl` and no other unique header pairs are available except `Set-Cookie`, with a value of `tdsess=deleted; expires=Thu, 01-Jan-1970 00:00:01 GMT` from `loginUrl`.

Now that `responseA` from the `loginUrl` `<form>` elements attribute name has been collected as `username` and `password`, this information will be used to create the `paramsCorrect` and `paramsIncorrect` parameter strings, which will be posted to `postUrl`:

```
responseA = pq(response.text)
username = responseA.find('input[id="usr"]').attr('name')
password = responseA.find('input[id="pwd"]').attr('name')

#Welcome : Success
paramsCorrect = {username: 'admin', password: '12345'} #Success
print(paramsCorrect)
processParams(paramsCorrect)
```

A successful form submission with the provided `paramsCorrect` parameter string will result in the following output:

```
{'pwd': '12345', 'usr': 'admin'}
Confirm Login : WELCOME :)
```

The preceding output is extracted from the response of `postUrl`, which in this test case is actually a redirected page with a URL of `http://testing-ground.scraping.pro/login?mode=welcome`:

Successful form submission with valid login credentials

Let's continue with form submission, but with invalid credentials.
The `paramsIncorrect` phrase contains an invalid value for `password`:

```
paramsIncorrect = {username: 'admin', password: '123456'} #Access Denied
print(paramsIncorrect)
processParams(paramsIncorrect)
```

The preceding code will result in the following output:

```
{'pwd': '123456', 'usr': 'admin'}
Confirm Login : ACCESS DENIED!
```

The preceding output can also be found in the `loginUrl` itself, and no redirection takes place this time:

Access Denied! (processed with wrong credentials)

As you can see, user authentication and form submission work in tandem. With the use of proper login credentials and by being able to handle the form submission process using Python, we can obtain a successful output or deal with the related output that's returned from a website.

In the next section, we will be performing form submission and user authentication by handling cookies that contain a session.

Working with cookies and sessions

In this section, we will be handling form processing for user authentication and managing cookies and sessions for `http://quotes.toscrape.com/login` from `http://toscrape.com`

 In order to log in, you need to log in with a CSRF token (any username/password works).

Let's set up the code. The `pyquery` and `requests` libraries need to be imported and the required URLs will be collected and used. The `getCustomHeaders()` function, together with the `cookieHeader` argument, is used to set the cookie value for the URL request headers. The `responseCookies()` function, together with the `response` argument, displays the `headers` and `cookies`, and also returns the `Set-Cookie` value from `cookies`:

```
from pyquery import PyQuery as pq
import requests
mainUrl = "http://toscrape.com/"
loginUrl = "http://quotes.toscrape.com/login"
quoteUrl = "http://quotes.toscrape.com/"

def getCustomHeaders(cookieHeader):
    return {
        'Host': 'quotes.toscrape.com',
        'User-Agent': 'Mozilla/5.0 (Windows NT 10.0; Win64; x64; rv:65.0)
Gecko/20100101 Firefox/65.0',
        'Accept':
'text/html,application/xhtml+xml,application/xml;q=0.9,image/webp,*/*;q=0.8
',
        'Referer': 'http://quotes.toscrape.com/login',
        'Content-Type': 'application/x-www-form-urlencoded',
        'Cookie': cookieHeader
    }

def responseCookies(response):
    headers = response.headers
    cookies = response.cookies
    print("Headers: ", headers)
    print("Cookies: ", cookies)
    return headers['Set-Cookie']

if __name__ == '__main__':
```

 For more information on HTTP and HTTP headers, please visit `Chapter 1`, *Web Scraping Fundamentals*, the *Understanding Web Development and Technologies* and *HTTP* sections. For more details on cookies, please visit `https://www.aboutcookies.org/` or `allaboutcookies.org`.

Now, let's begin by loading `mainUrl` and `loginUrl`, respectively:

```
requests.get(mainUrl)
response = requests.get(loginUrl)
```

The following screenshot shows what a login page looks like when using `loginUrl`:

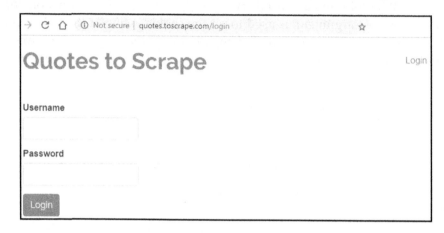

Login page from http://quotes.toscrape.com/login

As soon as `loginUrl` is loaded, we can inspect or use browser-based developer tools to find the request headers and confirm whether any cookies exist. We receive the following output:

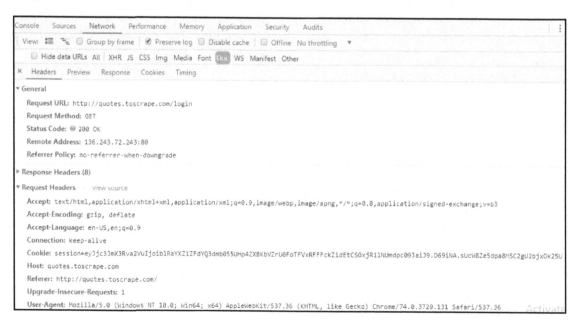

Network panel Doc-based headers tab from browser developer tools

The following code accepts cookies from `response` and is used in headers:

```
setCookie = responseCookies(response)
print("Set-Cookie: ",setCookie)
```

As we can see from the preceding screenshot, **Request Headers** contains key=Cookie with a value beginning with `sessio=....`, also known as the session ID. This information is found in both `response.headers` and `response.cookies`, and the `responseCookies()` function returns the cookie value from `response.headers` before printing the details:

```
Headers: {'Set-Cookie':
session=eyJjc3JmX3Rva2VuIjoicUlPVGNnQ2FKZmJaS3NOdmlIREFWbVdvWGtMakJkVX11U3B
ScmVZTWhRd0d6dEZueFBsRSJ9.D68Log.3ANox76h0whpTRjkqNo7JRgCtWI; HttpOnly;
Path=/',...,'Content-Encoding':'gzip','Content-Type':'text/html;
charset=utf-8',......}

Cookies: <RequestsCookieJar[<Cookie
session=eyJjc3JmX3Rva2VuIjoicUlPVGNnQ2FKZmJaS3NOdmlIREFWbVdvWGtMakJkVX11U3B
ScmVZTWhRd0d6dEZueFBsRSJ9.D68Log.3ANox76h0whpTRjkqNo7JRgCtWI for
quotes.toscrape.com/>]>

Set-Cookie:
session=eyJjc3JmX3Rva2VuIjoicUlPVGNnQ2FKZmJaS3NOdmlIREFWbVdvWGtMakJkVX11U3B
ScmVZTWhRd0d6dEZueFBsRSJ9.D68Log.3ANox76h0whpTRjkqNo7JRgCtWI; HttpOnly;
Path=/
```

 A session ID is a unique number that a website's server assigns to a specific user for a certain duration or for a session. This ID can be stored in certain <form> fields or cookies, or even appended to a URL query string.

Now that we've received the cookie-based session value, we need to maintain this value so that we have a successful login procedure.

Let's collect the `<form>`-based fields and more information on form submission:

```
  ↳ ⟦ ⟧    Elements   Console   Sources   Network   Performance   Memory   Application   Security   Audits
<!doctype html>
<html lang="en">
▶ <head>…</head>
▼ <body>
  ▼ <div class="container">
      ::before
    ▶ <div class="row header-box">…</div>
    ▼ <form action="/login" method="post" accept-charset="utf-8">
        <input type="hidden" name="csrf_token" value="jJgAHDQykMBnCFsPIZOoqdbflYRzXtSuiEmwKeGavVWxpNLUhrcT"> == $0
      ▼ <div class="row">
          ::before
        ▼ <div class="form-group col-xs-3">
            <label for="username">Username</label>
            <input type="text" class="form-control" id="username" name="username">
          </div>
          ::after
        </div>
      ▼ <div class="row">
          ::before
        ▼ <div class="form-group col-xs-3">
            <label for="username">Password</label>
            <input type="password" class="form-control" id="password" name="password">
          </div>
          ::after
        </div>
        <input type="submit" value="Login" class="btn btn-primary">
      </form>
      ::after
    </div>
    ▶ <footer class="footer">…</footer>
  </body>
html   body   div.container   form   input
```

Elements panel from Browser Developer Tools with page source

As we can see from the preceding screenshot, `<form>` is using HTTP POST to submit form fields to `loginUrl`, and there's also a hidden `<input>` field with `csrf_token`, along with the fields accepting the login credentials.

 Cross-Site Request Forgery (CSRF) or session riding is a security measure that is used to identify each individual request between a user and a website. Generally, `CSRF_TOKEN` or a token is used to manage such a mechanism. A token is a random string generated by websites when a request to the page is made by a user. A token value is required to process any form of HTTP request to the website. The token value keeps changing for each successful request. An HTML `<form>` containing a token value can be processed with either an updated or deleted token, which are not accepted by websites.

In this example, `username` and `password` are open string values, and `test` has been used for both:

```
responseA = pq(response.text)
csrf_token = responseA.find('input[name="csrf_token"]').attr('value')
username = responseA.find('input[id="username"]').attr('name')
password = responseA.find('input[id="password"]').attr('name')

params = {username: 'test', password: 'test', 'csrf_token': csrf_token}
print(params)
```

The form fields with the existing value and name are collected and `params` is configured, which results in the following output:

```
{'password':'test','username':'test','csrf_token':'jJgAHDQykMBnCFsPIZOoqdbf
lYRzXtSuiEmwKeGavVWxpNLUhrcT'}
```

> The parameters to be submitted via a form action are built using the `name` attribute of the `<form>` element as a key and default, respectively, and is required to receive values as their value.

The `requests.post()` phrase implements a HTTP `POST` request to `loginURL` with the `params` and `customHeaders` that have been setup. A `customHeaders` is created with the `setCookie` value that we received earlier:

```
customHeaders = getCustomHeaders(setCookie)
response = requests.post(loginUrl, data=params, headers=customHeaders)
setCookie = responseCookies(response)
#print("Set-Cookie: ",setCookie)

responseB = pq(response.text)
logoutText = responseB.find('a[href*="logout"]').text()
logoutLink = responseB.find('a[href*="logout"]').attr('href')

print("Current Page : ",response.url)
print("Confirm Login : ", responseB.find('.row h2').text())
print("Logout Info : ", logoutText," & ",logoutLink)
```

Finally, we receive a successful output, along with the redirected URL and information regarding the logout:

```
Current Page : http://quotes.toscrape.com/
Confirm Login : Top Ten tags
Logout Info : Logout & /logout
```

The following screenshot shows the successful authentication with the information verified:

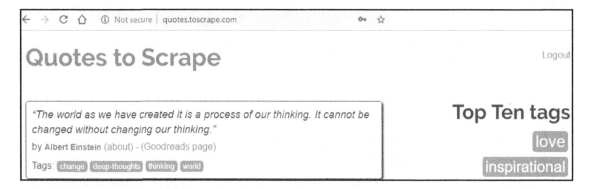

Successful authentication verified with information from http://quotes.toscrape.com/

 Empty `customHeaders` or `customHeaders` without a `key` named `Cookie` will not be successful in the authentication process. Similarly, `csrf_token` is also required as the parameter. A posted, updated, or empty `csrf_token` will not be successful in the authentication process, even when `customHeaders` is provided with the required `key:value` pairs of information.

Summary

In this chapter, we have explored some basic measures and techniques that are relevant to security concerns, faced often, and are challenging with regards to web scraping.

Maintaining security measures between a user and a website is quite a challenging and hazardous task. Different security concern exist and need to be managed. Various new concepts exist on the web that need to be processed effectively and legally so that we can perform web scraping activities.

In the next chapter, we will be using the Python programming language to interact with the web API for data extraction.

Further reading

- **AJAX:** `http://api.jquery.com/jquery.ajax/`, `https://www.w3schools.com/js/js_ajax_intro.asp`
- **Browser developer tools:** `https://developers.google.com/web/tools/chrome-devtools/`, `https://developer.mozilla.org/son/docs/Tools`
- **Cookies:** `https://www.aboutcookies.org/`, `http://www.allaboutcookies.org/`
- **CSRF:** `https://www.owasp.org/index.php/Cross-Site_Request_Forgery_(CSRF)`
- **HTML forms:** `https://www.w3schools.com/html/html_forms.asp`, `https://developer.mozilla.org/en-US/docs/Learn/HTML/Forms`
- **HTTP:** `https://www.w3.org/Protocols/`
- **HTTP headers:** `http://jkorpela.fi/http.html`
- **HTTP session:** `https://developer.mozilla.org/en-US/docs/Web/HTTP/Session`
- **Web scraping sandbox:** `http://toscrape.com/`
- **Web scraper testing ground:** `http://testing-ground.scraping.pro/`

7
Data Extraction Using Web-Based APIs

Web-based APIs allow users to interact with information on the web. API deals directly with data that's in a formatted pattern easy to use and maintain. Some APIs also require user authentication before they can provide data to the user. This chapter will cover the use of Python and some web APIs to interact with, and extract data from, the available API. Generally, APIs provide data in an exchangeable document format, such as JSON, CSV, and XML.

In this chapter, we will cover the following topics:

- Introduction to web APIs
- Accessing web APIs using the Python programming language
- Processing and extracting data via web APIs

Technical requirements

A web browser (Google Chrome or Mozilla Firefox) is required for this chapter. We will be using the following Python libraries:

- `requests`
- `json`
- `collections`

If these libraries don't exist on your current Python setup, refer to Chapter 2, *Python and the Web – Using urllib and Requests*, in the *Setting things up* section to learn how to download them.

The code files for this chapter are available in this book's GitHub repository: `https://github.com/PacktPublishing/Hands-On-Web-Scraping-with-Python/tree/master/Chapter07`.

Introduction to web APIs

A web-based application programming information, or **web-based API**, is an interface provided by a website to return information for the request that's received. A web API (or API) is actually a web service that's provided by websites to users or third-party web applications or automated scripts in order to share and exchange information.

Generally, this is a **user interface** (UI) that's processed via a web browser for retrieving certain information from requests that have been made to a website or web server. Websites with large amount of information of any type can provide a web API to their user, which facilitates information sharing.

 API in the field of software applications is known for its set of facilities, such as methods and libraries, which can be used to further enhance, build, or develop applications. This is also known as a developer API.

Web APIs are not dependent on any programming languages. They enable easy access to web-based information in a raw format, and usually return a structured response in JSON, XML, or CSV format.

They work on the HTTP principle (request and response cycle), but accept only sets of a predefined format of requests and parameters to generate a response. In terms of security concerns, many APIs also provide authentication tools, such as an API key, which is required to make a request to a website.

REST and SOAP

API is a service that's provided by web servers that are based on software architecture or principles. **Simple Object Access Protocol (SOAP)** and **Representational State Transfer (REST)** are methods for accessing web services. While REST is an architecture, SOAP is a protocol based on web standards. We will be dealing with the REST API in upcoming sections.

REST

REST (https://www.ics.uci.edu/~fielding/pubs/dissertation/rest_arch_style.htm) is a style of software architecture based on a set of defining and addressing network principles. REST is a software architecture, not a set of standards. REST uses standard HTTP protocol and methods such as GET, POST, PUT, and DELETE to provide services. It is stateless, multilayered, and also supports caching.

Web APIs are generally classed as RESTful web services; they provide an interface to the user and other resources for communication. RESTful web services (REST APIs or web APIs) (https://restfulapi.net/) is the service provided by the web for adapting to the REST architecture.

Services that are provided via REST don't need to be adapted to the new standards, development, or frameworks. Most of the time, it will be using a GET request, along with query strings that have been issued to APIs, searching for their response. HTTP status codes (https://restfulapi.net/http-status-codes/) (404, 200, 304) are often tracked to determine the response of an API. Responses can also be obtained in various formats, such as JSON, XML, and CSV.

In terms of choosing between REST and SOAP, REST is more easy and efficient when it comes to processing compared to SOAP, and is being provided to the public by a large number of websites.

SOAP

SOAP (https://www.w3.org/TR/soap/is) is a set of standards specified by W3C and also represents alternative to REST when it comes to web services. SOAP uses HTTP and **SMTP (Simple Mail Transfer Protocol)**, and is used to exchange documents over the internet, as well as via remote procedures.

SOAP uses XML as a messaging service and is also known as an XML-based protocol. SOAP requests contain XML documents (with an envelope and body) that describes the methods and parameters that are sent to a server. The server will execute the method that's received, along with parameters, and send an SOAP response back to the program initiating the request.

SOAP is highly extensible and includes built-in error handling. It also works with other protocols, such as SMTP. SOAP is also independent to platforms and programming languages, and is mostly implemented in distributed enterprise environments.

Benefits of web APIs

Day by day, information requirements are growing, along with their availability across the web. Information sources, their availability, facilities, and technologies to share and exchange have become a global demand. The API is one of the preferred data sources and can be used to retrieve data.

API is not only a way of communicating with a user via a web browser – you can also use systems. APIs allow communication between systems and devices, such as mobiles, despite their underlying system or programming languages. Many mobile apps generate requests to certain APIs and display related information that has been retrieved from responses. APIs are not just a simple service for retrieving data; they are used to exchange and process information and even communicate between systems across different platforms and services.

From a web scraping perspective, responses or data that's available through APIs are preferred over data that's retrieved using scraping scripts. This is due to the following reasons:

- An API's returned data is completely specific to the requests being performed, along with the filters or parameters that have been applied to it.
- Tasks such as parsing HTML or XML using Python libraries, such as `BeautifulSoup`, `pyquery`, and `lxml`, isn't always required.
- The format of the data is structured and easy to handle.
- Data cleaning and processing for final listings will be more easy or might not be required.
- There will be significant reductions in processing time (compared to coding, analyzing the web, and applying XPath and CSS selectors to retrieve data).
- They are easy to process.

There are also certain factors to be considered before adapting completely to the web API from a scraping point of view, including the following:

- Not all websites provide users with access to web APIs.
- Responses from APIs are specific to the set of predefined parameters. This might restrict the exact requests based on requirements that can be made, and restrict the availability of data to be obtained immediately.
- Responses that are returned are limited to a certain volume, such as the number of records returned per request and the maximum number of requests allowed.
- Although data will be available in a structured format, it can be distributed across key-value pairs, which might require some additional merging tasks.

Given these points, we can see that the web API is the preferred choice for obtaining information from websites.

Accessing web API and data formats

In this section, we will be exploring various APIs that are available on the web, send requests to them, and receive responses, before explaining how they work via the Python programming language.

Let's consider the following sample URL, `https://www.someexampledomain.com`. The API it provides comes with parameters, locators, and authentication. By using these, we can access the following resources:

- `https://api.someexampledomain.com`
- `https://api.someexampledomain.com/resource?key1=value1&key2=value2`
- `https://api.someexampledomain.com/resource?api_key=ACCESS_KEY&key1=value1&key2=value2`
- `https://api.someexampledomain.com/resource/v1/2019/01`

Parameters or collections of key-value pairs are actually sets of predefined variables that are provided by the web. Usually, the API provides some sort of documentation or basic guidelines regarding its usage, HTTP methods, available keys and types, or permitted values that the key can receive, along with other information on the features that are supported by the API, as shown in the following screenshot:

Sunset and sunrise times API

We offer a **free API** that provides **sunset and sunrise times** for a given **latitude and longitude**.

Please note that **attribution is required** if you use our API. Check "Usage limits and attribution" section below for more information.

API documentation

Ours is a very simple REST api, you only have to do a GET request to **https://api.sunrise-sunset.org/json**.

Parameters

- **lat** (float): Latitude in decimal degrees. Required.
- **long** (float): Longitude in decimal degrees. Required.
- **date** (string): Date in YYYY-MM-DD format. Also accepts other date formats and even relative date formats. If not present, date defaults to current date. Optional.
- **callback** (string): Callback function name for JSONP response. Optional.
- **formatted** (integer): 0 or 1 (1 is default). Time values in response will be expressed following ISO 8601 and day_length will be expressed in seconds. Optional.

Sample requests

These are three sample requests for getting sunset and sunrise information from our API for a given location:

```
https://api.sunrise-sunset.org/json?lat=36.7201600&lng=-4.4203400
https://api.sunrise-sunset.org/json?lat=36.7201600&lng=-4.4203400&date=today
https://api.sunrise-sunset.org/json?lat=36.7201600&lng=-4.4203400&date=2019-03-03
https://api.sunrise-sunset.org/json?lat=36.7201600&lng=-4.4203400&formatted=0
```

API details and links from https://sunrise-sunset.org/api

End users and systems can only use the API with the features and functions that the provider permits.

The following a number of actual API links and example calls that show the formats and parameters that are used in URLs:

- `http://api.walmartlabs.com/v1/reviews/33093101?apiKey={apiKey}`
  `lsPublisherId={Your LinkShare Publisher Id}format=json`
- `https://api.nasa.gov/neo/rest/v1/feed?start_date=START_DATEend_date=`
  `END_DATEapi_key=API_KEY`

- `https://api.sunrise-sunset.org/json?lat=36.7201600lng=-4.4203400date=today`

- `https://api.twitter.com/1.1/search/tweets.json?q=nasaresult_type=popular`

- `http://api.geonames.org/postalCodeSearchJSON?postalcode=9011maxRows=10 username=demo`

- `http://api.geonames.org/postalCodeSearch?postalcode=9011maxRows=10 username=demo`

- `https://api.nytimes.com/svc/mostpopular/v2/viewed/1.json?api-key=yourkey`

- `https://maps.googleapis.com/maps/api/staticmap?center=Brooklyn+Bridge,New+York,NYzoom=13size=600x300maptype=roadmap markers=color:blue%7Clabel:S%7C40.702147,-74.015794markers=color:green%7Clabel:G%7C40.711614,-74.012318markers=color:red%7Clabel:C%7C40.718217,-73.998284key=YOUR_API_KEY`

Parameters such as `key`, `api_key`, `apiKey` and `api-key` are required for security and tracking measures and need to be obtained before you process any API requests.

The API links and example calls in this section are linked to the resources they are listed on. For example, `https://api.twitter.com/1.1/search/tweets.json?q=nasa&result_type=popular` is listed on `https://developer.twitter.com/en/docs/tweets/search/api-reference/get-search-tweets`.

Making requests to the web API using a web browser

Obtaining information about the parameters to be applied through query strings and obtaining the API key, if required, is the preliminary step in gaining API access. Most of the public or free APIs are quite straightforward and easy to manage in comparison to developer APIs that are provided by Google, Twitter, and Facebook.

API requests can be made by using a web browser. However, in this section, we will try to display some general cases that can be encountered while accessing APIs, while also exhibiting some important properties of the RESTful API.

Case 1 – accessing a simple API (request and response)

In this section, we will be using the following URL: https://api.sunrise-sunset.org/json?lat=27.717245lng=85.323959date=2019-03-04.

Let's process a request through a simple API in order to obtain the sunrise and sunset timings (available in UTC) for Kathmandu, Nepal. Query strings require values for lat (latitude), lng (longitude), and date for the chosen location. As we can see in the following screenshot, the response that we obtained is in JSON format (formatted using a browser extension), and its a successful request was verified by using a browser-based developer tool with **Request Method** and **HTTP Status Code** (200, that is, OK or Success):

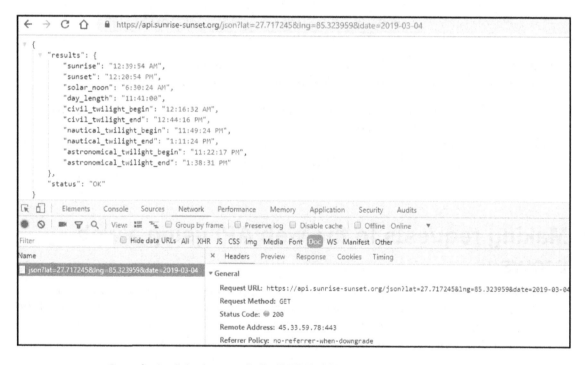

Response from https://api.sunrise-sunset.org/json?lat=27.717245&lng=85.323959&date=2019-03-04 with Status Code

The response is returned in a raw format or JSON format, as shown in the following code. The JSON response, when obtained normally, is processed using the Python `json` library. In the following code, the API request has been processed using the `requests` library. `requests` provide various features for dealing with HTTP; for example, the HTTP status code can be obtained by using `status_code`. Headers are obtained by using `headers`. Here, we are interested in `status_code` and `headers`, and, in particular, `Content-Type`, so that we can plan further processing and the use of libraries that might be required:

```python
import requests
url =
'https://api.sunrise-sunset.org/json?lat=27.7172&lng=85.3239&date=2019-03-0
4'

results = requests.get(url) #request url
print("Status Code: ", results.status_code)
print("Headers-ContentType: ", results.headers['Content-Type'])
print("Headers: ", results.headers)

jsonResult = results.json() #read JSON content
print("Type JSON Results",type(jsonResult))
print(jsonResult)
print("SunRise & Sunset: ",jsonResult['results']['sunrise']," &
",jsonResult['results']['sunset'])
```

As we can see, `status_code` is 200 (that is, OK) and `Content-Type` is of the JSON type. This gives us confirmation that we can use JSON-related libraries to move forward. However, in this case, we are using the `json()` function from the `requests` library, which reduces our dependence on extra libraries and converts the response object into a `dict` object. With the `dict` we received, we can access the desired elements by using a `key:value` pair:

```
Type Results <class 'requests.models.Response'>
Status Code: 200
Headers-ContentType: application/json

Headers: {'Access-Control-Allow-Origin':'*','Content-
Type':'application/json','Vary':'Accept-Encoding',
'Server':'nginx','Connection':'keep-alive','Content-
Encoding':'gzip','Transfer-Encoding':'chunked','Date': 'Mon, 04 Mar 2019
07:48:29 GMT'}

Type JSON Results <class 'dict'>

{'status':'OK','results':{'civil_twilight_end':'12:44:16
PM','astronomical_twilight_end':'1:38:31 PM',
'civil_twilight_begin':'12:16:32 AM','sunrise':'12:39:54
```

```
AM',......,'sunset':'12:20:54 PM','solar_noon': '6:30:24
AM','day_length':'11:41:00'}}

SunRise & Sunset: 12:39:54 AM & 12:20:54 PM
```

Case 2 – demonstrating status codes and informative responses from the API

In this section, we will be using the following URL: `https://api.twitter.com/1.1/search/tweets.json?q=`.

In this section, we will be processing an API request from Twitter. The URL to be requested is `https://api.twitter.com/1.1/search/tweets.json?q=`. By using this URL, we can easily identify that the query string, `q`, is empty, and that the value that's expected by the Twitter API is not provided. The complete URL should have been something along the lines of `https://api.twitter.com/1.1/search/tweets.json?q=nasaresult_type=popular`.

The response that was returned was for an incomplete API call, and can be seen in the following screenshot, along with the HTTP status code (`400` or `Bad Request`) and a message that was returned by the API stating **errors** with **"message" : "Bad Authentication data"**. For more information on the Twitter API's **Search** option, please refer to `https://developer.twitter.com/en/docs/tweets/search/api-reference/get-search-tweets`:

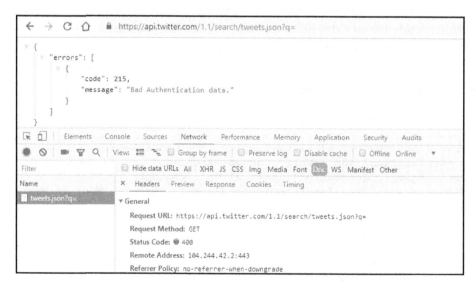

Incomplete request made to Twitter API

The response that was returned by Twitter API is actually information, not an error. Such informative responses make the API more scalable and easy to debug when they're used by other resources. It's also an appreciated characteristic of RESTful web services. This kind of information can be easily overcome by deploying API parameters and other requirements.

The following code will make a request to Twitter with an empty query string and identify the responses:

```
import requests
import json
url = 'https://api.twitter.com/1.1/search/tweets.json?q='

results = requests.get(url)
print("Status Code: ", results.status_code)
print("Headers: Content-Type: ", results.headers['Content-Type'])

jsonResult = results.content      #jsonResult = results.json()
print(jsonResult)

jsonFinal = json.loads(jsonResult.decode())
print(jsonFinal) #print(json.loads(requests.get(url).content.decode()))

if results.status_code==400:
    print(jsonFinal['errors'][0]['message'])
else:
    pass
```

The preceding code uses the json Python library to load the decoded jsonResult that was obtained by using the loads() function. We can also use json() from requests, as we did in case 1. jsonFinal is now a Python dictionary object and can be explored so that we can find its 'key:value'. The final output is as follows:

```
Status Code: 400
Headers: Content-Type: application/json; charset=utf-8

b'{"errors":[{"code":215,"message":"Bad Authentication data."}]}'
{'errors': [{'message': 'Bad Authentication data.', 'code': 215}]}

Bad Authentication data.
```

Case 3 – demonstrating RESTful API cache functionality

In this section, we will be using the following URL: `https://api.github.com/`.

GitHUb (`https://github.com/`) is a place for developers and their code repositories. The GitHub API is quite famous among developers, all of which come from various programming backgrounds. As we can see in the following screenshot, the response is obtained in JSON. The request was a success since the HTTP status code that was returned was 200, that is, OK or Success:

Response from https://api.github.com with HTTP Status Code 200

As you can see, we made a basic call to `https://api.github.com`. The content that was returned contains links for the API, along with some parameters to be supplied for specific calls, such as `{/gist_id}`, `{/target}`, and `{query}`.

Let's send a request to the API again, but this time without any changes or updates in the parameter values. The content that we will receive will be similar to the previous response, but there will be a difference in the HTTP Status Code; that is, we will get 304 Not Modified in comparison to 200 OK:

HTTP Status code 304 for https://api.github.com

This HTTP status code (304 or Not Modified) demonstrates REST's caching functionality. Since the response doesn't have any updates or updated content, the client-side caching functionality comes into play. This helps with processing time, as well as bandwidth time and usage. The cache is one of the important properties of RESTful web services. The following is the Python code revealing the cache property of the RESTful API, which was obtained by passing external headers that were supplied to the headers parameter while making a request with requests.get():

```
import requests
url = 'https://api.github.com'

#First Request
results = requests.get(url)
print("Status Code: ", results.status_code)
print("Headers: ", results.headers)

#Second Request with 'headers'
etag = results.headers['ETag']
print("ETag: ",etag)

results = requests.get(url, headers={'If-None-Match': etag})
print("Status Code: ", results.status_code)
```

requests is used to call url twice in the code. We can also see that the second request has been supplied with etag for header information, that is, If-None-Match. This particular header checks for the response header that was obtained using the ETag key as an HTTP Response Header. ETag is used for tracking purposes and normally identifies the resources that exist. This exhibits the cache ability. For more information on ETag, please refer to https://developer.mozilla.org/en-US/docs/Web/HTTP/Headers/ETag.

ETag is collected from `results.headers` and forwarded with second request that was made by obtaining HTTP `Status Code: 304`. The following code shows the output:

```
Status Code: 200
Headers: Content-Type: application/json; charset=utf-8
Headers: {'X-GitHub-Request-Id': 'A195:073C:37F223:79CCB0:5C8144B4',
'Status': '200 OK','ETag': 'W/"7dc470913f1fe9bb6c7355b50a0737bc"',
'Content-Encoding': 'gzip','Date': 'Thu, 07 Mar 2019 16:20:05
GMT',........, 'Content-Type': 'application/json; charset=utf-8', .....,
'Server': 'GitHub.com'}

ETag: W/"7dc470913f1fe9bb6c7355b50a0737bc"
Status Code: 304
```

In this section, we have learned about various APIs, accessing them via the use of features, and demonstrated a number of important concepts that are relevant to web scraping methods. In the next section, we will be scraping data with the use of APIs.

Web scraping using APIs

In this section, we will be requesting APIs and collecting the required data through them. Technically, data that's obtained through an API isn't similar to performing a scraping activity since we can't only extract data that's required from the API and process it further.

Example 1 – searching and collecting university names and URLs

In this example, we will be using an API provided by HIPO (https://hipolabs.com/) to search for universities: http://universities.hipolabs.com/search?name=Wales.

This API uses a query parameter called `name`, which will look for a university name. We will also provide an additional parameter, `country`, with country names such as United States, and United Kingdom. This API can be requested from the following URLs, while more information can be found at https://github.com/hipo/university-domains-list:

- http://universities.hipolabs.com
- http://universities.hipolabs.com/search?name=Wales
- http://universities.hipolabs.com/search?name=Medicinecountry=United Kingdom

Let's import the required libraries and use the `readUrl()` function to request the API and return the JSON response, as shown in the following code:

```
import requests
import json
dataSet = []

def readUrl(search):
    results = requests.get(url+search)
    print("Status Code: ", results.status_code)
    print("Headers: Content-Type: ", results.headers['Content-Type'])
    return results.json()
```

With the JSON response returned, the required values can be retrieved with the keys and index that we have found, as shown in the following screenshot:

```
"web_pages": [
    "http://www.wales.ac.uk/"
],
"alpha_two_code": "GB",
"state-province": null,
"country": "United Kingdom",
"domains": [
    "wales.ac.uk"
],
"name": "University of Wales"


"web_pages": [
    "http://www.uwic.ac.uk/"
],
"alpha_two_code": "GB",
"state-province": null,
"country": "United Kingdom",
"domains": [
    "uwic.ac.uk"
],
"name": "University of Wales Institute, Cardiff"
```

JSON (formatted) obtained from the API

`name` and `url` are traversed and appended to `dataSet`:

```
url = 'http://universities.hipolabs.com/search?name='
jsonResult = readUrl('Wales') # print(jsonResult)

for university in jsonResult:
    name = university['name']
```

```
    url = university['web_pages'][0]
    dataSet.append([name,url])

print("Total Universities Found: ",len(dataSet))
print(dataSet)
```

The final output is as follows:

```
Status Code: 200
Headers: Content-Type: application/json
Total Universities Found: 10

[['University of Wales', 'http://www.wales.ac.uk/'],
['University of Wales Institute, Cardiff', 'http://www.uwic.ac.uk/'],
.......,
['University of Wales, Lampeter', 'http://www.lamp.ac.uk/'],
['University of Wales, Bangor', 'http://www.bangor.ac.uk/']]
```

Example 2 – scraping information from GitHub events

In this example, we will be collecting information regarding `type` (type of event), `created_at` (date of event created), `id` (event identification code), and `repo` (repository name) across pages. We will be using the following URL: `https://api.github.com/events`.

GitHub `Events` lists public activities that have been performed within the past 90 days. These events are provided in pages, with 30 items per page, and a maximum of 300 being shown. Various sections exist inside events, all of which reveal the description about the `actor`, `repo`, `org`, `created_at`, `type`, and more.

 For more details, please refer to the following link: `https://developer.github.com/v3/activity/events/`.

Here is the code we will be using:

```
if __name__ == "__main__":
    eventTypes=[]
    #IssueCommentEvent,WatchEvent,PullRequestReviewCommentEvent,CreateEvent
    for page in range(1, 4): #First 3 pages
        events = readUrl('events?page=' + str(page))
        for event in events:
            id = event['id']
```

```
            type = event['type']
            actor = event['actor']['display_login']
            repoUrl = event['repo']['url']
            createdAt = event['created_at']
            eventTypes.append(type)
            dataSet.append([id, type, createdAt, repoUrl, actor])

    eventInfo = dict(Counter(eventTypes))
    print("Individual Event Counts:", eventInfo)
    print("CreateEvent Counts:", eventInfo['CreateEvent'])
    print("DeleteEvent Counts:", eventInfo['DeleteEvent'])

print("Total Events Found: ", len(dataSet))
print(dataSet)
```

The preceding code gives us the following output:

```
Status Code: 200
Headers: Content-Type: application/json; charset=utf-8
. . . . . . . . . . . . . .
Status Code: 200
Headers: Content-Type: application/json; charset=utf-8

Individual Event Counts: {'IssueCommentEvent': 8, 'PushEvent': 42,
'CreateEvent': 12, 'WatchEvent': 9, 'PullRequestEvent': 10, 'IssuesEvent':
2, 'DeleteEvent': 2, 'PublicEvent': 2, 'MemberEvent': 2,
'PullRequestReviewCommentEvent': 1}

CreateEvent Counts: 12
DeleteEvent Counts: 2
Total Events Found: 90

[['9206862975', 'PushEvent', '2019-03-08T14:53:46Z', 'https://api.github.com/r
epos/CornerYoung/MDN', 'CornerYoung'], 'https://api.github.com/repos/OUP/INTE
GRATION-ANSIBLE', 'peter-
masters'],....................,'2019-03-08T14:53:47Z', 'https://api.github.
com/repos/learn-co-curriculum/hs-zhw-shoes-layout', 'maxwellbenton']]
```

The Counter class from the collections Python module is used to obtain the individual count of elements from eventTypes:

```
from collections import Counter
```

Summary

APIs provide several benefits, all of which we have covered in this chapter. RESTful web services are growing in demand and will contribute to data requests and responses in the future more than ever before. Structured, easy access, parameter-based filters make APIs more convenient to use, and are excellent at saving time.

In the next chapter, we will be learning about Selenium and how to use it to scrape data from the web.

Further reading

- Fielding, Roy Thomas. *Architectural Styles and the Design of Network-based Software Architectures*. Doctoral dissertation, University of California, Irvine, 2000
- REST: https://www.ics.uci.edu/~fielding/pubs/dissertation/rest_arch_style.htm
- SOAP: https://www.w3.org/TR/soap/
- A simple SOAP client: https://www.ibm.com/developerworks/xml/library/x-soapcl/index.html

- RESTful API HTTP Status Codes: https://restfulapi.net/http-status-codes/
- 304 Not Modified: What It Is and How to Fix It: https://airbrake.io/blog/http-errors/304-not-modified
- ETag: https://developer.mozilla.org/en-US/docs/Web/HTTP/Headers/ETag
- Types of Numeric Data: https://www.stat.berkeley.edu/~spector/extension/python/notes/node22.html

8
Using Selenium to Scrape the Web

So far, we have learned how to use a number of data finding techniques and how to access web content by implementing various Python libraries for web scraping.

Selenium is a web application testing framework, which automates the browsing action and can be used for both easy and complex web scraping activities. Selenium provides a web browser as an interface or automated tool. Dynamic or secure web content that uses JavaScript, cookies, scripts, and so on are loaded, tested, and even scraped with the help of Selenium.

There is so much to learn about the Selenium framework. In this chapter, we will be covering the major concepts of the framework that are relevant to web scraping.

This chapter will cover the following topics:

- Introduction to Selenium
- Using Selenium for web scraping

Technical requirements

A web browser (Google Chrome or Mozilla Firefox) is required for this chapter, and we will be using the following Python libraries:

- `selenium` (Python library)
- `re`

If these libraries are not present in your current Python setup, then you can set them up or install them by referring to the *Setting things up* section in `Chapter 2`, *Python and the Web – Using urllib and Requests*.

In addition to the Python libraries and web browsers mentioned, we will be using WebDriver for Google Chrome.

Code files are available online at `https://github.com/PacktPublishing/Hands-On-Web-Scraping-with-Python/tree/master/Chapter08`.

Introduction to Selenium

As I mentioned, Selenium is a web application framework that can be used for web scraping activities. It can also be used as a browser automation tool.

The automation of tasks or activities related to web applications, such as those in the following list, involves those tasks being performed without the direct involvement of human beings:

- Browsing
- Clicking links
- Saving screenshots
- Downloading images
- Filling out HTML `<form>` templates and many more activities

Selenium provides a web browser as an interface or automated tool. With the automation of the browsing action, Selenium can also be used in web scraping. Dynamic or secure web services that use JavaScript, cookies, scripts, and so on are loaded, tested, and even crawled and scraped with the help of Selenium.

Selenium is open source and can be accessed across multiple platforms. Various web browsers can be used for testing using libraries that are available for programming languages such as Java, and Python. Libraries are used to create scripts that interact with Selenium to perform browser-based automation.

Although using Selenium in application testing has many advantages when it comes to actions such as crawling and scraping, it also has its disadvantages, such as time and memory consumption. Selenium is extendable and effective, but is slow in performing its actions, and consumes large amounts of memory space.

 For more detailed information on Selenium, please visit `https://www.seleniumhq.org/`.

In the following section, we will set up Selenium WebDriver and test the setup with a Python library, which can be found at `https://selenium-python.readthedocs.io/`.

 Selenium is a web testing framework, whereas Selenium (`https://pypi.org/project/selenium/`) is a Python library that binds Selenium WebDriver or is used to create scripts to interact with Selenium.

Application testing is performed to ensure that the requirements are met by the application and that bugs and errors are detected to ensure a quality product. It can be conducted either manually (with the help of users) or by using automated tools (such as Selenium). Testing web-based applications is done prior to the launch of the application over the internet.

Selenium projects

Selenium consists of multiple components or tools that are also known as Selenium projects, which makes it a complete framework for web-based application testing. We will now look at some of the major components of these Selenium projects.

Selenium WebDriver

Selenium WebDriver is a component of Selenium that is used to automate the browser. Automating the browser can be conducted by providing commands with various language bindings available for Java, Python, JavaScript, and so on by using third-party drivers such as Google Chrome driver, Mozilla Gecko driver, and Opera (`https://github.com/mozilla/geckodriver/`). Selenium WebDriver has no external dependency on any other software or servers.

WebDriver is an object-oriented API with updated features that overcomes and addresses the limitations of previous Selenium versions and Selenium **Remote Control** (**RC**). Please visit the Selenium WebDriver web page (`https://www.seleniumhq.org/projects/webdriver/`) for more information.

Selenium RC

Selenium RC is a server that is programmed in Java. It uses HTTP to accept commands for the browser and is used to test complex AJAX-based web applications.

Selenium RC has been officially deprecated following the release of Selenium 2 (Selenium version 2). However, WebDriver contains the major features of Selenium RC. Please visit `https://www.seleniumhq.org/projects/remote-control/` for more information.

Selenium Grid

Selenium Grid is also a server that allows tests to run parallel on multiple machines across multiple browsers and operating systems, distributing the system load and cutting down performance issues, such as time consumption.

Complex tests were used to process Selenium RC and Selenium Grid together. Since the release of version 2.0, the Selenium server now has built-in support for WebDriver, Selenium RC, and Selenium Grid. Please visit the Selenium Grid web page (`https://www.seleniumhq.org/projects/grid/`) for more information.

Selenium IDE

An open source Selenium **integrated development environment (IDE)** is used to build test cases with Selenium. It's basically a web browser extension available with features such as the ability to record and play back web automation through a **graphical user interface (GUI)**.

The following are a few key features of the Selenium IDE:

- Extendable and easy to use for debugging
- Resilient tests
- Cross-browser support
- Can create scripts that can run commands and support control-flow structures

Please visit the Selenium IDE web page (`https://www.seleniumhq.org/selenium-ide/`) for more information and installation procedures. Please visit the Selenium projects web page (`https://www.seleniumhq.org/projects/`) for more information on Selenium components.

Now that we know what Selenium is used for and some of its major components, let's look at how we can install and perform general tests using Selenium WebDriver.

Setting things up

For the successful implementation of browser automation and application testing using Selenium, WebDriver needs to be set up. Let's go through the following steps to set up WebDriver for Google Chrome:

1. Visit `https://www.seleniumhq.org/`:

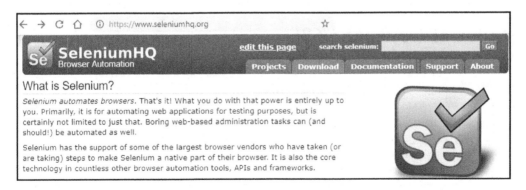

SeleniumHQ Browser Automation main page

2. Click **Download** (or browse to `https://www.seleniumhq.org/download/`).

3. Under the **Third Party Drivers, Bindings, and Plugins** section, click **Google Chrome Driver** (or browse to `https://sites.google.com/a/chromium.org/chromedriver/`):

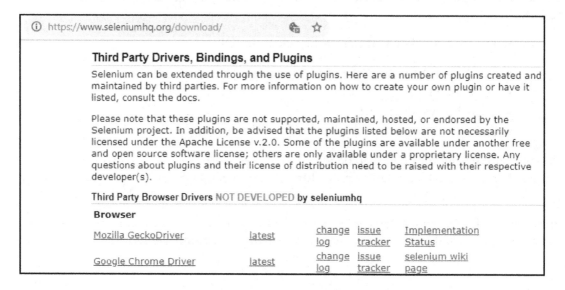

Third -party drivers, Selenium

4. From **ChromeDriver - WebDriver for Chrome** (`https://sites.google.com/a/chromium.org/chromedriver`), download the latest stable release of ChromeDriver, appropriate to the platform:

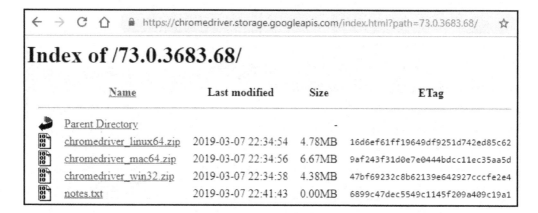

ChromeDriver listings

5. Unzip the downloaded `chromedriver*.zip`. An application file named `chromedriver.exe` should appear. We can place the `.exe` file on the main folder containing the codes.

 We will be using Google Chrome and ChromeDriver throughout the chapter; for details about using other browsers, or more information on Selenium, please visit SeleniumHQ. For more information on the installation, please refer to `https://selenium-python.readthedocs.io/installation.html`.

Now that we have completed the setup for WebDriver and the Selenium Python library, let's verify this setup through the Python IDE. As shown in the following screenshot, `selenium` contains the `webdriver` module, with submodules such as `Chrome`, `Android`, `Firefox`, `Ie`, and `Opera`. The current version is `3.14.1`:

```
>>> from selenium import webdriver
>>> dir(webdriver)
['ActionChains', 'Android', 'BlackBerry', 'Chrome', 'ChromeOptions', 'DesiredCapabilities', 'Edge', 'Fire
fox', 'FirefoxOptions', 'FirefoxProfile', 'Ie', 'IeOptions', 'Opera', 'PhantomJS', 'Proxy', 'Remote', 'Sa
fari', 'TouchActions', 'WebKitGTK', 'WebKitGTKOptions', '__builtins__', '__cached__', '__doc__', '__file
__', '__loader__', '__name__', '__package__', '__path__', '__spec__', '__version__', 'android', 'blackberr
y', 'chrome', 'common', 'edge', 'firefox', 'ie', 'opera', 'phantomjs', 'remote', 'safari', 'support', 'we
bkitgtk']
>>> webdriver.__version__
'3.14.1'
```

Printing the selenium.webdriver version

We will be using Selenium with Google Chrome, so let's explore the contents of `Chrome` inside `webdriver`:

```
>>> dir(webdriver.Chrome)
['__class__', '__delattr__', '__dict__', '__dir__', '__doc__', '__enter__', '__eq__', '__exit__', '__form
at__', '__ge__', '__getattribute__', '__gt__', '__hash__', '__init__', '__init_subclass__', '__le__', '__
lt__', '__module__', '__ne__', '__new__', '__reduce__', '__reduce_ex__', '__repr__', '__setattr__', '__si
zeof__', '__str__', '__subclasshook__', '__weakref__', '_unwrap_value', '_web_element_cls', '_wrap_value'
, 'add_cookie', 'application_cache', 'back', 'close', 'create_options', 'create_web_element', 'current_ur
l', 'current_window_handle', 'delete_all_cookies', 'delete_cookie', 'desired_capabilities', 'execute', 'e
xecute_async_script', 'execute_cdp_cmd', 'execute_script', 'file_detector', 'file_detector_context', 'fin
d_element', 'find_element_by_class_name', 'find_element_by_css_selector', 'find_element_by_id', 'find_ele
ment_by_link_text', 'find_element_by_name', 'find_element_by_partial_link_text', 'find_element_by_tag_nam
e', 'find_element_by_xpath', 'find_elements', 'find_elements_by_class_name', 'find_elements_by_css_select
or', 'find_elements_by_id', 'find_elements_by_link_text', 'find_elements_by_name', 'find_elements_by_part
ial_link_text', 'find_elements_by_tag_name', 'find_elements_by_xpath', 'forward', 'fullscreen_window', 'g
et', 'get_cookie', 'get_cookies', 'get_log', 'get_network_conditions', 'get_screenshot_as_base64', 'get_s
creenshot_as_file', 'get_screenshot_as_png', 'get_window_position', 'get_window_rect', 'get_window_size',
'implicitly_wait', 'launch_app', 'log_types', 'maximize_window', 'minimize_window', 'mobile', 'name', 'or
ientation', 'page_source', 'quit', 'refresh', 'save_screenshot', 'set_network_conditions', 'set_page_load
_timeout', 'set_script_timeout', 'set_window_position', 'set_window_rect', 'set_window_size', 'start_clie
nt', 'start_session', 'stop_client', 'switch_to', 'switch_to_active_element', 'switch_to_alert', 'switch_
to_default_content', 'switch_to_frame', 'switch_to_window', 'title', 'window_handles']
```

Exploring Chrome from Selenium WebDriver.

As shown in the preceding screenshot, there are a number of functions that will be called and used to implement the browser automation. You can also see that there are many function names that begin with `find_element*`, similar to the traversing and parsing functions that we used and learned about in earlier chapters on the scraping activity.

In the next section, we will learn about `selenium.webdriver`.

Exploring Selenium

In this section, we will use and introduce various properties for `webdriver` and `webdriver.Chrome`, while looking at some real cases. The following sections will illustrate the use of Selenium and explore its major properties.

Accessing browser properties

In this section, we will demonstrate the use of Selenium and Chrome WebDriver to load Google Chrome with URLs and access certain browser-based features.

To begin with, let's import `webdriver` from `selenium` and set a path to `chromedriver.exe`—let's call it `chromedriver_path`. The path created will be required to load Google Chrome. Depending on the application location, the complete path to `chromedriver.exe` should be mentioned, and is required for successful implementation:

```
from selenium import webdriver
import re

#setting up path to 'chromedriver.exe'
chromedriver_path='chromedriver' #C:\\Users\\....\\...\chromedriver.exe
```

The `selenium.webdriver` is used to implement various browsers, in this case, Google Chrome. The `webdriver.Chrome()` phrase is provided with the path of Chrome WebDriver so that `chromedriver_path` can be used for execution.

The phrase `driver`, which is an object of the
`selenium.webdriver.chrome.webdriver.WebDriver` class, is created using
`webdriver.Chrome()`, which will now provide access to the various attributes and
properties from `webdriver`:

```
driver = webdriver.Chrome(executable_path=chromedriver_path)
```

`chromedriver.exe` will be instantiated at this instance or upon creation of the
`driver` object. The Terminal screen and an empty new window of Google Chrome will be
loaded, as shown in the following screenshot:

The Terminal screen and empty browser page

If you encounter any error in executing the code so far, please go through the following
steps, and then execute the code again:

1. Obtain the latest ChromeDriver and replace the existing one
2. Update and verify the `PATH` of `chromedriver_path`

The new window from Google Chrome is then provided with a URL using the
`get()` function from `webdriver`.

The `get()` phrase accepts the URL that is to be loaded on the browser. Let's provide
`https://www.python.org` as an argument to `get()`; the browser will start loading the
URL, as shown in the following screenshot:

```
driver.get('https://www.python.org')
```

As you can see in the following screenshot, a notice is displayed just below the address bar with the message **Chrome is being controlled by automated test software**. This message also confirms the successful execution of the `selenium.webdriver` activity, and it can be provided with further codes to act on or automate the page that has been loaded:

Chrome browser loaded with https://www.python.org

Upon successful loading of the page, we can access and explore its properties using `driver`. To illustrate this, let's extract or print the title from the HTML `<title>` tag and print the current URL that is accessible:

```
print("Title: ",driver.title) #print <title> text
Title:  Welcome to Python.org

print("Current Page URL: ",driver.current_url) #print current url, loaded
in the browser
Current Page URL:  https://www.python.org/
```

As seen in the preceding code, the page title is available using `driver.title`, and the current page URL is found with `driver.current_url`. The `current_url` phrase can be used to verify whether any URL redirection has taken place after loading the initial URL. Let's save a page screenshot with a condition that is verified using `search()` from the Python library, `re`:

```
#check if pattern matches the current url loaded

if re.search(r'python.org',driver.current_url):
    driver.save_screenshot("pythonorg.png") #save screenshot with provided
name
    print("Python Screenshot Saved!")
```

The `save_screenshot()` phrase is provided with the filename as an argument for the image, and it creates a PNG image. The image will be saved at the current code location; the full destination or desired path can also be provided.

To explore further, let's collect the web cookies from `https://www.python.org`. The `get_cookies()` phrase is used to retrieve cookies, as follows:

```
#get cookie information
cookies = driver.get_cookies()
print("Cookies obtained from python.org")
print(cookies)

Cookies obtained from python.org
[{'domain': '.python.org', 'expiry': 1619415025, 'httpOnly': False, 'name':
'__utma', 'path': '/', 'secure': False, 'value':
'32101439.1226541417.1556343026.1556343026.1556343026.1'},........
{'domain': '.python.org', 'expiry': 1556343625, 'httpOnly': False, 'name':
'__utmt', 'path': '/', 'secure': False, 'value': '1'}]
```

The page source can be obtained using `driver.page_source`.

To obtain the page source manually, right-click on the page and click **View page source**, or press *Ctrl + U*:

```
print(driver.page_source) #page source
```

The page can be reloaded or refreshed using `driver.refresh()`.

To refresh the page source manually, right-click on the page and click **Reload**, or press *Ctrl + R*:

```
driver.refresh() #reload or refresh the browser
```

With the features that were accessed using `driver` in the preceding code, let's continue loading, taking screenshots, and accessing cookies from `https://www.google.com` using the following code:

```
driver.get('https://www.google.com')
print("Title: ",driver.title)
print("Current Page URL: ",driver.current_url)

if re.search(r'google.com',driver.current_url):
    driver.save_screenshot("google.png")
    print("Google Screenshot Saved!")

cookies = driver.get_cookies()
```

The action performed with `http://google.com` will take place on the same browser window that was used for accessing `http://python.org`. With this, we can now perform actions using the browser history (that is, we will use the **Back** and **Forward** buttons that are available in the web browser) and retrieve the URL, as shown in the following code:

```
print("Current Page URL: ",driver.current_url)

driver.back() #History back action
print("Page URL (Back): ",driver.current_url)

driver.forward() #History forward action
print("Page URL (Forward): ",driver.current_url)
```

In the preceding code, `back()` takes the browser back a page, whereas `forward()` moves it a step forward along the browser history. The output received is as follows:

```
Current Page URL: https://www.google.com/
Page URL (Back): https://www.python.org/
Page URL (Forward): https://www.google.com/
```

Following successful execution of the code, it is recommended that you close and quit the driver to free up system resources. We can perform the termination actions using the following functions:

```
driver.close() #close browser
driver.quit()  #quit webdriver
```

The preceding code contains the following two phrases:

- `close()` terminates the loaded browser window
- `quit()` ends the WebDriver application

The complete code we have executed so far in this particular section is as follows:

```
from selenium import webdriver
import re
chrome_path='chromedriver'
driver = webdriver.Chrome(executable_path=chrome_path)
#print(type(driver))
driver.get('https://www.python.org')
print("Title: ",driver.title)
print("Current Page URL: ",driver.current_url)

if re.search(r'python.org',driver.current_url):
    driver.save_screenshot("pythonorg.png")
    print("Python Screenshot Saved!")
cookies = driver.get_cookies()
```

```
print(driver.page_source)
driver.refresh()

driver.get('https://www.google.com')
print("Title: ",driver.title)
print("Current Page URL: ",driver.current_url)
if re.search(r'google.com',driver.current_url):
    driver.save_screenshot("google.png")
    print("Google Screenshot Saved!")
cookies = driver.get_cookies()

print("Current Page URL: ",driver.current_url)
driver.back()
print("Page URL (Back): ",driver.current_url)
driver.forward()
print("Page URL (Forward): ",driver.current_url)

driver.close()
driver.quit()
```

The preceding code demonstrates the use of `selenium.webdriver` and its various properties. In the next section, we will demonstrate the use of `webdriver` and web elements (elements from the web page).

Locating web elements

In this section, we will perform a search on `http://automationpractice.com` to obtain a list of products that match the search query, illustrating the use of `selenium.webdriver`. Web elements are elements that are listed in a web page or that are found in a page source. We also look at a class called `WebElement`, used as `selenium.webdriver.remote.webelement.WebElement`.

 The automation practice website (`http://automationpractice.com/`) is a sample e-commerce website from `http://www.seleniumframework.com` that you can use for practice.

To begin with, let's import `webdriver` from `selenium`, set a path to `chromedriver.exe`, create an object of `webdriver`—that is, `driver`, as implemented in the previous section, *Accessing browser properties*—and load the URL, `http://automationpractice.com`:

```
driver.get('http://automationpractice.com')
```

The new Google Chrome window will be loaded with the URL provided. Find the search (input) box just above **Cart**, as shown in the following screenshot:

Inspecting elements (search box) from http://automationpractice.com

To continue searching through the script, we need to identify the element with the HTML <input>. Please refer to the *Using web browser developer tools for accessing web content* section in `Chapter 3`, *Using LXML, XPath, and CSS Selectors*.

In our case, the search box can be identified by the attributes shown in the preceding screenshot, or even by using the XPath or CSS selectors:

- id="search_query_top"
- name="search_query"
- class="search_query"

The `selenium.webdriver` provides lots of locators (methods that are used to locate elements) that can be applied conveniently as applicable to the cases encountered.

Locators return single, multiple, or lists of WebElement instances, written as `selenium.webdriver.remote.webelement.WebElement`. The following are a few locators, along with a brief description:

- `find_element_by_id()`: This finds an element by its `id` attribute. This method returns a single WebElement.
- `find_element_by_name()`: This finds a single element by its `name` attribute. Multiple WebElements can be found or located using `find_elements_by_name()`.
- `find_element_by_tag_name()`: This finds a single element by the name of its HTML tag. Multiple WebElements can be located using `find_elements_by_tag_name()`.
- `find_element_by_class_name()`: This finds a single element by its class attribute. Multiple WebElements can be located using `find_elements_by_class_name()`.
- `find_element_by_link_text()`: This finds a single element by a link identified by the link text. Multiple WebElements can be located using `find_elements_by_link_text()`.
- `find_element_by_partial_link_text()`: This finds a single element by a link identified by the partial text the element is carrying. Multiple WebElements can be located using `find_elements_by_partial_link_text()`.
- `find_element_by_xpath()`: This finds a single element by providing an XPath expression. Multiple WebElements can be located using `find_elements_by_xpath()`.
- `find_element_by_css_selector()`: This finds a single element by providing CSS selectors. Multiple WebElements can be located using `find_elements_by_css_selector()`.

Now, let's find the input box using `find_element_by_id()`:

```
searchBox = driver.find_element_by_id('search_query_top')
#searchBox = driver.find_element_by_xpath('//*[@id="search_query_top"]')
#searchBox = driver.find_element_by_css_selector('#search_query_top')
```

As you can see in the preceding code, `searchBox` can be located using any convenient locators that are provided with their respective arguments.

The WebElement that is obtained can be accessed for the following properties and general methods, as well as many more:

- `get_attribute()`: This returns the attribute value for the key argument provided, such as `value`, `id`, `name`, and `class`.
- `tag_name`: This returns the HTML tag name of a particular WebElement.
- `text`: This returns the text of the WebElement.
- `clear()`: This clears the text of HTML form elements.
- `send_keys()`: This is used to fill with text and provide the key effect, such as pressing ENTER, BACKSPACE, and DELETE, available from the `selenium.webdriver.common.keys` module in `selenium.webdriver.common` to the HTML form elements.
- `click()`: This performs the clicking action to the WebElement. This is used for HTML elements such as **Submit Button**.

In the following code, we will be using the functions and properties listed previously in `searchBox`:

```
print("Type :",type(searchBox))
<class 'selenium.webdriver.remote.webelement.WebElement'>

print("Attribute Value :",searchBox.get_attribute("value")) #is empty
Attribute Value :

print("Attribute Class :",searchBox.get_attribute("class"))
Attribute Class : search_query form-control ac_input

print("Tag Name :",searchBox.tag_name)
Tag Name : input
```

Let's clear the text inside `searchBox` and input the text `Dress` to be searched. We also need to submit the button located on the right-hand side of the `searchBox` and click it to execute the search using the WebElement method, `click()`:

```
searchBox.clear()
searchBox.send_keys("Dress")
submitButton = driver.find_element_by_name("submit_search")
submitButton.click()
```

The browser will process the search action for the submitted text `Dress` and load the results page.

Now that the search action is complete, to verify the successful search, we will extract information regarding the product numbers and count using the following code:

```
#find text or provided class name
resultsShowing = driver.find_element_by_class_name("product-count")
print("Results Showing: ",resultsShowing.text)

Results Showing: Showing 1-7 of 7 items

#find results text using XPath
resultsFound =
driver.find_element_by_xpath('//*[@id="center_column"]//span[@class="headin
g-counter"]')
print("Results Found: ",resultsFound.text)

Results Found: 7 results have been found.
```

With the number of items and the count of the products that were found, this conveys a successful message to our search process. Now, we can proceed with looking for products using XPath, CSS selectors, and so on:

```
#Using XPath
products =
driver.find_elements_by_xpath('//*[@id="center_column"]//a[@class="product-
name"]')

#Using CSS Selector
#products = driver.find_elements_by_css_selector('ul.product_list
li.ajax_block_product a.product-name')

foundProducts=[]
for product in products:
    foundProducts.append([product.text,product.get_attribute("href")])
```

From the preceding code, `products` obtained is iterated and an individual item is added to the Python list `foundProducts`. `product` is an object of WebElement, in other words, `selenium.webdriver.remote.webelement.WebElement,` while properties are collected using `text` and `get_attribute()`:

```
print(foundProducts)

[['Printed Summer Dress',
'http://automationpractice.com/index.php?id_product=5&controller=product&se
arch_query=Dress&results=7'],
['Printed Dress',
'http://automationpractice.com/index.php?id_product=4&controller=product&se
arch_query=Dress&results=7'],
```

```
['Printed Summer Dress',
'http://automationpractice.com/index.php?id_product=6&controller=product&se
arch_query=Dress&results=7'],
['Printed Chiffon Dress',
'http://automationpractice.com/index.php?id_product=7&controller=product&se
arch_query=Dress&results=7'],['PrintedDress',
'http://automationpractice.com/index.php?id_product=3&controller=product&se
arch_query=Dress&results=7'],
['Faded Short Sleeve T-shirts',
'http://automationpractice.com/index.php?id_product=1&controller=product&se
arch_query=Dress&results=7'],['Blouse',
'http://automationpractice.com/index.php?id_product=2&controller=product&se
arch_query=Dress&results=7']]
```

In this section, we explored the various properties and methods from `selenium.webdriver` that are used to deal with the browser, use HTML forms, read page content, and so on. Please visit `https://selenium-python.readthedocs.io` for more detailed information on Python Selenium and its modules. In the next section, we will use most of the methodologies that were used in the current section to scrape information from a web page.

Using Selenium for web scraping

Selenium is used to test web applications. It is mostly used to perform browser automation using various programming language-based libraries and browser drivers. As we saw in a previous section, *Exploring Selenium*, we can navigate and locate elements in a page using Selenium and perform crawling and scraping-related activities.

Let's look at a few examples of scraping contents from web pages using Selenium.

Example 1 – scraping product information

In this example, we will continue using the search results obtained from `foundProducts` in the *Exploring Selenium* section.

We will extract some specific information from each individual product link found in `foundProducts`, listed as follows:

- `product_name` : Product name
- `product_price`: Listed price
- `image_url`: URL of product's main image

- `item_condition`: Condition of product
- `product_description`: Short description of product

Each individual product link from `foundProducts` is loaded using `driver.get()`:

```
dataSet=[]
if len(foundProducts)>0:
    for foundProduct in foundProducts:
        driver.get(foundProduct[1])

        product_url = driver.current_url
        product_name =
driver.find_element_by_xpath('//*[@id="center_column"]//h1[@itemprop="name"
]').text
        short_description =
driver.find_element_by_xpath('//*[@id="short_description_content"]').text
        product_price =
driver.find_element_by_xpath('//*[@id="our_price_display"]').text
        image_url =
driver.find_element_by_xpath('//*[@id="bigpic"]').get_attribute('src')
        condition =
driver.find_element_by_xpath('//*[@id="product_condition"]/span').text
        dataSet.append([product_name,product_price,condition,short_description,imag
e_url,product_url])
print(dataSet)
```

Targeted fields or information to be extracted are obtained using XPath, and are appended to the `dataSet`. Please refer to the *Using web browser developer tools for accessing web content* section in `Chapter 3`, *Using LXML, XPath, and CSS Selectors*.

The output from `dataSet` is obtained as follows:

```
[['Printed Summer Dress','$28.98','New','Long printed dress with thin
adjustable straps. V-neckline and wiring under the bust with ruffles at the
bottom of the dress.',
'http://automationpractice.com/img/p/1/2/12-large_default.jpg',
'http://automationpractice.com/index.php?id_product=5&controller=product&se
arch_query=Dress&results=7'],
['Printed Dress','$50.99','New','Printed evening dress with straight
sleeves with black .............,
['Blouse','$27.00','New','Short sleeved blouse with feminine draped sleeve
detail.',
'http://automationpractice.com/img/p/7/7-large_default.jpg','http://automat
ionpractice.com/index.php?id_product=2&controller=product&search_query=Dres
s&results=7']]
```

Finally, system resources are kept free using `close()` and `quit()`. The complete code for this example is listed as follows:

```python
from selenium import webdriver
chrome_path='chromedriver'
driver = webdriver.Chrome(executable_path=chrome_path)
driver.get('http://automationpractice.com')

searchBox = driver.find_element_by_id('search_query_top')
searchBox.clear()
searchBox.send_keys("Dress")
submitButton = driver.find_element_by_name("submit_search")
submitButton.click()

resultsShowing = driver.find_element_by_class_name("product-count")
resultsFound =
driver.find_element_by_xpath('//*[@id="center_column"]//span[@class="headin
g-counter"]')

products =
driver.find_elements_by_xpath('//*[@id="center_column"]//a[@class="product-
name"]')
foundProducts=[]
for product in products:
    foundProducts.append([product.text,product.get_attribute("href")])

dataSet=[]
if len(foundProducts)>0:
    for foundProduct in foundProducts:
        driver.get(foundProduct[1])
        product_url = driver.current_url
        product_name =
driver.find_element_by_xpath('//*[@id="center_column"]//h1[@itemprop="name"
]').text
        short_description =
driver.find_element_by_xpath('//*[@id="short_description_content"]').text
        product_price =
driver.find_element_by_xpath('//*[@id="our_price_display"]').text
        image_url =
driver.find_element_by_xpath('//*[@id="bigpic"]').get_attribute('src')
        condition =
driver.find_element_by_xpath('//*[@id="product_condition"]/span').text
dataSet.append([product_name,product_price,condition,short_description,imag
e_url,product_url])

driver.close()
driver.quit()
```

In this example, we performed HTML `<form>`- based action and extracted the required details from each individual page. Form processing is one of the major tasks performed during the testing of a web application.

Example 2 – scraping book information

In this example, we will automate the browser to process the category and pagination link from the main URL provided. We are interested in extracting details from the **Food and Drink** category across multiple pages from `http://books.toscrape.com/index.html`.

An individual page from the category contains listings of products (**Books**), with certain information listed as follows:

- `title`: Title of the book listed
- `titleLarge`: Title of the book listed (complete title, found as a value to the `title` attribute)
- `price`: Listed book price
- `stock`: Stock information relating to the listed book
- `image`: URL of book image
- `starRating`: Rating (number of stars found)
- `url`: URL of each listed book.

A similar example was also shown in `Chapter 3`, *Using LXML, XPath and CSS Selectors* in the section named *Web Scraping Using LXML*, under the name *Example 2 – Looping with XPath and scraping data from multiple pages*. There, we used the Python library `lxml`.

With `selenium.webdriver` imported and the Chrome driver path set up, let's start loading `http://books.toscrape.com/index.html`. As the main page gets loaded, we will see various categories appear, listed one below the other.

The targeted category contains the text **Food and Drink**, and can be found using `find_element_by_link_text()` (we can use any applicable `find_element...` methods to find the particular category). The element found is processed further with `click()`—clicking on the element returned. This action will load the particular category URL in the browser:

```
driver.get('http://books.toscrape.com/index.html')

driver.find_element_by_link_text("Food and Drink").click()
```

```
print("Current Page URL: ", driver.current_url)
totalBooks =
driver.find_element_by_xpath("//*[@id='default']//form/strong[1]")
print("Found: ", totalBooks.text)
```

To deal with multiple pages that are found during iteration, `NoSuchElementException` from `selenium.common.exceptions` will be imported:

```
from selenium.common.exceptions import NoSuchElementException
```

As we will be using the pagination button **next**, `NoSuchElementException` will be helpful in dealing with the condition if no further **next** or pages are found.

As seen in the following code, the pagination option **next** is located in the page and processed with the `click()` action. This action will load the URL it contains to the browser, and the iteration will continue until **next** is not located or found in the page, caught by the `except` block in the code:

```
try:
    #Check for Pagination with text 'next'
    driver.find_element_by_link_text('next').click()
    continue
except NoSuchElementException:
    page = False
```

The complete code for this example is listed as follows:

```
from selenium import webdriver
from selenium.common.exceptions import NoSuchElementException
chrome_path = 'chromedriver'
driver = webdriver.Chrome(executable_path=chrome_path)
driver.get('http://books.toscrape.com/index.html')

dataSet = []
driver.find_element_by_link_text("Food and Drink").click()
totalBooks =
driver.find_element_by_xpath("//*[@id='default']//form/strong[1]")

page = True
while page:
    listings =
driver.find_elements_by_xpath("//*[@id='default']//ol/li[position()>0]")
    for listing in listings:
url=listing.find_element_by_xpath(".//article[contains(@class,'product_pod'
)]/h3/a"). get_attribute('href')
title=listing.find_element_by_xpath(".//article[contains(@class,'product_po
d')]/h3/a").text
```

```
titleLarge=listing.find_element_by_xpath(".//article[contains(@class,'produ
ct_pod')]/h3/a"). get_attribute('title')
price=listing.find_element_by_xpath(".//article/div[2]/p[contains(@class,'p
rice_color')]").text
stock=listing.find_element_by_xpath(".//article/div[2]/p[2][contains(@class
,'availability')]"). text
image=listing.find_element_by_xpath(".//article/div[1][contains(@class,'ima
ge_container')]/a/img") .get_attribute('src')
starRating=listing.find_element_by_xpath(".//article/p[contains(@class,'sta
r-rating')]"). get_attribute('class')
dataSet.append([titleLarge,title,price,stock,image,starRating.replace('star
-rating ',''),url])

    try:
        driver.find_element_by_link_text('next').click()
        continue
    except NoSuchElementException:
        page = False

driver.close()
driver.quit()
```

Finally, upon completion of the iteration, `dataSet` will contain the listing data for all pages, as follows:

```
[['Foolproof Preserving: A Guide to Small Batch Jams, Jellies, Pickles,
Condiments, and More: A Foolproof Guide to Making Small Batch Jams,
Jellies, Pickles, Condiments, and More', 'Foolproof Preserving: A Guide
...','£30.52','In stock',
'http://books.toscrape.com/media/cache/9f/59/9f59f01fa916a7bb8f0b28a4012179
a4.jpg','Three','http://books.toscrape.com/catalogue/foolproof-preserving-a
-guide-to-small-batch-jams-jellies-pickles-condiments-and-more-a-foolproof-
guide-to-making-small-batch-jams-jellies-pickles-condiments-and-
more_978/index.html'], ['The Pioneer Woman Cooks: Dinnertime: Comfort
Classics, Freezer Food, 16-Minute Meals, and Other Delicious Ways to Solve
Supper!', 'The Pioneer Woman Cooks: ...', '£56.41', 'In stock',
'http://books.toscrape.com/media/cache/b7/f4/b7f4843dbe062d44be1ffcfa16b2fa
a4.jpg', 'One',
'http://books.toscrape.com/catalogue/the-pioneer-woman-cooks-dinnertime-com
fort-classics-freezer-food-16-minute-meals-and-other-delicious-ways-to-
solve-supper_943/index.html'],................,
['Hungry Girl Clean & Hungry: Easy All-Natural Recipes for Healthy Eating
in the Real World', 'Hungry Girl Clean & ...', '£33.14', 'In stock',
'http://books.toscrape.com/media/cache/6f/c4/6fc450625cd672e871a6176f74909b
e2.jpg', 'Three',
'http://books.toscrape.com/catalogue/hungry-girl-clean-hungry-easy-all-natu
ral-recipes-for-healthy-eating-in-the-real-world_171/index.html']]
```

In this section, we explored the methods and properties from `selenium.webdriver` and implemented them for web scraping activity.

Summary

In this chapter, we learned about Selenium and using the Python library for Selenium to perform browser automation, the scraping of web content, browser-based activities, and HTML `<form>` processing. Selenium can be used to process multiple activities, and it's one of the major advantages that Selenium holds over Python-dedicated libraries, such as `lxml`, `pyquery`, `bs4`, and `scrapy`.

In the next chapter, we will learn more about web-scraping techniques using regular expressions.

Further reading

- **SeleniumHQ:** https://www.seleniumhq.org/
- **Selenium with Python:** https://selenium-python.readthedocs.io/
- **Python Selenium:** http://pypi.python.org/pypi/selenium

Using Regex to Extract Data

9

If these libraries don't exist in your current Python setup, refer to Chapter 2, *Python and the Web – Using urllib and Requests*, the *Setting things up* section, for more information on their installation and how to set them up. So far, we have learned about web technologies, data finding techniques, and how to access web content using Python libraries.

Regular Expressions (**Regex** or **regex**) is actually a pattern that's built using predefined commands and formats to match the desired content. Regex provides a great value during data extraction when there is no particular layout or markup patterns to be chosen and can be applied with other techniques such as XPath, and CSS selectors.

Complex web content and data in general text or character format might require the use of Regex to complete activities, such as matching and extraction, plus function replacing, splitting, and so on.

In this chapter, we will learn about the following topics:

- Overview of Regex
- Using Regex to extract data

Technical requirements

A web browser (Google Chrome or Mozilla Firefox) is required for this chapter. We will be using the following Python libraries:

- `requests`
- `re`
- `bs4`

If these libraries don't exist in your current Python setup, refer to `Chapter 2`, *Python and the Web – Using urllib and Requests,* the *Setting things up* section, for more information on their installation and how to set them up.

The code files for this chapter are available in this book's GitHub repository: `https://github.com/PacktPublishing/Hands-On-Web-Scraping-with-Python/tree/master/Chapter09`.

Those of you who are already using `re` can refer to the *Using regular expressions to extract data* section.

Overview of regular expressions

Regular expressions are used to match patterns found in text or strings. Regex can be used for testing and finding patterns as desired against text or web content. Regex contains various ways to define patterns and special notations, such as *escape codes* to apply some predefined rules. For more information on Regex, please refer to the *Further reading* section.

There are various cases where Regex can be quite effective and quick for obtaining the desired results. Regex can be applied to content (text or web sources) alone and can be used to target specific information patterns that aren't easily extractable while using XPath, CSS selectors, BS4, PyQuery, and so on.

Sometimes, cases may arise that will demand Regex and XPath or CSS selectors to be used together in order to obtain the desired output. This output can then be tested using Regex in order to find patterns or to clean and manage data. Code editors, document writers, and readers also provide embedded Regex-based utilities.

Regex can be applied to any text or strings of characters, HTML sources, and so on that contain proper or improper formatting. Regex can be used for various applications, such as the following:

- Content based on a particular pattern
- Page links
- Image titles and links
- Texts inside links
- Matching and validating email addresses
- Matching a postal code or zip code from address strings
- Validating phone numbers, and so on

Using tools such as searching, finding, splitting, substituting, matching, and iterating, are applicable with or without other technology interference.

In the following sections, we will be using the `re` Python module and exploring its methods, which we can then apply to Regex.

Regular expressions and Python

`re` is a standard Python library that's used to deal with Regex. Every default Python installation contains the `re` library. If the library doesn't exist, please refer to Chapter 2, *Python and the Web – Using urllib and Requests*, the *Setting things up* section, to learn how to set it up.

 >>> in code represents the use of the Python IDE. It accepts the code or instructions it's given and displays the output on the next line.

Let's begin by importing `re` using the Python IDE and listing its properties using the `dir()` function:

```
>>> import re
>>> print(dir(re)) #listing features from re
```

The following is the output of the preceding command:

```
['A', 'ASCII', 'DEBUG', 'DOTALL', 'I', 'IGNORECASE', 'L', 'LOCALE', 'M',
'MULTILINE', 'S', 'Scanner', 'T', 'TEMPLATE', 'U', 'UNICODE', 'VERBOSE',
'X', '_MAXCACHE', '__all__', '__builtins__', '__cached__', '__doc__',
'__file__', '__loader__', '__name__', '__package__', '__spec__', '__versio
n__', '_alphanum_bytes', '_alphanum_str', '_cache', '_cache_repl',
'_compile', '_compile_repl', '_expand', '_locale', '_pattern_type',
'_pickle', '_subx', 'compile', 'copyreg', 'error', 'escape', 'findall',
'finditer', 'fullmatch', 'match', 'purge', 'search', 'split',
'sre_compile', 'sre_parse', 'sub', 'subn', 'sys', 'template']
```

As we can see from the preceding output, there are various functions available in `re`. We will be using a few of these functions from a content extraction perspective, and we will explain the basics of Regex fundamentals by using examples such as the following:

```
>>> sentence = """Brief information about Jobs in Python. Programming and
Scripting experience in some language (such as Python R, MATLAB, SAS,
Mathematica, Java, C, C++, VB, JavaScript or FORTRAN) is expected.
Participants should be comfortable with basic programming concepts like
variables, loops, and functions."""
```

`sentence` we declared previously contains brief information regarding Python jobs and job descriptions. We will be using this sentence to explain basic Regex functionalities.

The `split()` function explodes the string and returns the list of individual words, which are separated by the *space* character by default. We can also split the string object using `re.split()`. In this case, `split()` accepts the Regex pattern to split the sentence, for example, `re.split(r'\s+', sentence)`:

```
>>> splitSentence = sentence.split() #split sentence or
re.split(r'\s', sentence)

>>> print("Length of Sentence: ", len(sentence), '& splitSentence:
', len(splitSentence))
Length of Sentence: 297 & splitSentence: 42

>>> print(splitSentence) #List of words obtained using split()

['Brief', 'information', 'about', 'Jobs', 'in', 'Python.', 'Programming',
'and', 'Scripting', 'experience', 'in', 'some', 'language', '(such', 'as',
'Python', 'R,', 'MATLAB,', 'SAS,', 'Mathematica,', 'Java,', 'C,', 'C++,',
'VB,', 'JavaScript', 'or', 'FORTRAN)', 'is', 'expected.', 'Participants',
'should', 'be', 'comfortable', 'with', 'basic', 'programming', 'concepts',
'like', 'variables,', 'loops,', 'and', 'functions.']
```

The length of `sentence` and the Python `splitSentence` list object is obtained and printed using the preceding code. These counts of element and character will be helpful while comparing answers that are returned from the following examples:

```
>>> matches = re.findall(r"([A-Z+]+)\,",sentence) #finding pattern with [A-
Z+] and comma behind
>>> print("Findall found total ",len(matches)," Matches >> ",matches)

Findall found total  6  Matches >>  ['R', 'MATLAB', 'SAS', 'C', 'C++',
'VB']


>>> matches = re.findall(r"([A-Z]+)\,",sentence) #finding pattern with [A-
Z] and comma behind
>>> print("Findall found total ",len(matches)," Matches >> ",matches)

Findall found total 5 Matches >> ['R', 'MATLAB', 'SAS', 'C', 'VB']
```

`re.findall()` accepts a pattern to search and the content to look for regarding the provided pattern. Normally, patterns can be provided directly to functions as an argument and as a *raw* string preceded with `r`, such as `r'([A-Z]+)'`, or a variable containing a *raw* string.

In the preceding code, we can see similar patterns with certain additional characters provided, but they differ in output. A general explanation is provided for some of these patterns, as follows:

- `[A-Z]`: Square brackets in the pattern match a set of characters and are case-sensitive. Here, it matches characters from `A` to `Z` but not `a` to `z`. We can provide a set of characters such as `[A-Za-z0-9]`, which matches any characters from `A` to `Z` and `a` to `z`, as well as numeric characters from `0` to `9`. Additional characters, if required, can be passed inside the set as `[A-Z+]`; the `+` character can exist with `A` to `Z` of characters, for example, C++ or C.
- `()`: Round brackets in the pattern hold the group of values that were matched.
- `+` (used for repetition): Found outside of the character set, it matches one or more occurrences of the pattern it follows. `[A-Z]+` will match at least one or more combinations that's found with the `A` to `Z` characters, for example, `R` and `MATLAB` from the preceding code. There are a few more characters for specifying repetition or occurrences, also known as Regex quantifiers:
    - `*` matches zero or more occurrences of the patterns
    - `?` matches zero or one occurrence of the pattern
    - `{m,n}` matches the minimum, `m`, and maximum, `n`, numbers of repetition, respectively:

- {2,5}: Minimum 2 or maximum 5
- {2,}: Minimum 2 or could be more
- {,5}: Maximum 5
- {3}: 3 occurrences

- \, (comma): In Regex, characters other than [A-Za-z0-9] are normally written as escaped characters in order to mention that particular character (\, for comma, \. for period, \? for question mark, and so on).

Regex quantifiers are also categorized as follows:

- **Greedy quantifiers**: These match any element as many times as possible.
- **Lazy or non-greedy quantifiers**: These match any element as few times as possible. Normally, a greedy quantifier is converted into a lazy quantifier by adding ? to it.

Patterns such as ([A-Z+]+)\, match the set of characters from A to Z and + that can exist in at least one or more characters, followed by ,. In sentence in the preceding code, we can find R, MATLAB, SAS, Mathematica, Java, C, C++, VB, and JavaScript (there's also FORTRAN), that is, names followed by , (but not in the case of FORTRAN; this is why it's been excluded in the output for provided patterns).

In the following code, we are trying to matchFORTRAN that was found in sentence, which is being omitted with the patterns we tried in the code previously:

```
>>> matches = re.findall(r"\s*([\sorA-Z+]+)\)",sentence) #r'\s*([A-Z]+)\)'
matches 'FORTRAN'
>>> print("Findall found total ",len(matches)," Matches >> ",matches)

Findall found total  1  Matches >>  ['or FORTRAN']

>>> fortran = matches[0] # 'or FORTRAN'
>>> if re.match(r'or',fortran):
        fortran = re.sub(r'or\s*','',fortran) #substitute 'or ' with empty
string
>>> print(fortran)

FORTRAN

>>> if re.search(r'^F.*N$',fortran):  #using beginning and end of line
searching pattern
        print("True")

True
```

As shown in the preceding code block, the Python library, `re`, possesses various functions, which are as follows:

- `re.match()`: This matches a pattern provided at the start of the string and returns the matched object.
- `re.sub()`: This finds a pattern and substitutes it with the provided string. It works similar to find and replace in text.
- `re.search()`: This matches a pattern in the string and returns the matched object that's found.
- `\s`: This represents the *space*, *tab*, and *newline characters*. Here, `[\sorA-Z+]+\)` is matching one or more characters, including `A-Z`, `o`,`r`, `\s`, and `+`, followed by `\)` (closing parenthesis). There are a few more escape codes found in Regex, as follows:
    - `\d`: Matches a digit
    - `\D`: Matches a non-digit
    - `\s`: Matches whitespace
    - `\S`: Matches non-whitespace
    - `\w`: Matches alphanumeric characters
    - `\W`: Matches non-alphanumeric characters
    - `\b`: Matches a word boundary
    - `\B`: Matches a non-word boundary
- `^`: This matches the start of the string.

> **Note:** `r'[^a-z]'` (the caret or `^`), when used inside a character set, acts as negation. Here, this means *except* or *exclude* `[a-z]`.

- `$`: This matches the end of the string.
- `|`: This implements the logical expression, OR, in the pattern. For example, `r'a|b'` will match any true expression, that is, a or b.

The following code shows the use of some of these Regex patterns and the `findall()` function, along with their output:

```
>>> matches  = re.findall(r'\s(MAT.*?)\,',sentence,flags=re.IGNORECASE)
>>> print("(MAT.*?)\,: ",matches)   #r'(?i)\s(MAT.*?)\,' can also be used

(MAT.*?)\,: ['MATLAB', 'Mathematica']
```

```
>>> matches = re.findall(r'\s(MAT.*?)\,',sentence) #findall with 'MAT'
case-sensitive
>>> print("(MAT.*?)\,: ",matches)

(MAT.*?)\,: ['MATLAB']

>>> matches = re.findall(r'\s(C.*?)\,',sentence)
>>> print("\s(C.*?)\,: ",matches)

\s(C.*?)\,: ['C', 'C++']
```

The following functions were found in the preceding code:

- re functions also support an optional *flags* argument. There's also an abbreviation for these flags (i for re.IGNORECASE, s for re.DOTALL, and M for re.MULTILINE). These can be used in patterns by including them at the beginning of the expressions. For example, r'(?i)\s(MAT.*?)\, will return [MATLAB, Mathematica]. The following are some other re functions that were found in the code:

    - re.IGNORECASE : Ignores the case-sensitivity found in the pattern that's provided
    - re.DOTALL : Allows . (period) to match a newline, and works with strings containing multiple lines
    - re.MULTILINE : Works with multiline strings and searches for patterns, including newline ("\n")

- . or period: This matches any single character but not the newline ("\n"). It's used in patterns mostly with repetition characters. A period or . is required to be matched in the string, and should be used as \.:

```
>>> matchesOne = re.split(r"\W+",sentence)  #split by word, \w
(word characters, \W - nonword)
>>> print("Regular Split '\W+' found total: ",len(matchesOne
),"\n",matchesOne)

Regular Split '\W+' found total: 43
['Brief', 'information', 'about', 'Jobs', 'in', 'Python',
'Programming', 'and', 'Scripting', 'experience', 'in', 'some',
'language', 'such', 'as', 'Python', 'R', 'MATLAB', 'SAS',
'Mathematica', 'Java', 'C', 'C', 'VB', 'JavaScript', 'or',
'FORTRAN', 'is', 'expected', 'Participants', 'should', 'be',
'comfortable', 'with', 'basic', 'programming', 'concepts', 'like',
'variables', 'loops', 'and', 'functions', '']

>>> matchesTwo = re.split(r"\s",sentence) #split by space
```

```
>>> print("Regular Split '\s' found total: ",len(matchesTwo),"\n",
matchesTwo)

Regular Split '\s' found total: 42
['Brief', 'information', 'about', 'Jobs', 'in', 'Python.',
'Programming', 'and', 'Scripting', 'experience', 'in', 'some',
'language', '(such', 'as', 'Python', 'R,', 'MATLAB,', 'SAS,',
'Mathematica,', 'Java,', 'C,', 'C++,', 'VB,', 'JavaScript', 'or',
'FORTRAN)', 'is', 'expected.', 'Participants', 'should', 'be',
'comfortable', 'with', 'basic', 'programming', 'concepts', 'like',
'variables,', 'loops,', 'and', 'functions.']
```

- re.split(): This splits the provided content based on the pattern and returns a list with results. A split() also exists, which can be used with a string to explode with the default or provided characters. It's used in a similar fashion to splitSentence, from earlier in this section.

You are suggested to compare the results of matchesOne and matchesTwo from this section.

In code below we are trying to apply the regex pattern for the value found inside datetime attribute. Pattern defined will be compiled and then used to search in the code block:

```
>>> timeDate= '''<time datetime="2019-02-11T18:00:00+00:00"></time>
<time datetime="2018-02-11T13:59:00+00:00"></time>
<time datetime="2019-02-06T13:44:00.000002+00:00"></time>
<time datetime="2019-02-05T17:39:00.000001+00:00"></time>
<time datetime="2019-02-04T12:53:00+00:00"></time>'''

>>> pattern = r'(20\d+)([-]+)(0[1-9]|1[012])([-]+)(0[1-9]|[12][0-9]|3[01])'
>>> recompiled = re.compile(pattern)  # <class '_sre.SRE_Pattern'>
>>> dateMatches = recompiled.search(timeDate)
```

- re.compile(): This is used to compile a Regex pattern and receive a pattern object (_sre.SRE_Pattern). The object that's received can be used with other Regex features.

Group matches can be individually explored by using the group() method, as shown in the following code:

```
>>> print("Group : ",dateMatches.group())
Group : 2019-02-11
```

```
>>> print("Groups : ",dateMatches.groups())
Groups : ('2019', '-', '02', '-', '11')

>>> print("Group 1 : ",dateMatches.group(1))
Group 1 : 2019

>>> print("Group 5 : ",dateMatches.group(5))
Group 5 : 11
```

As we can see, though the pattern has been searched against multiline timeDate, it results in a single group; an individual group can be returned using the index too. An re-related match object contains the groups() and group() functions; groups(0) results in the same output as groups(). Individual elements in groups() will require an index starting from 1.

- re.finditer(): This is used to iterate over resulting matches that are obtained for the pattern or pattern object found in the content that's provided. It returns a match (_sre.SRE_Match) object that's found from re.match().

re.match() returns an object that contains various functions and attributes that are used in code examples. These are as follows:

- start(): Returns the starting character index that matches the expression
- end(): Returns the ending character index that matches the expression
- span(): Returns the starting and ending character indexes of the matching expression
- lastindex: Returns the index of the last matched expression
- groupdict(): Returns the matching group dictionary with a pattern string and matched values
- groups(): Returns all matching elements
- group(): Returns an individual group and can be accessed with the group name
- lastgroup: Returns the name of the last group

```
>>> for match in re.finditer(pattern, timeDate): # <class '_sre.SRE_Match'>
        #for match in re.finditer(recompiled, timeDate):
        s = match.start()
        e = match.end()
        l = match.lastindex
        g = match.groups()

        print('Found {} at {}:{}, groups{}
lastindex:{}'.format(timeDate[s:e], s, e,g,l))
```

```
Found 2019-02-11 at 16:26, groups('2019', '-', '02', '-', '11') lastindex:5
Found 2018-02-11 at 67:77, groups('2018', '-', '02', '-', '11') lastindex:5
Found 2019-02-06 at 118:128, groups('2019', '-', '02', '-', '06')
lastindex:5
Found 2019-02-05 at 176:186, groups('2019', '-', '02', '-', '05')
lastindex:5
Found 2019-02-04 at 234:244, groups('2019', '-', '02', '-', '04')
lastindex:5
```

Patterns can also specify string names for the groups they are in; for example,
r'(?P<year>[0-9]{4})' matches the year group. Using group-based patterns in Regex
helps us to read the pattern and manage the output more accurately; this means that we
don't have to worry about indexing.

Let's consider the patterns pDate (implementing group(), groupdict(), start(),
end(), lastgroup, and lastindex) with a group name and code that are exhibiting the
outputs for date and time, respectively:

```
>>> pDate = r'(?P<year>[0-9]{4})(?P<sep>[-
])(?P<month>0[1-9]|1[012])-(?P<day>0[1-9]|[12][0-9]|3[01])'
>>> recompiled = re.compile(pDate) #compiles the pattern

>>> for match in re.finditer(recompiled,timeDate): #apply pattern
on timeDate
        s = match.start()
        e = match.end()
        l = match.lastindex

        print("Group ALL or 0: ",match.groups(0)) #or
match.groups() that is all
        print("Group Year: ",match.group('year')) #return year
        print("Group Month: ",match.group('month')) #return month
        print("Group Day: ",match.group('day')) #return day

        print("Group Delimiter: ",match.group('sep')) #return
seperator
        print('Found {} at {}:{}, lastindex:
{}'.format(timeDate[s:e], s, e,l))

        print('year :',match.groupdict()['year']) #accessing
groupdict()
        print('day :',match.groupdict()['day'])

        print('lastgroup :',match.lastgroup) #lastgroup name
```

The preceding code results in the following output:

```
Group ALL or 0: ('2019', '-', '02', '11')
Group Year: 2019
Group Month: 02
Group Day: 11
Group Delimiter: -
Found 2019-02-11 at 16:26, lastindex: 4
year : 2019
day : 11
lastgroup : day
```

The following code shows the use of pTime (implementing span()):

```
>>> pTime =
r'(?P<hour>[0-9]{2})(?P<sep>[:])(?P<min>[0-9]{2}):(?P<sec_mil>[0-9.:+]+)'
>>> recompiled = re.compile(pTime)

>>> for match in re.finditer(recompiled,timeDate):
        print("Group String: ",match.group()) #groups
        print("Group ALL or 0: ",match.groups())

        print("Group Span: ",match.span()) #using span()
        print("Group Span 1: ",match.span(1))
        print("Group Span 4: ",match.span(4))

        print('hour :',match.groupdict()['hour']) #accessing groupdict()
        print('minute :',match.groupdict()['min'])
        print('second :',match.groupdict()['sec_mil'])

        print('lastgroup :',match.lastgroup) #lastgroup name
```

The preceding code will result in the following output:

```
Group String: 12:53:00+00:00
Group ALL or 0: ('12', ':', '53', '00+00:00')
Group Span: (245, 259)
Group Span 1: (245, 247)
Group Span 4: (251, 259)
hour : 12
minute : 53
second : 00+00:00
lastgroup : sec_mil
```

In this section, we have covered a general introduction to Regex and the features of the re Python library, along with some practical examples. Please refer to the *Further reading* section for more information regarding Regex. In the next section, we will be applying Regex to extract data from web-based content.

Using regular expressions to extract data

Now that we've covered the basics and had an overview of Regex, we will use Regex to scrape (extract) data in bulk in a similar manner to using XPath, CSS selectors, pyquery, bs4, and so on by choosing between the implementation of Regex, XPath, pyquery, and more. This depends on the requirements and feasibility of web access and the availability of the content.

It's not always a requirement that the content should be unstructured to apply Regex and extract data. Regex can be implemented for both structured and unstructured web content that's found in order to extract the desired data. In this section, we'll explore a few examples while using Regex and its various properties.

Example 1 – extracting HTML-based content

In this example, we will be using the HTML content from the regexHTML.html file and apply a Regex pattern to extract information such as the following:

- HTML elements
- The element's attributes (key and values)
- The element's content

This example will provide you with a general overview of how we can deal with various elements, values, and so on that exist inside web content and how we can apply Regex to extract that content. The steps we will be applying in the following code will be helpful for processing HTML and similar content:

```
<html>
<head>
    <title>Welcome to Web Scraping: Example</title>
    <style type="text/css">
        ....
    </style>
</head>
<body>
    <h1 style="color:orange;">Welcome to Web Scraping</h1>
     Links:
    <a href="https://www.google.com" style="color:red;">Google</a>
    <a class="classOne" href="https://www.yahoo.com">Yahoo</a>
    <a id="idOne" href="https://www.wikipedia.org"
style="color:blue;">Wikipedia</a>
    <div>
        <p id="mainContent" class="content">
```

```
            <i>Paragraph contents</i>
            <img src="mylogo.png" id="pageLogo" class="logo"/>
        </p>
        <p class="content" id="subContent">
            <i style="color:red">Sub paragraph content</i>
            <h1 itemprop="subheading">Sub heading Content!</h1>
        </p>
    </div>
</body>
</html>
```

The preceding code is the HTML page source we will be using. The content here is structured, and there are numerous ways that we can deal with it.

In the following code, we will be using functions such as the following:

- read_file(): This will read the HTML file and return the page source for further processing.
- applyPattern(): This accepts a pattern argument, that is, the Regex pattern for finding content, which is applied to the HTML source using re.findall() and prints information such as a list of searched elements and their counts.

To begin with, let's import re and bs4:

```
import re
from bs4 import BeautifulSoup

def read_file():
    ''' Read and return content from file (.html). '''
    content = open("regexHTML.html", "r")
    pageSource = content.read()
    return pageSource

def applyPattern(pattern):
    '''Applies regex pattern provided to Source and prints count and
contents'''
    elements = re.findall(pattern, page) #apply pattern to source
    print("Pattern r'{}' ,Found total: {}".format(pattern,len(elements)))
    print(elements) #print all found tags
    return

if __name__ == "__main__":
    page = read_file() #read HTML file
```

Here, `page` is an HTML page source that's read from an HTML file using `read_file()`. We have also imported `BeautifulSoup` in the preceding code to extract individual HTML tag names and just to compare the implementation of code and results found by using `soup.find_all()` and a Regex pattern that we will be applying:

```
soup = BeautifulSoup(page, 'lxml')
print([element.name for element in soup.find_all()])
['html', 'head', 'title', 'style', 'body', 'h1', 'a', 'a', 'a', 'div', 'p',
'i', 'img', 'p', 'i', 'h1']
```

For finding all of the HTML tags that exist inside `page`, we used the `find_all()` method with `soup` as an object of `BeautifulSoup` using the `lxml` parser.

 For more information on Beautiful Soup, please visit *Chapter 5, Web Scraping using Scrapy and Beautiful Soup*, the *Web scraping using Beautiful Soup* section.

Here, we are finding all HTML tag names that don't have any attributes. `\w+` matches any word with one or more character:

```
applyPattern(r'<(\w+)>') #Finding Elements without attributes

Pattern r'<(\w+)>' ,Found total: 6
['html', 'head', 'title', 'body', 'div', 'i']
```

Finding all HTML tags or elements that don't end with > or contain some attributes can be found with the help of the space character, that is, `\s`:

```
applyPattern(r'<(\w+)\s') #Finding Elements with attributes

Pattern r'<(\w+)\s' ,Found total: 10
['style', 'h1', 'a', 'a', 'a', 'p', 'img', 'p', 'i', 'h1']
```

Now, by combining all of these patterns, we are listing all HTML tags that were found in the page source. The same result was also obtained in the previous code by using `soup.find_all()` and the `name` attribute:

```
applyPattern(r'<(\w+)\s?') #Finding all HTML element

Pattern r'<(\w+)\s?' ,Found total: 16
['html', 'head', 'title', 'style', 'body', 'h1', 'a', 'a', 'a', 'div', 'p',
'i', 'img', 'p', 'i', 'h1']
```

Let's find the attribute's name, as found in the HTML element:

```
applyPattern(r'<\w+\s+(.*?)=') #Finding attributes name

Pattern r'<\w+\s+(.*?)=' ,Found total: 10
['type', 'style', 'href', 'class', 'id', 'id', 'src', 'class', 'style',
'itemprop']
```

As we can see, there were only 10 attributes listed. In the HTML source, a few tags contain more than one attribute, such as `<a href="https://www.google.com"` `style="color:red;">Google</a>`, and only the first attribute was found using the provided pattern.

Let's rectify this. We can select words with the = character after them by using the `r'(\w+)='` pattern, which will result in all of the attributes found in the page source being returned:

```
applyPattern(r'(\w+)=') #Finding names of all attributes

Pattern r'(\w+)=' ,Found total: 18
['type', 'style', 'href', 'style', 'class', 'href', 'id', 'href', 'style',
'id', 'class', 'src', 'id', 'class', 'class', 'id', 'style', 'itemprop']
```

Similarly, let's find all of the values for the attributes we've found. The following code lists the values of the attributes and compares the 18 attributes we listed previously. Only 9 values were found. With the pattern we used here, `r'=\"(\w+)\"'` will only find the word characters. Some of the attribute values contained non-word characters, such as `<a href="https://www.google.com" style="color:red;">`:

```
applyPattern(r'=\"(\w+)\"')

Pattern r'=\"(\w+)\"' ,Found total: 9
['classOne', 'idOne', 'mainContent', 'content', 'pageLogo', 'logo',
'content', 'subContent', 'subheading']
```

Here, the complete attribute values are listed by using the proper pattern we analyzed. The content attribute values also contained non-word characters such as ;, /, :, and .. In Regex, we can include such characters in the pattern individually, but this approach may not be appropriate in all cases.

In this case, the pattern that includes \w and the non-whitespace character, \S, fits perfectly, that is, `r'=\"([\w\S]+)\"`:

```
applyPattern(r'=\"([\w\S]+)\"')

Pattern r'=\"([\w\S]+)\"' ,Found total: 18
```

```
['text/css', 'color:orange;', 'https://www.google.com', 'color:red;',
'classOne', 'https://www.yahoo.com', 'idOne', 'https://www.wikipedia.org',
'color:blue;', 'mainContent', 'content', 'mylogo.png', 'pageLogo', 'logo',
'content', 'subContent', 'color:red', 'subheading']
```

Finally, let's collect all of the text inside the HTML elements that are found in-between the opening and closing HTML tags:

```
applyPattern(r'\>(.*)\<')
Pattern r'\>(.*)\<' ,Found total: 8
['Welcome to Web Scraping: Example', 'Welcome to Web Scraping', 'Google',
'Yahoo', 'Wikipedia', 'Paragraph contents', 'Sub paragraph content', 'Sub
heading Content!']
```

While applying Regex to the content, preliminary analysis for the type of content and the values to be extracted is compulsory. This will help to obtain the required results and can be done in one attempt.

Example 2 – extracting dealer locations

In this example, we will be extracting content from `http://godfreysfeed.com/dealersandlocations.php`. This website contains dealer locations information, which is shown in the screenshot that follows:

```
import re
import requests

def read_url(url):
    '''
Handles URL Request and Response
Loads the URL provided using requests and returns the text of page source
    '''
    pageSource = requests.get(url).text
    return pageSource

if __name__ == "__main__":
```

For this and the other examples in this section, we will be using the `re` and `requests` libraries in order to retrieve the page source, that is, `pageSource`. Here, we will be using the `read_url()` function to do so.

Godfreysfeed Dealers front page

You can either perform form submission with `zipcode` or extract content from the map.

By analyzing the page source, we will find that there's no HTML elements with dealers' information. Implementing Regex fits this case perfectly. Here, dealers' information is found inside JavaScript code with variables such as `latLng` and `infoWindowContent`, as shown in the following screenshot:

Godfreysfeed Dealers page source

We will now proceed with loading the page source for the desired URL and implementing Regex to find data:

```
dataSet=list() #collecting data extracted
sourceUrl = 'http://godfreysfeed.com/dealersandlocations.php'
page = read_url(sourceUrl) #load sourceUrl and return the page source
```

With the page source obtained from `read_url()`, let's do a basic analysis and build a pattern to collect latitude and longitude information. We will need two distinct patterns for the dealer's address and coordinate values, respectively. Output from both patterns can be combined to obtain the final results:

```
#Defining pattern matching latitude and longitude as found in page.
pLatLng= r'var latLng = new
google.maps.LatLng\((?P<lat>.*)\,\s*(?P<lng>.*)\)\;'

#applying pattern to page source
latlngs = re.findall(pLatLng,page)
print("Findall found total LatLngs: ", len(latlngs))

#Print coordinates found
print(latlngs)
```

By using the `pLatLng` pattern, a total of 55 coordinate values were found:

```
Findall found total LatLngs: 55

[('33.2509855','-84.2633946'),('31.0426107','-84.8821949'),('34.8761989','-
83.9582412'),('32.43158','-81.749293'),('33.8192864','-83.4387722'),('34.29
59968','-83.0062267'),
('32.6537561','-83.7596295'),('31.462497','-82.5866503'),('33.7340136','-82
.7472304')
,........................................................................,
('32.5444125','-82.8945945'),('32.7302168','-82.7117232'),('34.0082425','-8
1.7729772'),
('34.6639864',
'-82.5126743'),('31.525261','-83.06603'),('34.2068698','-83.4689814'),
('32.9765932','-84.98978'),('34.0412765','-83.2001394'),('33.3066615','-83.
6976187'),
('31.3441482','-83.3002373'),('30.02116','-82.329495'),('34.58403','-83.760
829')]
```

Now that we have the dealer's coordinates, let's find out the dealer's name, address, and more:

```
#Defining pattern to find dealer from page.
pDealers = r'infoWindowContent = infoWindowContent\+\s*\"(.*?)\"\;'
```

```
#applying dealers pattern to page source
dealers = re.findall(pDealers, page)
print("Findall found total Address: ", len(dealers))

#Print dealers information found
print(dealers)
```

There was also a total of 55 pieces of address-based information, which was found by using the pDealers pattern. Note that the dealer's content is in HTML format and that further implementation of Regex will be required to obtain individual titles such as name, address, and city:

Findall found total Address: 55

```
["<strong><span style='color:#e5011c;'>Akins Feed &
Seed</span></strong><br><strong>206 N Hill Street
</strong><br><strong>Griffin,
GA</strong><br><strong>30223</strong><br><br>", "<strong><span
style='color:#e5011c;'>Alf&apos;s Farm and
Garden</span></strong><br><strong>101 East 1st
Street</strong><br><strong>Donalsonville,
GA</strong><br><strong>39845</strong><br><br>", "<strong><span
style='color:#e5011c;'>American Cowboy Shop</span></strong><br><strong>513
D Murphy Hwy</strong><br><strong>Blairsville,
GA</strong><br><strong>30512</strong><br><br>",...........................
...... ...............................,"<strong><span
style='color:#e5011c;'>White Co. Farmers Exchange
</span></strong><br><strong>951 S Main St</strong><br><strong>Cleveland,
GA</strong><br><strong>30528 </strong><br><br>"]
```

Now that we have results from both latlngs and dealers, let's collect the individual portions of the dealer's address. Raw data for the dealers contains some HTML tags, and has been used to split and clean the dealer's address information. Since re.findall() returns the Python list, indexing can also be useful for retrieving address components:

```
d=0 #maintaining loop counter
for dealer in dealers:
    dealerInfo = re.split(r'<br>',re.sub(r'<br><br>','',dealer))
    #extract individual item from dealerInfo
    name = re.findall(r'\'>(.*?)</span',dealerInfo[0])[0]
    address = re.findall(r'>(.*)<',dealerInfo[1])[0]
    city = re.findall(r'>(.*),\s*(.*)<',dealerInfo[2])[0][0]
    state = re.findall(r'>(.*),\s*(.*)<',dealerInfo[2])[0][1]
    zip = re.findall(r'>(.*)<',dealerInfo[3])[0]
    lat = latlngs[d][0]
    lng = latlngs[d][1]
    d+=1
```

```
#appending items to dataset
dataSet.append([name,address,city,state,zip,lat,lng])
```

```
print(dataSet)  #[[name,address, city, state, zip, lat,lng],]
```

Finally, `dataSet` will contain an individual dealer's information that's been merged from `dealers` and `latlngs` in the listing:

```
[['Akins Feed & Seed', '206 N Hill Street', 'Griffin', 'GA', '30223',
'33.2509855', '-84.2633946'], ['Alf&apos;s Farm and Garden', '101 East 1st
Street', 'Donalsonville', 'GA', '39845', '31.0426107',
'-84.8821949'],.................................,
['Twisted Fitterz', '10329 Nashville Enigma Rd', 'Alapaha', 'GA', '31622',
'31.3441482', '-83.3002373'],
['Westside Feed II', '230 SE 7th Avenue', 'Lake Butler', 'FL', '32054',
'30.02116', '-82.329495'],
['White Co. Farmers Exchange', '951 S Main St', 'Cleveland', 'GA', '30528',
'34.58403', '-83.760829']]
```

In this example, we tried to extract data using different patterns and retrieved a dealer's information from the URL provided.

Example 3 – extracting XML content

In this example, we will be extracting contents from the `sitemap.xml` file, which can be downloaded from `https://webscraping.com/sitemap.xml`:

```
▼<urlset xmlns="https://www.sitemaps.org/schemas/sitemap/0.9">
  ▼<url>
     <loc>https://webscraping.com</loc>
  </url>
  ▼<url>
     <loc>https://webscraping.com/about</loc>
  </url>
  ▼<url>
     <loc>https://webscraping.com/blog</loc>
  </url>
  ▼<url>
     <loc>https://webscraping.com/blog/10/</loc>
  </url>
  ▼<url>
     <loc>https://webscraping.com/blog/11/</loc>
  </url>
  ▼<url>
     <loc>https://webscraping.com/blog/12/</loc>
  </url>
  ▼<url>
```

The sitemap.xml file from https://webscraping.com

By analyzing the XML content, we can see that different types of URLs exist as child nodes, that is, `<loc>`. From these URLs, we will be extracting the following:

- Blog URLs (URLs with a `/blog/` string, such as `https://webscraping.com/blog/Why-Python/`)
- Titles obtained from the blog URLs (*Why-Python*)
- Category URLs (URLs with a `/category/` string, such as `https://webscraping.com/blog/category/beautifulsoup`)
- Category titles obtained from category URLs (*beautifulsoup*)

 Blog titles and category titles that are obtained from code are retrieved from the URL or representations of the real content that's available from the URL. Actual titles might be different.

To begin with, let's import the `re` Python library and read the file's contents, as well as create a few Python lists in order to collect relevant data:

```
import re

filename = 'sitemap.xml'
dataSetBlog = [] # collect Blog title information from URLs except
'category'
dataSetBlogURL = [] # collects Blog URLs
dataSetCategory = [] # collect Category title
dataSetCategoryURL = [] # collect Category URLs

page = open(filename, 'r').read()
```

From the XML content, that is, `page`, we need to find the URL pattern. `pattern` used in code matches and returns all of the URLs inside the `<loc>` node. `urlPatterns` (`<class 'list'>`) is a Python list object that contains searched URLs and is iterated to collect and process the desired information:

```
#Pattern to be searched, found inside <loc>(.*)</loc>
pattern = r"loc>(.*)</loc"

urlPatterns = re.findall(pattern, page) #finding pattern on page

for url in urlPatterns: #iterating individual url inside urlPatterns
```

Now, let's match a `url`, such as `https://webscraping.com/blog/Google-App-Engine-limitations/`, which contains a `blog` string and append it to `dataSetBlogURL`. There are also few other URLs, such as `https://webscraping.com/blog/8/`, which will be ignored while we extract `blogTitle`.

Also, any `blogTitle` that's found as text equal to `category` will be ignored. The `r'blog/([A-Za-z0-9\-]+)` pattern matches alphabetical and numerical values with the `-` character:

```
if re.match(r'.*blog', url): #Blog related
    dataSetBlogURL.append(url)
    if re.match(r'[\w\-]', url):
        blogTitle = re.findall(r'blog/([A-Za-z0-9\-]+)', url)
        if len(blogTitle) > 0 and not re.match('(category)', blogTitle[0]):
            #blogTitle is a List, so index is applied.
            dataSetBlog.append(blogTitle[0])
```

Here's the output for `dataSetBlogURL`:

```
print("Blogs URL: ", len(dataSetBlogURL))
print(dataSetBlogURL)

Blogs URL: 80
['https://webscraping.com/blog', 'https://webscraping.com/blog/10/',
'https://webscraping.com/blog/11/', ........,
'https://webscraping.com/blog/category/screenshot',
'https://webscraping.com/blog/category/sitescraper',
'https://webscraping.com/blog/category/sqlite',
'https://webscraping.com/blog/category/user-agent',
'https://webscraping.com/blog/category/web2py',
'https://webscraping.com/blog/category/webkit',
'https://webscraping.com/blog/category/website/',
'https://webscraping.com/blog/category/xpath']
```

`dataSetBlog` will contain the following titles (URL portion). The `set()` method, when applied to `dataSetBlog`, will return unique elements from `dataSetBlog`. As shown in the following code, there's no duplicate title inside `dataSetBlog`:

```
print("Blogs Title: ", len(dataSetBlog))
print("Unique Blog Count: ", len(set(dataSetBlog)))
print(dataSetBlog)
#print(set(dataSetBlog)) #returns unique element from List similar to
dataSetBlog.


Blogs Title: 24
Unique Blog Count: 24
```

```
['Android-Apps-Update', 'Apple-Apps-Update', 'Automating-CAPTCHAs',
'Automating-webkit', 'Bitcoin', 'Client-Feedback', 'Fixed-fee-or-hourly',
'Google-Storage', 'Google-interview', 'How-to-use-proxies', 'I-love-AJAX',
'Image-efficiencies', 'Luminati', 'Reverse-Geocode', 'Services', 'Solving-
CAPTCHA', 'Startup', 'UPC-Database-Update', 'User-agents', 'Web-Scrapping',
'What-is-CSV', 'What-is-web-scraping', 'Why-Python', 'Why-web']
```

Now, let's extract information that's relevant to the URL by using `category`. The `r'.*category'` Regex pattern, which matches `url` from the iteration, is collected or appended to `datasetCategoryURL`. `categoryTitle` is extracted from `url` that matches the `r'category/([\w\s\-]+)` pattern and is added to `dataSetCategory`:

```
if re.match(r'.*category', url): #Category Related
    dataSetCategoryURL.append(url)
    categoryTitle = re.findall(r'category/([\w\s-]+)', url)
    dataSetCategory.append(categoryTitle[0])

print("Category URL Count: ", len(dataSetCategoryURL))
print(dataSetCategoryURL)
```

`dataSetCategoryURL` will result in the following values:

```
Category URL Count: 43
['https://webscraping.com/blog/category/ajax',
'https://webscraping.com/blog/category/android/',
'https://webscraping.com/blog/category/big picture',
'https://webscraping.com/blog/category/business/',
'https://webscraping.com/blog/category/cache',
'https://webscraping.com/blog/category/captcha',
...............................,
'https://webscraping.com/blog/category/sitescraper',
'https://webscraping.com/blog/category/sqlite',
'https://webscraping.com/blog/category/user-agent',
'https://webscraping.com/blog/category/web2py',
'https://webscraping.com/blog/category/webkit',
'https://webscraping.com/blog/category/website/',
'https://webscraping.com/blog/category/xpath']
```

Finally, the following output displays the title that was retrieved from `dataSetCategory`, as well as its counts:

```
print("Category Title Count: ", len(dataSetCategory))
print("Unique Category Count: ", len(set(dataSetCategory)))
print(dataSetCategory)
#returns unique element from List similar to dataSetCategory.
#print(set(dataSetCategory))
```

```
Category Title Count: 43
Unique Category Count: 43

['ajax', 'android', 'big picture', 'business', 'cache', 'captcha',
'chickenfoot', 'concurrent', 'cookies', 'crawling', 'database',
'efficiency', 'elance', 'example', 'flash', 'freelancing', 'gae', 'google',
'html', 'image', 'ip', 'ir', 'javascript', 'learn', 'linux', 'lxml',
'mobile', 'mobile apps', 'ocr', 'opensource', 'proxies', 'python', 'qt',
'regex', 'scrapy', 'screenshot', 'sitescraper', 'sqlite', 'user-agent',
'web2py', 'webkit', 'website', 'xpath']
```

From these example cases, we can see that, by using Regex, we can write patterns that target specific data from sources such as web pages, HTML, or XML.

Regex features such as searching, splitting, and iterating can be implemented with the help of various functions from the re Python library. Although Regex can be implemented on any type of content, unstructured content is preferred. Structured web content with elements that carry attributes are preferred when using XPath and CSS selectors.

Summary

In this chapter, we learned about regular expressions and their implementation by using the re Python library.

So far, we've learned about various scraping-based tools and techniques. Regex can provide more flexibility when it comes to extraction tasks and can be used with other tools.

In the next chapter, we will be learning about further steps and topics that could be beneficial in a learning context, such as managing scraped data, visualization and analysis, and an introduction to machine learning and data mining, as well as exploring some related resources.

Further reading

- Regular Expression HOWTO: `https://docs.python.org/2/howto/regex.html`
- Regular Expressions – JavaScript: `https://developer.mozilla.org/en-US/docs/Web/JavaScript/Guide/Regular_Expressions`
- Python Regular Expressions: `https://developers.google.com/edu/python/regular-expressions`
- Online Regex Tester and Debugger: `https://regex101.com/`
- *Regular Expressions Cookbook: 2nd Edition, 2012* by Jan Goyvaerts and Steven Levithan
- Regular Expressions References: `https://regexone.com/references/python`
- Regular Expressions – Information: `http://www.regular-expressions.info/python.html`

Section 4: Conclusion

In this section, you will learn about certain topics that are applicable to collected or scraped data and you will learn about some advanced concepts, that are worth knowing from an information and career perspective.

This section consists of the following chapter:

- Chapter 10, *Next Steps*

10
Next Steps

So far, we have explored various tools and techniques regarding web scraping via the use of the Python programming language.

Web scraping, or web harvesting, is done in order to extract and collect data from websites. Web scraping comes in handy in terms of model development, which requires data to be collected on the fly that's true, relevant to the topic, and accurate. This is desirable as it takes less time compared to implementing datasets. The data that's collected is stored in various formats, such as JSON, CSV, XML, and more, is written to databases for later use, and is also made available online as datasets.

Websites also provide web APIs with a user interface to interact with information on the web. This data can be used for research, analysis, marketing, **machine learning** (**ML**) models, information building, knowledge discovery, and more in the field of computer science, management, medicine, and more. We can also perform analysis on the data that's obtained through APIs and publicly, or freely, available datasets and generate an outcome, but this process isn't classed as web scraping.

In this chapter, we will learn about topics that are applicable to collected or scraped data and learn about some advanced concepts that are worth knowing about from an information and career perspective:

- Managing scraped data
- Analysis and visualization using pandas and matplotlib
- ML
- Data mining
- What's next?

Technical requirements

A web browser (Google Chrome or Mozilla Firefox) is required. We will be using the following Python libraries in this chapter:

- pandas
- matplotlib
- csv
- json

If these libraries don't exist in your current Python setup, refer to Chapter 2, *Python and the Web – Using urllib and Requests,* in the *Setting things up* section, for instructions on installing them and setting them up.

The code files for this chapter are available in this book's GitHub repository: https://github.com/PacktPublishing/Hands-On-Web-Scraping-with-Python/tree/master/Chapter10.

Managing scraped data

In this section, we will explore some tools and learn more about handling and managing the data that we have scraped or extracted from certain websites.

Data that's collected from websites using scraping scripts is known as raw data. This data might require some additional tasks to be performed on top of it before it can be processed further so that we can gain an insight on it. Therefore, raw data should be verified and processed (if required), which can be done by doing the following:

- **Cleaning**: As the name suggests, this step is used to remove unwanted pieces of information, such as space and whitespace characters, and unwanted portions of text. The following code shows some relevant steps that were used in examples in previous chapters, such as Chapter 9, *Using Regex to Extract Data*, and Chapter 3, *Using LXML, XPath, and CSS Selectors*. Functions such as sub() (that is, re.sub()), strip(), and replace() are used in many places and can also be used for the purpose of cleaning:

```
dealerInfo = re.split(r'<br>', re.sub(r'<br><br>', '', dealer))

stock = list(map(lambda stock:stock.strip(),availability))

availability = stockPath(row)[0].strip()

article['lastUpdated'] = article['lastUpdated'].replace('This page
was last edited on', '')

title = row.find(attrs={'itemprop':'text'}).text.strip()

re.sub(r'or\s*','',fortran)

dealerInfo = re.split(r'<br>',re.sub(r'<br><br>','',dealer))
```

- **Formatting**: This step is used to obtain the desired format from the data. For example, we might require fixed decimal places in the price that's received, we may need to convert or round up large floating values into fixed decimal places, split large strings into smaller units, and more, and then write them to datasets. There may also be cases where decimal numbers or integers are extracted as strings and need to be formatted. Normally, converting data types and presenting data is considered formatting:

```
>>> price = 1234.567801
>>> newprice = round(price,2)
>>> print(newprice)
1234.57

>>> totalsum="200.35"
>>> print(type(totalsum))
<class 'str'>
```

```
#For large precision use:
https://docs.python.org/2/library/decimal.html
>>> totalsum = float(totalsum)
>>> print(type(totalsum))
<class 'float'>

>>> totalsum
200.35

>>> ratings = 5.5
>>> print(int(rating))
5
```

These additional steps can also be performed within the scripts while we are extracting particular data, and has been done in the examples we've looked at throughout the book. In many cases, cleaning and formatting works together, or is done side by side.

Writing to files

We have needed to extract lines of data throughout this book. You may have noticed that, in most of these examples, we used a dataset (a Python list object that was used to collect data) that was appended with various fields in a Python list, as shown in the following code (collected from various examples of this book):

```
dataSet.append([year,month,day,game_date,team1,team1_score,team2,team2_scor
e,game_status])
..
dataSet.append([title,price,availability,image.replace('../../../..',baseUr
l),rating.replace('star-rating ','')])
...
dataSet.append([link, atype, adate, title, excerpt,",".join(categories)])
...
dataSet.append([titleLarge, title, price, stock, image,
starRating.replace('star-rating ', ''), url])
```

With the availability of such a dataset, we can write this information to external files, as well as to the database. Before we write the dataset to the files, column names that describe the data from the dataset are needed. Consider the following code, where keys is a separate list containing a string title, that is, the name of the columns to the respective list item appended to the dataset:

```
keys = ['year','month','day','game_date','team1', 'team1_score', 'team2',
'team2_score', 'game_status']
......
```

```
dataSet.append([year,month,day,game_date,team1,team1_score,team2,team2_scor
e,game_status])
```

Let's consider the following example, which contains `colNames` with the column to be used, and `dataSet` with the cleaned and formatted data:

```
import csv
import json

colNames = ['Title','Price','Stock','Rating']
dataSet= [['Rip it Up and ...', 35.02, 'In stock', 5],['Our Band Could Be
...', 57.25, 'In stock', 4],
    ['How Music Works', 37.32, 'In stock', 2],['Love Is a Mix ...', 18.03,
'Out of stock',1],
    ['Please Kill Me: The ...', 31.19, 'In stock', 4],["Kill 'Em and Leave:
...", 45.0, 'In stock',5],
    ['Chronicles, Vol. 1', 52.60, 'Out of stock',2],['This Is Your Brain
...', 38.4, 'In stock',1],
    ['Orchestra of Exiles: The ...', 12.36, 'In stock',3],['No One Here
Gets ...', 20.02, 'In stock',5],
    ['Life', 31.58, 'In stock',5],['Old Records Never Die: ...', 55.66, 'Out
of Stock',2],
    ['Forever Rockers (The Rocker ...', 28.80, 'In stock',3]]
```

Now we will write the preceding `dataSet` to the CSV file. The first line of the CSV file should always contain the column names. In this case, we will use `colNames` for the columns:

```
fileCsv = open('bookdetails.csv', 'w', newline='', encoding='utf-8')
writer = csv.writer(fileCsv) #csv.writer object created

writer.writerow(colNames)    #write columns from colNames
for data in dataSet:         #iterate through dataSet and write to file
    writer.writerow(data)

fileCsv.close() #closes the file handler
```

The preceding code will result in the `bookdetails.csv` file, which has the following content:

```
Title,Price,Stock,Rating
Rip it Up and ...,35.02,In stock,5
Our Band Could Be ...,57.25,In stock,4
..........
Life,31.58,In stock,5
Old Records Never Die: ...,55.66,Out of Stock,2
Forever Rockers (The Rocker ...,28.8,In stock,3
```

Similarly, let's create a JSON file with `colNames` and `dataSets`. JSON is similar to Python dictionary, where each data or value possesses a key; that is, it exists in a key-value pair:

```
finalDataSet=list() #empty DataSet

for data in dataSet:
    finalDataSet.append(dict(zip(colNames,data)))

print(finalDataSet)

[{'Price': 35.02, 'Stock': 'In stock', 'Title': 'Rip it Up and ...',
'Rating': 5}, {'Price': 57.25, 'Stock': 'In stock', ..........'Title': 'Old
Records Never Die: ...', 'Rating': 2}, {'Price': 28.8, 'Stock': 'In stock',
'Title': 'Forever Rockers (The Rocker ...', 'Rating': 3}]
```

As we can see, `finalDataSet` is formed by appending data from `dataSet` and by using the `zip()` Python function. `zip()` combines each individual element from the list. This zipped object is then converted into a Python dictionary. For example, consider the following code:

```
#first iteration from loop above dict(zip(colNames,data)) will generate
{'Rating': 5, 'Title': 'Rip it Up and ...', 'Price': 35.02, 'Stock': 'In
stock'}
```

Now, with the available `finalDataSet`, we can dump or add the data to a JSON file using the `dump()` function from the `json` module:

```
with open('bookdetails.json', 'w') as jsonfile:
    json.dump(finalDataSet,jsonfile)
```

The preceding code will result in the `bookdetails.json` file. Its content is as follows:

```
[
    {
        "Price": 35.02,
        "Stock": "In stock",
        "Title": "Rip it Up and ...",
        "Rating": 5
    },
    ................
    {
        "Price": 28.8,
        "Stock": "In stock",
        "Title": "Forever Rockers (The Rocker ...",
        "Rating": 3
    }
]
```

In this section, we have covered the basic steps for managing raw data. The files we have obtained can be shared and exchanged easily across various independent systems, used as models for ML, and can be imported as data sources in applications. Furthermore, we can also use **Database Management Systems (DBMS)** such as MySQL, PostgreSQL, and more to store data and execute **Structured Query Language (SQL)** using the necessary Python libraries.

Analysis and visualization using pandas and matplotlib

In this section, we will be exploring a few basic concepts with regard to analyzing data using pandas and plotting general charts using matplotlib.

pandas is one of the most popular data analysis libraries in recent times. Data analysis and visualization are major tasks and can be performed with the help of pandas and other libraries such as matplotlib.

For more details and documentation on pandas and matplotlib, please visit their official sites at `https://pandas.pydata.org/` and `https://matplotlib.org/`.

pandas is also termed and used as a raw spreadsheet. It supports mathematical, statistical and query-type statements, and allows you to read from and write to various files. It is also popular among developers and analysts since it has easy functions and properties available that can help you handle data that's in a row and column structure:

```
>>> import pandas
>>> print(dir(pandas))
['Categorical', 'CategoricalIndex', 'DataFrame', 'DateOffset', 'DatetimeIndex', 'ExcelFile', 'ExcelWriter', 'Expr',
'Float64Index', 'Grouper', 'HDFStore', 'Index', 'IndexSlice', 'Int64Index', 'MultiIndex', 'NaT', 'Panel', 'Panel4D',
'Period', 'PeriodIndex', 'RangeIndex', 'Series', 'SparseArray', 'SparseDataFrame', 'SparseList', 'SparseSeries', 'Sp
arseTimeSeries', 'Term', 'TimeGrouper', 'TimeSeries', 'Timedelta', 'TimedeltaIndex', 'Timestamp', 'WidePanel', '_bu
iltins__', '__cached__', '__doc__', '__docformat__', '__file__', '__loader__', '__name__', '__package__', '__path__'
, '__spec__', '__version__', '_join', '_np_version_under1p10', '_np_version_under1p11', '_np_version_under1p12', '_n
p_version_under1p8', '_np_version_under1p9', '_period', '_sparse', '_testing', '_version', '_window', 'algos', 'api'
, 'bdate_range', 'compat', 'computation', 'concat', 'core', 'crosstab', 'cut', 'date_range', 'datetime', 'datetools'
, 'describe_option', 'eval', 'ewma', 'ewmcorr', 'ewmcov', 'ewmstd', 'ewmvar', 'ewmvol', 'expanding_apply', 'expandin
g_corr', 'expanding_count', 'expanding_cov', 'expanding_kurt', 'expanding_max', 'expanding_mean', 'expanding_median'
, 'expanding_min', 'expanding_quantile', 'expanding_skew', 'expanding_std', 'expanding_sum', 'expanding_var', 'facto
rize', 'fama_macbeth', 'formats', 'get_dummies', 'get_option', 'get_store', 'groupby', 'hashtable', 'index', 'indexe
s', 'infer_freq', 'info', 'io', 'isnull', 'json', 'lib', 'lreshape', 'match', 'melt', 'merge', 'merge_asof', 'merge_
ordered', 'msgpack', 'notnull', 'np', 'offsets', 'ols', 'option_context', 'options', 'ordered_merge', 'pandas', 'par
ser', 'period_range', 'pivot', 'pivot_table', 'plot_params', 'pnow', 'qcut', 'read_clipboard', 'read_csv', 'read_exc
el', 'read_fwf', 'read_gbq', 'read_hdf', 'read_html', 'read_json', 'read_msgpack', 'read_pickle', 'read_sas', 'read_
sql', 'read_sql_query', 'read_sql_table', 'read_stata', 'read_table', 'reset_option', 'rolling_apply', 'rolling_corr
', 'rolling_count', 'rolling_cov', 'rolling_kurt', 'rolling_max', 'rolling_mean', 'rolling_median', 'rolling_min', '
rolling_quantile', 'rolling_skew', 'rolling_std', 'rolling_sum', 'rolling_var', 'rolling_window', 'scatter_matrix',
'set_eng_float_format', 'set_option', 'show_versions', 'sparse', 'stats', 'test', 'timedelta_range', 'to_datetime',
'to_msgpack', 'to_numeric', 'to_pickle', 'to_timedelta', 'tools', 'tseries', 'tslib', 'types', 'unique', 'util', 'va
lue_counts', 'wide_to_long']
```

Exploring pandas using the Python IDE

In this section, we will be reading data from the `bookdetails.csv` file and conducting analysis and visualization using the file's data. Let's import the libraries that are required, that is, pandas and `matplotlib.pyplot`. We will be using the `pd` and `plt` aliases, respectively, and reading the data from the file:

```
import pandas as pd
import matplotlib.pyplot as plt

dataSet = pd.read_csv('bookdetails.csv') #loads the file content as
dataframe.

print(type(dataSet)) #<class 'pandas.core.frame.DataFrame'>
```

As we can see, the `read_csv()` function reads the content from a CSV file and generates a DataFrame object. pandas also supports various data files via the use of functions such as `read_html()`, `read_excel()`, `read_json()`, and `read_sql_table()`.

Here, `dataSet` is an object of the pandas DataFrame. The DataFrame represents a two-dimensional tabular structure with rows, columns, and indexes. Query-level analysis, conditional statements, filtering, grouping, and more are supported by DataFrames against data in rows and columns:

```
print(dataSet)
```

The following screenshot displays the content that's now available in `dataSet`:

```
                             Title  Price           Stock  Rating
0               Rip it Up and ...  35.02        In stock       5
1           Our Band Could Be ...  57.25        In stock       4
2               How Music Works  37.32        In stock       2
3               Love Is a Mix ...  18.03   Out of stock       1
4           Please Kill Me: The ...  31.19        In stock       4
5           Kill 'Em and Leave: ...  45.00        In stock       5
6               Chronicles, Vol. 1  52.60   Out of stock       2
7           This Is Your Brain ...  38.40        In stock       1
8       Orchestra of Exiles: The ...  12.36        In stock       3
9               No One Here Gets ...  20.02        In stock       5
10                           Life  31.58        In stock       5
11          Old Records Never Die: ...  55.66   Out of Stock       2
12  Forever Rockers (The Rocker ...  28.80        In stock       3
```

Dataset contents from a CSV file

Row indexes are also shown, all of which start with 0 (zero). The general statistical output can be obtained by using the `describe()` function:

```
print(dataSet.describe())
#print(dataSet.describe('price') will only generate values for column price
        Price      Rating
count 13.000000   13.000000
```

```
mean    35.633077    3.230769
std     14.239014    1.535895
min     12.360000    1.000000
25%     28.800000    2.000000
50%     35.020000    3.000000
75%     45.000000    5.000000
max     57.250000    5.000000
```

As we can see, by default, `describe()` selects the columns that are applicable to statistical functions and returns calculations with the following functions:

- `count`: Number of rows

- `mean`: Average value for the related column

- `min`: Minimum value found

- `max`: Maximum value found

- `std`: Calculated standard deviation

- `25%`: Returns the 25th percentile

- `50%`: Returns the 50th percentile

- `75%`: Returns the 75th percentile

In the following code, we are selecting an individual column called `Price` as `price_group`. All of the columns from the dataset can be listed using `dataSet.columns`. Multiple columns can be selected by using the following `dataSet[['Price', 'Rating']]` format:

```
print(dataSet.columns)
Index(['Title', 'Price', 'Stock', 'Rating'], dtype='object')

print(sum(dataSet['Price']))
463.23

print(sum(dataSet['Rating']))
42

print(dataSet['Price'][0:5])
0  35.02
1  57.25
```

```
2 37.32
3 18.03
4 31.19
Name: Price, dtype: float64
```

The following code shows the individual data for the `Price` column:

```
#dataSet[['Price','Rating']] will select both column
price_group = dataSet[['Price']] #selecting 'Price' column only.
print(price_group)

Index(['Title', 'Price', 'Stock', 'Rating'], dtype='object')
   Price
0 35.02
1 57.25
2 37.32
.....
11 55.66
12 28.80
```

pandas DataFrames also accept conditions or filtering actions being used on columns. As you can see, the filter is applied to `Rating` for values that are `>=4.0`, and only `Title` and `Price` are going to be returned:

```
print(dataSet[dataSet['Rating']>=4.0][['Title','Price']])

     Title              Price
0  Rip it Up and ...    35.02
1  Our Band Could Be ... 57.25
4  Please Kill Me: The ...31.19
5  Kill 'Em and Leave: ...45.00
9  No One Here Gets ...  20.02
10 Life                 31.58
```

Similarly, string-based filters can also be applied. `Stock`, which contains the `Out` text, is filtered, and the output returns all the columns that satisfy the `Out` text. The `contains()` function accepts regular expressions and strings:

```
print(dataSet[dataSet.Stock.str.contains(r'Out')])

     Title              Price Stock        Rating
3  Love Is a Mix ...    18.03 Out of stock 1
6  Chronicles, Vol. 1   52.60 Out of stock 2
11 Old Records Never Die: ...55.66 Out of Stock 2

#will return only column 'Price'
#print(dataSet[dataSet.Stock.str.contains(r'Out')]['Price'])
```

The between() function is supplied with values that refer to Rating to filter and return Title of the books:

```
print(dataSet[dataSet.Rating.between(3.5,4.5)]['Title'])

1 Our Band Could Be ...
4 Please Kill Me: The ...
```

Since we have the price_group data, we can call the plot() function on the data with the help of the show() function:

```
bar_plot = price_group.plot()    #default plot
bar_plot.set_xlabel("No of Books") #set X axis: label
bar_plot.set_ylabel("Price") #set Y axis: label
plt.show() #displays the plot or chart created
```

The preceding code will generate a line chart with default properties, such as colors and legend placements, as follows:

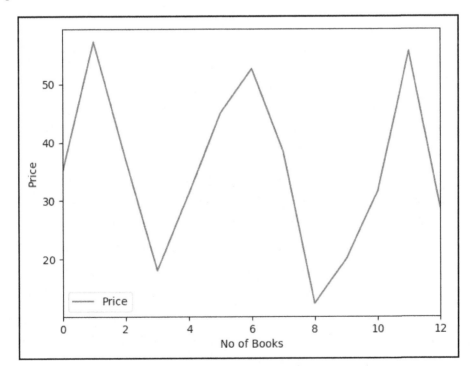

Default line chart for the Price column

We can also change the kind of chart, that is, line, bar, and more.

Visit matplotlib at `https://matplotlib.org/gallery/index.html` to find out more about various functional chart types and their additional associated properties.

In the following code, `kind='bar'` overwrites the default line type:

```
bar_plot = price_group.plot(kind='bar') #kind='bar'
bar_plot.set_xlabel("No of Books")  #Label for X-Axis
bar_plot.set_ylabel("Price") #label for Y-Axis
plt.show()
```

The preceding code generates the following bar chart:

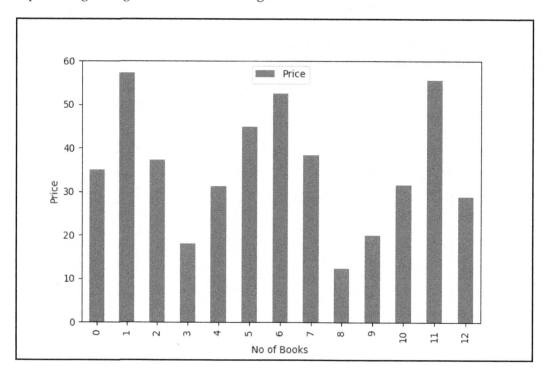

Bar chart for the Price column

So far, we have used a basic chart type with a single column. In the following code, we are plotting a bar chart with the `Price` and `Rating` values:

```
price_group = dataSet[['Price','Rating']]  #obtain both columns
#title: generates a title for plot
bar_plot = price_group.plot(kind='bar',title="Book Price ad Rating")
```

```
bar_plot.set_xlabel("No of Books")
bar_plot.set_ylabel("Price")
plt.show()
```

We receive the following output:

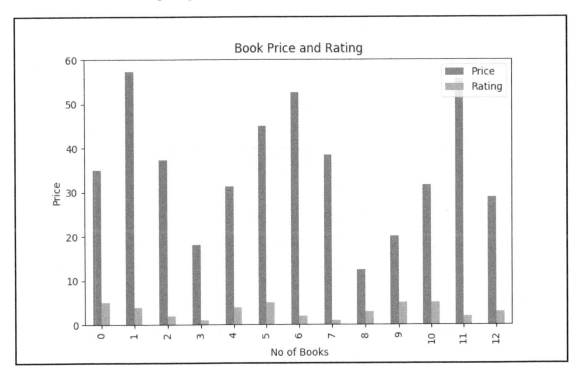

Bar chart with Price and Rating columns

So far, we have successfully plotted line and bar charts. The following code plots a pie chart for the first six items from the Price column and labels them with the first six Title available from dataSet:

```
prices = dataSet['Price'][0:6] #Price from first 6 items
labels = dataSet['Title'][0:6] #Book Titles from first 6 items
legends,ax1 = plt.pie(prices, labels=labels, shadow=True, startangle=45)
plt.legend(legends, prices, loc="best") #legend built using Prices
plt.show()
```

The values from `Price` are used as legends. We receive the following output:

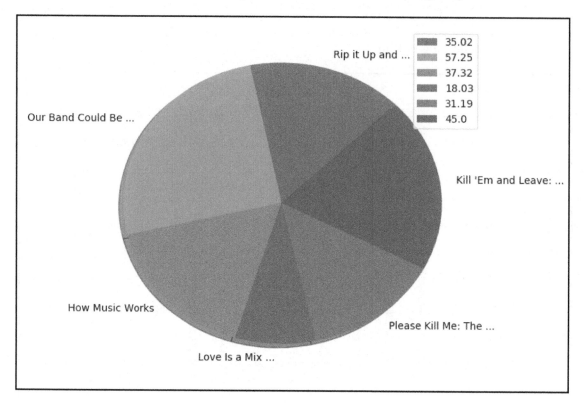

Pie chart with Price and Title column data

There's a lot more to explore in terms of using pandas and matplotlib. In this section, we have displayed the basic features that are available from both libraries. Now, we will look at ML.

Machine learning

ML is a branch of **artificial intelligence (AI)** that deals with the study of mathematical and statistical algorithms to process and develop an automated system that can learn from data with minimal human involvement. ML predictions and decision-making models are dependent on data. Web scraping is one of the resources that makes data available to ML models.

Nowadays, many recommendation engines implement ML in order to serve the marketing ads and recommendations such as Google AdSense and AdWords in real time. The process that's implemented in ML is similar to that of data mining and predictive modeling. Both of these concepts seek patterns while skimming through data and modifying the program's actions as per the requirements. Therefore, ML is a handy tool when it comes to exploring the field of business, marketing, retail, stock prices, video surveillance, face recognition, medical diagnosis, weather prediction, online customer support, online fraud detection, and more.

With new and improved ML algorithms, data capture methods, and faster computer and networking, the field of ML is accelerating.

ML and AI

AI is a broad spectrum that covers a wide range of topics, such as neural networks, expert systems, robotics, fuzzy logic, and more. ML is a subset of AI. It explores the idea of building a machine that learns on its own, thus surpassing the need for constant speculation. Therefore, ML has led to a major breakthrough for achieving AI.

ML incorporates the use of several algorithms, thus allowing software to provide accurate results. Making a useful prediction from a set of parsed data is what the concept of ML aims to do. The foremost benefit of ML is that it can tirelessly learn and predict without the need for a hardcoded software regime. Training includes feeding huge datasets as input. This allows an algorithm to learn, process, and make predictions, which are provided as output.

Several important parameters are employed when measuring the potential of any model. Accuracy is one of them, and is an important parameter in measuring the success of any developed model. In ML, 80% accuracy is a success. If the model has 80% accuracy, then we are saving 80% of our time and increasing productivity. However, it is not always the best metric for accessing classification models if the data is unbalanced.

In general, accuracy is termed as an intuitive measure. While employing accuracy, equal cost is assigned to false positives and false negatives. For imbalanced data (such as 94% falling in one instance and 6% in other), there are many great ways to decrease the cost; make a vague prediction that every instance belongs to the majority class, prove that the overall accuracy is 94%, and complete the task. In the same line, problems arise if what we are talking about, such as a disease, is rare and lethal. The cost of failing to properly examine the disease of a sick person is higher than the cost of pushing a healthy individual to more tests.

All in all, there are no best metrics. It is common for two people to choose different metrics to reach their goal.

Python and ML

A Dutch programmer (Guido Van Rossum) launched Python as his side project but did not realize that it would accelerate his height of success. Python is widely adapted among developers when it comes to speedy prototyping. It is gaining popularity among all the ML tools that are available for its readability, versatility, and easiness.

As ML engineers, computer vision engineers, data scientists, or data engineers, we have to juggle with the ideas of linear algebra and calculus, which often get complex once we dive deeper. However, Python comes to the rescue with its quick implementation, thus bypassing the hurdle of the maximum effort. Quick validation of this idea makes the Python programming language more desirable.

Data is everything for ML. Raw data is unstructured, large, incomplete, and has missing values. Data cleaning is one of the most crucial steps of ML so that we can move on with our data. There are many essential libraries available in Python that make the implementation of ML simpler. Various open source repositories in Python help bring changes to the existing method. Web scraping is one of these methods that deals with data that exists on the web, which it then processes further as input to ML models.

The following are some of the most common and widely used libraries that are worth looking at if we decide to work with Python and ML:

- **scikit-learn**: Used for working with classical ML algorithms

- **NumPy (numerical Python)**: Designed to work for scientific computing

- **SciPy**: Contains modules for linear algebra, optimization, integration, and statistics

- **pandas**: Used for data aggregation, manipulation, and visualization

- **matplotlib** and **Seaborn**: For data visualization

- **Bokeh** and **Plotly**: For interactive visualization

- **TensorFlow** and **Theano**: Used for deep learning

- **Beautiful Soup, LXML, PyQuery** and **Scrapy**: Used to withdraw data from HTML and XML documents

Once we have a basic understanding of Python, these libraries can be imported and implemented. Alternatively, we can also apply these functionalities from scratch, which is what most developers do.

Python requires less writing and debugging in terms of code, which saves time compared to other programming languages. This is exactly what AI and ML programmers want: a focus on understanding the architectural aspect rather than spending all of their time on debugging. Thus, Python can be easily handled by people with less knowledge in programming due to syntax that provides human-level readability.

Apart from Python, there are several other tools for ML, such as Microsoft Excel, SAS, MATLAB, and R. These tools are often overlooked due to a lack of adequate community services and because they are incapable of handling large datasets. MATLAB also provides sophisticated libraries and packages for image processing and analysis. In comparison to Python, the execution time is moderate and the functionality is limited to prototyping, not deployment.

R is another tool that's used for statistical analysis. Python performs data manipulation by providing various development tools that can be collaborated with other systems. However, R only works on a particular form of dataset, and so the predefined functions require the predefined input. R provides a primitive ground to the data, which Python allows us to explore the data.

Types of ML algorithms

In general, there are three types of ML algorithms, as shown here:

- Supervised learning:

    - Classification

    - Regression

- Unsupervised learning:

    - Association

    - Clustering

- Reinforcement learning

Supervised learning

Supervised learning is about observing or directing the execution of something. The input that's given to the model is the prediction we want to make. The labeled data is the explicit prediction given for the particular instances of the input. Supervised learning requires labeled data, which requires some expertise. However, these conditions are not always met. We don't always posses the labeled dataset. For example, fraud prediction is one of the rapidly unfolding fields where the attacker is constantly looking for available exploits. These new attacks can't possibly be maintained under a dataset with labelled attacks.

Mathematically, the mapping functions of the input to the output can be expressed as $Y = f(X)$. Here, Y is the output variable and X is the input variable.

Classification

Classification determines or categorizes a model based on its attributes, and is the process of identifying the genre to which a new observation belongs to, as per the membership category, which is known in advance. It is a technique of determining which class a dependent variable belongs to based on one or more independent variables. The output variable in the classification problem is either a group or a category.

Some examples include, credit scoring (differentiating between high risk and low risk based on earning and saving), medical diagnosis (predicting the risk of disease), web advertising (predicting whether a user will click on advertisements or not), and more.

The ability of the classification model can be determined by using model evaluation procedures and model evaluation metrics.

Model evaluation procedures

Model evaluation procedures help you find out how well a model will adapt to the sample data:

- **Training and testing the data**: The training data is used to train the model so that it fits the parameter. The testing data is a masked dataset for which a prediction has to be made.

- **Train and test split**: Typically, when the data is separated, most of the data is used for training, whereas a small portion of the data is used for testing.

- **K-fold cross-validation**: K-train and test splits are created and averaged together. The process runs k-times slower than train and test splits.

Model evaluation metrics

Model evaluation metrics are employed to quantify the performance of the model. The following metrics can be implemented in order to measure the ability of a classification predictive model.

Evaluation metrics are managed with the help of the following:

- **Confusion matrix**: This is a 2 x 2 matrix, also known as an error matrix. It helps picture the performance of an algorithm – typically a supervised learning one—with the help of classification accuracy, classification error, sensitivity, precision measures, and predictions. The choice of metrics depends on the business objective. Hence, it is necessary to identify whether false positives or false negatives can be reduced based on the requirements.

- **Logistic regression**: Logistic regression is a statistical model that aids in analyzing the dataset. It has several independent variables that are responsible for determining the output. The output is measured with diploid variables (involving two possible outcomes). The aim of logistic regression is to find the best-fitting model to describe the relationship between diploid variables (dependent variables) and a set of independent variables (predictors). Hence, it is also known as a predictive learning model.

- **Naives Bayes**: This works on the concept of conditional probability, as given by Bayes theorem. Bayes theorem calculates the conditional probability of an event based on the prior knowledge that might be in relation to the event. This approach is widely used in face recognition, medical diagnosis, news classification, and more. The Naives Bayes classifier is based on Bayes theorem, where the conditional probability of *A* given *B* can be calculated as follows:

```
P(A | B) = ( P(B | A) * P( A ))/ P( B )
Given:
P(A | B) = Conditional probability of A given B
P(B | A) = Conditional probability of B given A
P( A )= Probability of occurrence of event A
P( B )= Probability of occurrence of event B
```

- **Decision tree**: A decision tree is a type of supervised learning model where the final outcome can be viewed in the form of a tree. The decision tree includes leaf nodes, decision nodes, and the root node. The decision node has two or more branches, whereas the leaf node represents the classification or decision. The decision tree breaks down the dataset further into smaller subsets, thus incrementally developing the associated tree. It is simple to understand and can easily handle categorical and numerical datasets.

- **Random forest algorithm**: This algorithm is a supervised ML algorithm that is easy to use and provides great results, even without hyperparameter tuning. Due to its simplicity, it can be used for both regression and classification tasks. It can handle larger sets of data in order to maintain missing values. This algorithm is also considered the best at performing classification-related tasks compared to regression.

- **Neural network**: Although we already have linear and classification algorithms, a neural network is the state of art technique for many ML problems. A neural network is comprised of units, namely neurons, which are arranged into layers. They are responsible for the conversion of an input vector into some output. Each unit takes an input, applies a function, and passes the output to the next layer. Usually, nonlinear functions are applied to this algorithm.

- **Support Vector Machine (SVM) algorithm**: The SVM learning algorithm is a supervised ML model. It is used for both classification and regression analysis, and is widely known as a constrained optimization problem. SVM can be made more powerful using the kernel trick (linear, radial basis function, polynomial, and sigmoid). However, the limitations of the SVM approach lies in the selection of the kernel.

Regression

Regression is a statistical measurement that aids in estimating the relationship among variables. In general, classification focuses on the prediction of a label, whereas regression focuses on the prediction of a quantity. Regression is used in finance, investing, and other disciplines by managers to value their assets. In the same line, it attempts to determine the strength of the relationship between dependent variables and a series of other changing variables (independent variables); for example, the relationship between commodity prices and the businesses dealing in those commodities.

The regression model has two major characteristics. The output variable in the regression problem is a real value or quantitative in nature. The creation of the model takes past data into consideration. Mathematically, a predictive model maps the input variable (X) to the continuous output variable (Y). A continuous output variable is an integer or floating-point value.

The ability of the regression predictive model can be measured by calculating the **root mean square error** (**RMSE**). For example, in total, the regression prediction model made two predictions, that is, 1.5 and 3.3, where the expected values are 1.0 and 3.0. Therefore, RMSE can be calculated as follows:

```
RMSE = sqrt(average(error^2))
RMSE = sqrt(((1.0 - 1.5)^2 + (3.0 - 3.3)^2) / 2)
RMSE = sqrt((0.25 + 0.09) / 2)
RMSE = sqrt(0.17)
RMSE = 0.412
```

Unsupervised learning

Unsupervised learning is a class of ML techniques in which the data that's given as input isn't labeled. Moreover, only the input variables (X) are given, with no correspondence to the output variables (Y). In unsupervised learning, the algorithms are left in solitude to learn and explore on their own, with no real early expectations. This absence of labeling teaches us about the reconstruction of input data either using representation or embedding. It is beneficial when it comes to data mining and feature extraction.

Unsupervised learning allows you to discover hidden trends and patterns. Some real-world examples are predicting or understanding handwritten digits, nano camera fabrication technology, Planck quantum spectrum, and more.

Mathematically, unsupervised learning has an input value (X) with no corresponding output value. In comparison to supervised learning, the task processing of unsupervised learning is quite complex. The implementation of unsupervised learning can be found in automatic or self-driving cars, facial recognition programs, expert systems, bioinformatics, and more.

Association and clustering are two parts of unsupervised learning.

Association

This is a technique that's used to discover new patterns in huge datasets. Association is deliberated to identify strong rules from a dataset based on the degree of newsworthiness. During prolonged analysis of the data, more new rules are generated.

The association rule is largely employed in market basket analysis. This technique helps to determine the strength of association between the pairs of the product purchased and the frequency of cooccurrence in the observations.

Market basket analysis is one of the modeling techniques that's used by retailers to uncover associations between items. The theory elaborates around the fact that if we buy some items, we are more likely to buy similar items.

Mathematically, it is represented as $P(A \mid B)$, where a person who buys A also buys B. It can also be written as if $\{A\}$, then $\{B\}$. In other words, if there is a probability of A to occur, then there is also a probability of B to occur as well. For example, $P(milk \mid bread) = 0.7$.

Clustering

Cluster is the assembly of an object belonging to the same label, treated as one. Clustering is the technique of grouping an object to its corresponding category. This includes sorting several objects into their particular groups, where the capacity of association is at its maximum if it belongs to the same group, or minimum, otherwise.

One of the most popular clustering algorithms is the k-means clustering algorithm. This algorithm demands the predefined value of k. K represents the number of clusters we want to divide data into. The real performance is obtained when the cluster is hyperspherical, such as circles in a 2D space or spheres in a 3D space.

The main advantage of clustering is that it helps you figure out the distinct, useful feature from the data and that it is flexible to changes.

Reinforcement learning

Reinforcement learning is a part of ML that deals with taking necessary action in order to increase the reward for a particular situation. It employs several pieces of software and machines in order to find the best possible path for a specific situation.

Reinforcement learning is different from supervised learning. In supervised learning, training data is provided with a label, based on which it is trained. In the case of reinforcement learning, the reinforcement agent makes the decision to resolve the task that's been assigned to them.

There are two types of reinforcement learning:

- **Positive reinforcement**: Maximizes performance and sustains changes for a longer duration

- **Negative reinforcement**: Minimizes performance and sustains change for a shorter duration

Data mining

The process of discovering hidden or predictive information from large datasets or databases is known as data mining. Data mining is a form of analysis that's conducted on data to discover new patterns and facts. These facts are used to discover knowledge and is also considered as a step toward **knowledge discovery in databases** (KDD).

Various processes and steps from AI, ML, statistics, database management systems, and more are often combined to search for the new pattern. With growing volumes of data and ML algorithms, there is always a tendency of finding new or hidden facts in the database. Facts and patterns that are found or searched for are then used to predict a certain outcome, and can also be applied in many fields, such as statistics, data visualization, marketing, management, medical, decision making systems, and so on.

Data analysis and data mining are often compared or talked about in tandem. Data mining is considered a part of the data analysis process. We will need some predefined hypotheses while working with data analysis since it's the process of organizing data to develop models and determine some insights. In terms of applied practices, data mining is mainly conducted on structured data, whereas data analysis can be done on structured, unstructured, or semi-structured data.

Data mining is based on scientific and mathematical methods, whereas data analysis uses analytics models and intelligence systems. When looking from a distance, both data analysis and data mining are subsets of data science, where data mining implements predictive algorithms to discover patterns and data analysis implements activities to gain some insights from datasets.

A major benefit of data mining is being able to process huge volumes of data in a short amount of time. It can also be implemented across new or existing platforms, predict hidden patterns or help in discovering them, help in decision-making, knowledge discovery, and much more.

Tasks of data mining

In general, data mining tasks are segregated into two types, also known as data mining analytics or data mining modeling. Both can be further categorized, as shown here:

- Predictive:

    - Classification

    - Regression

    - Prediction

- Descriptive:

    - Clustering

    - Summarization

    - Association rules

Predictive

This uses statistical analysis and turns data into valuable information. It predicts the probable future outcome of occurring situations. Prediction-related techniques that generate output by analyzing current and historical facts fall under this model.

Classification

This is one of the most common mining techniques and classifies and categorizes samples before processing them to find facts. For more information on the classification and model evaluation procedure, please refer to the *Types of ML algorithms* section.

Regression

This technique is used to predict, forecast, and analyze information trends and the relationship between variables. For more information on regression, please refer to the *Types of ML algorithms* section.

Prediction

This technique analyzes past events and predicts the possible missing or future values by using references from other data mining techniques such as clustering, classification, and more.

Descriptive

Also known as the preliminary stage of data processing, it uses business intelligence and many other systems. This form of analytics is limited since it only analyzes past data and normally provides information about things that have already happened.

Clustering

Clustering is a technique that's used to identify data that's similar to each other. For more information on clustering, please refer to the *Types of ML algorithms* section.

Summarization

This provides a more compact representation of the dataset and includes visualization and report generation. Most management reporting regarding sales and marketing use this technique.

Association rules

For more information on association, please refer to the *Types of ML algorithms* section.

What's next?

Web scraping is dynamic, demanding, and also a challenging task. We need to obey the legal perspective, which is presented on a website's **Terms of Services (ToS)** and Privacy Policy before carrying this task forward. Python programming, with its supportive nature, easy syntax, short and readable code formation, and the availability of libraries and tools is one of the best languages to be used in web scraping.

Still, the challenges are there and general scripts might not be able to fulfill the demand that exists. Sometimes, a scraping task might be for a huge volume, and personal PCs or laptops won't be a place worth implementing when you consider time, machine resources, and more. There are a number of features and procedures that can make a scraping task more complicated and challenging. Let's go over some of them:

- The adoption of growing web-based security measures

- Dynamic loading of data and the involvement of scripting languages makes scraping complex

- Presence of CAPTCHA, which can be found at http://www.captcha.net/

- Blocking a user's IP address (for simultaneous requests)

- Blocking requests from certain parts of the world (using and switching proxies might help)

For such cases, we can get help from organizations who are doing scraping-related work. These organizations can help us with our demand of data by charging certain fees and providing us with a web interface where we can process our demand. Such companies may be searched for in Google as `Web Scraping Services` or `Web Scraping Softwares`. There's also various browser-based extensions available that can be found by searching for `Scraping Extensions`.

Summary

In this chapter, we have explored and learned about the basic concepts regarding data management by using files, analysis, and visualization using pandas and matplotlib. We also introduced ML and data mining, and we also explored some related resources that can be helpful for further learning and career development.

With this chapter, we come to the end of the book! Web scraping is a broad topic that is related directly or indirectly to a number of technologies and development techniques. Throughout this book, we have learned about numerous concepts in this domain by using the Python programming language. We can also explore more of the topics related to web scraping like ML, Data mining, Web scraping, AI and Python programming. These topics are worth exploring from a knowledge and career perspective.

Further reading

- *Artificial Intelligence: A Modern Approach,* at `http://aima.cs.berkeley.edu/`
- *Machine Learning,* at `http://www.cs.cmu.edu/~tom/mlbook.html`
- *Data Mining and Analysis, Fundamental Concepts and Algorithms,* at `http://www.dataminingbook.info/pmwiki.php`
- The Python data analysis library, at `https://pandas.pydata.org`
- matplotlib: Python plotting, at `https://matplotlib.org`
- File handling (Python), at `https://www.w3schools.com/python/python_file_handling.asp`
- *Introduction to Information Retrieval,* at `https://nlp.stanford.edu/IR-book/`
- SQLite, at `https://www.sqlite.org/index.html`
- MySQL, at `https://www.mysql.com/`
- PostgreSQL, at `https://www.postgresql.org/`
- CAPTCHA, at `http://www.captcha.net/`
- *Overview of the KDD Process,* at `http://www2.cs.uregina.ca/~dbd/cs831/notes/kdd/1_kdd.html`

Other Books You May Enjoy

If you enjoyed this book, you may be interested in these other books by Packt:

R Web Scraping Quick Start Guide
Olgun Aydin

ISBN: 9781789138733

- Write and create regEX rules
- Write XPath rules to query your data
- Learn how web scraping methods work
- Use rvest to crawl web pages
- Store data retrieved from the web
- Learn the key uses of Rselenium to scrape data

Python Web Scraping Cookbook
Michael Heydt

ISBN: 9781787285217

- Use a wide variety of tools to scrape any website and data—including BeautifulSoup, Scrapy, Selenium, and many more
- Master expression languages such as XPath, CSS, and regular expressions to extract web data
- Deal with scraping traps such as hidden form fields, throttling, pagination, and different status codes
- Build robust scraping pipelines with SQS and RabbitMQ
- Scrape assets such as images media and know what to do when Scraper fails to run
- Explore ETL techniques of build a customized crawler, parser, and convert structured and unstructured data from websites

Leave a review - let other readers know what you think

Please share your thoughts on this book with others by leaving a review on the site that you bought it from. If you purchased the book from Amazon, please leave us an honest review on this book's Amazon page. This is vital so that other potential readers can see and use your unbiased opinion to make purchasing decisions, we can understand what our customers think about our products, and our authors can see your feedback on the title that they have worked with Packt to create. It will only take a few minutes of your time, but is valuable to other potential customers, our authors, and Packt. Thank you!

Index

Made in the USA
Middletown, DE
07 February 2020